Women in Rock Memoirs

Women in Rock Memoirs

Music, History, and Life-Writing

Edited by
CRISTINA GARRIGÓS AND MARIKA AHONEN

OXFORD
UNIVERSITY PRESS

Oxford University Press is a department of the University of Oxford. It furthers
the University's objective of excellence in research, scholarship, and education
by publishing worldwide. Oxford is a registered trade mark of Oxford University
Press in the UK and certain other countries.

Published in the United States of America by Oxford University Press
198 Madison Avenue, New York, NY 10016, United States of America.

© Oxford University Press 2023

All rights reserved. No part of this publication may be reproduced, stored in
a retrieval system, or transmitted, in any form or by any means, without the
prior permission in writing of Oxford University Press, or as expressly permitted
by law, by license, or under terms agreed with the appropriate reproduction
rights organization. Inquiries concerning reproduction outside the scope of the
above should be sent to the Rights Department, Oxford University Press, at the
address above.

You must not circulate this work in any other form
and you must impose this same condition on any acquirer.

Library of Congress Cataloging-in-Publication Data
Names: Garrigós, Cristina, editor. | Ahonen, Marika, editor.
Title: Women in rock memoirs : music, history, and life-writing /
[edited by Cristina Garrigós, Marika Ahonen].
Description: [1.] | New York : Oxford University Press, 2023. |
Includes bibliographical references and index.
Identifiers: LCCN 2023017341 (print) | LCCN 2023017342 (ebook) |
ISBN 9780197659335 (paperback) | ISBN 9780197659328 (hardback) |
ISBN 9780197659359 (epub)
Subjects: LCSH: Women rock musicians—Biography—Authorship. |
Rock musicians—Biography—Authorship. | Women—Biography—Authorship. |
Autobiography—Authorship.
Classification: LCC ML82 .W667 2023 (print) | LCC ML82 (ebook) |
DDC 782.42166092/52—dc23/eng/20230526
LC record available at https://lccn.loc.gov/2023017341
LC ebook record available at https://lccn.loc.gov/2023017342

DOI: 10.1093/oso/9780197659328.001.0001

Paperback printed by Marquis Book Printing, Canada
Hardback printed by Bridgeport National Bindery, Inc., United States of America

Contents

Contributors   vii

Introduction: Female Musicians Writing Memoirs   1
Cristina Garrigós and Marika Ahonen

PART I: MEMORY, TRAUMA, AND WRITING

1. Childhood Trauma and the Musical In-Between in Memoirs by Astrid Swan and Dory Previn   23
Astrid Joutseno

2. The Monster in the House: Gender-Based Violence and Punk in Alice Bag's *Violence Girl: East L.A. Rage to Hollywood Stage. A Chicana Punk Story*   40
Cristina Garrigós

3. Memory and Writing in Kim Gordon's *Girl in a Band*   56
Ángel Chaparro Sainz

4. Memory, Truth, and Narrative Ethics in Christina Rosenvinge's *Debut*   72
Marika Ahonen

PART II: AUTHENTICITY, SEXUALITY, AND SEXISM

5. Jayne County, Laura Jane Grace, and the HerStory of Transgender Punks in America   89
Karen Fournier

6. A Portrait of the Artist as a Punk: Authenticity and the Woman Musician in Debbie Harry's *Face It*   106
Margaret Henderson

7. "Mothers aren't sexy," "What is that you're wearing?," "What's it like to be in an all-girl band?": Memoirs as Histories of 1980s Music Industry Sexism   122
Wayne Heisler Jr.

8. The Art of Performing Authenticity: A Study of Amanda
   Palmer's Memoirs 141
   Beatriz A. Medeiros

9. The Punk, the Rebel, and the Cowboy: Queering Masculine
   Spaces in Patti Smith's Memoirs 158
   Amy McCarthy

PART III: AGING, PERFORMANCE, AND THE IMAGE

10. Queens of Noise: Rewriting the "Rock Chick" Identity
    through *Neon Angel* and *Living Like a Runaway* 177
    Jacqueline Dickin

11. Humanizing Icon: Collaboration and Control in
    Grace Jones's *I'll Never Write My Memoirs* 192
    Satoko Naito

12. Power in the Eye of the Beholder: Authoring Text and
    Image in the Female Rock Memoir 208
    Silvia Hernández Hellín

13. Cosey Fanni Tutti, Age and Place 225
    Abigail Gardner

Index 243

Contributors

Marika Ahonen is a doctoral candidate in Cultural History at the University of Turku, Finland. Her doctoral dissertation examines the construction of narratives in popular music and the ethical questions raised in this context through the authorship and music of Spanish singer-songwriter Christina Rosenvinge (b. 1964). Overall, her research interests include the connection between popular music and identity, the relation of gender to agency, and the fields of narrative ethics and power mechanisms. She is also drawn to the areas of phenomenology and hermeneutics. In 2022, Ahonen won the ISCH (International Society for Cultural History) essay prize with the article "Sirens, Narrative Ethics, and Christina Rosenvinge's Mi Vida Bajo el Agua," published in the journal *Cultural History* 12, no. 1 (April 2023).

Ángel Chaparro Sainz is an Associate Professor at the University of the Basque Country, Spain. He holds a degree in English Philology and a PhD in North American Literature from that same university. He is a member of the research group REWEST. His book *Parting the Mormon Veil: Phyllis Barber's Writing* was published by the Biblioteca Javier Coy (University of Valencia) in 2013. More recently, he has coedited the volume *Transcontinental Reflections on the American West: Words, Images, Sounds beyond Borders* (2015). He has published in different collections and journals such as *Miscelánea, Lectora, Revista Canaria de Estudios Ingleses*, and *Women's Studies*.

Jacqueline Dickin is an adjunct Associate Lecturer in the field of Life-Writing at Flinders University, South Australia, where she is also a member of the Flinders Life Narrative Research Lab. Her work has been published in the *a.b: Auto/biography Studies* special issue "Comic Lives" (March 2023) and, with Kylie Cardell, in the forthcoming edited collection *Life Writing as World Literature* (Bloomsbury, 2023). She is currently working on a book that explores Australian popular memoir and the wellness empire during the COVID-19 pandemic.

Karen Fournier is an Associate Professor at the School of Music, Theatre, and Dance at the University of Michigan, Ann Arbor, where she also serves as the Director of Research. She has published widely on such topics as British punk, women in rock, and epistemology. Her first book, *The Words and Music of Alanis Morissette*, was published in 2015, and she has completed a second book on the role played by women in the early British punk movement.

Abigail Gardner is a Professor in Cultural Studies at the University of Gloucestershire, UK. She writes on music, gender, and aging. Key publications include *Listening, Belonging and Memory* (Bloomsbury, 2023), *Ageing and Contemporary Female Musicians* (Routledge, 2019), *PJ Harvey and Music Video Performance* (Routledge,

2015), and, with Ros Jennings, *Aging and Popular Music in Europe* (Routledge, 2019) and *Rock On: Women, Ageing and Popular Music* (Ashgate, 2012). She has led European projects on music and listening and produces community film and digital storytelling.

Cristina Garrigós is a Professor of American Literature at UNED (National University of Distance Education) in Spain. Her research interests include US contemporary literature, film, music, punk, memory, and gender studies. She is co-author of the book of interviews *God Save the Queens: Pioneras del Punk* (66rpm 2019) with Paula Guerra and Nuria Triana. She is the editor of *Punk Connections: A Transcultural Perspective* (University of Barcelona, 2017) with Nuria Triana-Toribio. She has published on authors such as Kathy Acker, Gloria Anzaldúa, Giannina Braschi, Helena María Viramontes, Don DeLillo, and Ruth Ozeki, among others. Her latest book is *Alzheimer's Disease in Contemporary US Fiction: Memory Lost* (Routledge, 2021). Her term as president of the Spanish Association for American Studies (SAAS) began in 2023.

Wayne Heisler Jr.'s research and writing focus on music and bodies, including choreomusical relationships in dance, opera, and gender and sexuality in music and dance performance. His current book project concerns choreographies of songs in the twentieth century. In addition to music and dance, Heisler has written about a range of popular artists: Chrissie Hynde, Cyndi Lauper, Kate Smith, and U2. He is a Professor of Historical and Cultural Studies in Music at the College of New Jersey, where his courses include "Gender, Sexuality, and Pop Music in the 1980s."

Margaret Henderson is an Associate Professor in Literature at the University of Queensland, Australia. She is the author of *Kathy Acker: Punk Writer* (Routledge, 2020) and *Marking Feminist Times: Remembering the Longest Revolution in Australia*, and coauthor (with Anthea Taylor) of *Postfeminism in Context: Women, Australian Popular Culture, and the Unsettling of Postfeminism*. She has published extensively on contemporary women's writing—including memoir, feminist material culture, and feminism and popular culture. She is currently writing a book on women's punk and post-punk memoirs.

Silvia Hernández Hellín earned her PhD in Literary Studies in 2021 from the University of Las Palmas de Gran Canaria (Spain), where she was awarded a BA in Modern Languages and an MA in Audiovisual and Literary Culture. She has worked as an adjunct professor of English at the University of Palmas de Gran Canaria and the University School of Tourism of Lanzarote. Her dissertation explores Patti Smith's autobiographical prose work, focusing on the theory of life-writing. Her research interests include life-writing, literature and film studies, and twentieth- and twenty-first-century US literature.

Astrid Joutseno's PhD *Life Writing from Birth to Death: How M/others Know* analyzes life-writing on mommy blogs. As Astrid Swan, the author has released seven albums.

In October 2021 she published *D/other*, examining mothers, children, and death within the structures of pop music. Dr. Joutseno/Swan was awarded the Teosto Award in 2018. She published a memoir, *Viimeinen kirjani: kirjoituksia elämästä*, in 2019.

Amy McCarthy is a PhD student at York St John University, UK, and specializes in women's rock music memoirs. She completed her master's degree at the University of Sheffield in 2018, where she wrote her dissertation on the female body in women's music memoirs. In 2018, she won the Wilko Johnson Writing Award for her music writing.

Beatriz A. Medeiros is a PhD candidate in communication and cultural studies under a cotutelle agreement between the Universidade Federal Fluminense (Brazil) and the University of Tübingen (Germany). Her research focuses on the networks of women in rock music and their strategies of survival in the male-dominated music industry. With a master's degree in Communication and a bachelor's degree in Media Studies, she is dedicated to studying the sociological practices of women in popular music, including their digital performances, from a decolonial and postcolonial perspective.

Satoko Naito teaches film, literature, and history as a docent at the Centre for East Asian Studies at the University of Turku, Finland, where she is also an affiliate scholar of SELMA. She received her PhD in Japanese literature from Columbia University (2010) and was an assistant professor of Japanese at the University of Maryland, College Park, before a family relocation to Finland. She has published articles dealing with Japanese literature, early modern women's education, and popular theater, and has contributed chapters to projects including *The Cambridge History of Japanese Literature* (eds. Haruo Shirane and Tomi Suzuki, with David Lurie, 2015) and *The Palgrave Encyclopedia of Medieval Women's Writing in the Global Middle Ages* (eds. Michelle M. Sauer, Diane Watt, and Liz Herbert McAvoy, 2022). Naito is also a host of the Nordic Asia Podcast on the New Books Network.

Introduction

Female Musicians Writing Memoirs

Cristina Garrigós and Marika Ahonen

The last decade has seen a significant rise in the number of published memoirs by women in rock. Patti Smith's *Just Kids* came out in 2010 to a positive reception,[1] and others soon followed, among them Cherie Currie's *Neon Angel: Memoir of a Runaway* (2011), Alice Bag's *Violence Girl: East L.A. Rage to Hollywood Stage. A Chicana Punk Story* (2011), Kim Gordon's *Girl in a Band* (2015), Lita Ford's *Living Like a Runaway* (2015), Carrie Brownstein's *Hunger Made Me a Modern Girl* (2016), Chrissie Hynde's *Reckless: My Life as a Pretender* (2016), Cosey Fanni Tutti's *Art, Sex, Music* (2017), and Viv Albertine's *Clothes, Clothes, Clothes. Music, Music, Music. Boys, Boys, Boys* (2016). More recently, Debbie Harry's *Face It* (2019), Liz Phair's *Horror Stories: A Memoir* (2019), Kathy Valentine's *All I Ever Wanted: A Rock 'n' Roll Memoir* (2020), and Jayne County's *Man Enough to Be a Woman: The Autobiography of Jayne County* (2021) can be added to the list.[2] This inventory is, as all lists are, incomplete. However, it proves that there is a new interest in the life-stories of women in rock. In fact, the abundance of works written by female artists telling the stories of how they became involved in the music world—some of them being what Lucy O'Brien has termed "women made of punk"[3]—has even led to the creation of a new genre, somewhat contestably labeled by Geoff Edgers the "Female Rock Memoir."[4]

---

[1] Patti Smith's *Just Kids* won the National Book Award (Nonfiction, 2010). It was also a *Los Angeles Times* Book Prize finalist (2010), *New York Times* bestseller (Nonfiction, 2020), and National Book Circle Awards Finalist (Autobiography/Memoir, 2010).

[2] All the books listed here were published after 2010, but, of course, a few memoirs were written by rock musicians earlier in the twentieth century, such as Lydia Lunch, *Paradoxia: A Predator's Diary* (New York: Akashic Books, 1997); and Grace Slick, *Somebody to Love: A Rock and Roll Memoir* (New York: Grand Central Publishing, 1999).

[3] Geoff Edgers, "Rise of the Female Rock Memoir," *Washington Post*, September 5, 2015.

[4] Lucy O'Brien. "The Woman Punk Made Me," in *Punk Rock: So What? The Cultural Legacy of Punk*, ed. Roger Sabin (London: Routledge, 1999), 186–198.

The commercial success of these memoirs attests to the rise of a genre in which women's voices have acquired a new significance, as even though the publication of memoirs written by rock musicians is a well-established trend, such memoirs have traditionally been written by men (such as those by Chuck Berry, Neil Young, Keith Richards, Richard Hell, and Bruce Springsteen, among others). When we consider that in the rock music world, attention has long been centered on men, this is hardly surprising. Female musicians have also written about their lives in the past, but the best-known books are by women working in jazz, blues, folk, and country, many of whom coauthored their books with men.[5] Before the publication of Patti Smith's memoirs, very few women in rock had had the chance to narrate their lives, or indeed to learn that there was an interested audience. However, along with Fourth Wave feminism, the #MeToo movement,[6] and the rise in Aging Studies, the time seems to be right for women who participated in rock music from the 1970s onward to narrate their own stories.

Women rockers, aware that their public persona had previously been structured mostly through interviews and images, now take up their pens or computer keyboards to deliver first-person narratives of their vision of themselves. In this volume we address the key question of how twenty-first-century female rock musicians, or female-identified rock musicians, narrate and remember their lives through memoir, and what type of knowledge these books afford.[7] Thus, in this volume we focus specifically on female-identified rock musicians by emphasizing an intersectional understanding of the topic. Our interest is in exploring the tension between the public persona and the private, in remembering and forgetting, and in the dynamic between telling and not telling that often structures these works.

Moreover, something shared by the writers of these memoirs is their age: as said above, most of the authors are mature women whose careers unfolded from the 1970s onward. By exploring their memories, we thus also come to an understanding of the development of rock music, and of the societies where they grew up as artists, from women's perspectives. Life-writing obviously

---

[5] E.g., Billie Holiday, *Lady Sings the Blues* (New York: Doubleday, 1956), written with William Dufty; Nina Simone, *I Put a Spell on You* (New York: Pantheon, 1992), written with Stephen Cleary, and Loretta Lynn, *Coal's Miner Daughter* (New York: Da Capo Press, 1976), written with George Vecsev.

[6] The MeToo movement was founded in 2006 by Tarana Burke to address the sexual harassment of women. The expression became popular in the social networks and in 2017 the hashtag #MeToo went viral after Harvey Weinstein's scandal. See https://metoomvmt.org/.

[7] This book does not include studies about other women in rock such as, for instance, groupies, as in Sally Mann Romano, *The Band's with Me: Tour 1964–1975* (San Francisco: Big Gorilla Books, 2018).

requires one to look back at one's individual memory, but it also implies an exercise of collective and cultural memory, one that allows us, the readers, to better understand the history of women in popular music.

Memoirs in the Context of Life-Writing and Celebrity Culture

Many authors have addressed the roles that women play in the popular music industry. Key studies on this topic include those by Helen Reddington, Sheila Whiteley, Lucy O'Brien, Gerri Hirshey, Norma Coates, and Marion Leonard, among others.[8] Like them, our focus is on women-identified musicians, but we are interested in exploring their voices as authors of their memoirs. That is, we are concerned with exploring the strategies and discourses of their life-writing and what these texts reveal about the history of women in rock. This book therefore offers a so far undeveloped perspective— not only an exploration of the role of women/LGYBTQ+ in music, but one carried out through studies of their memoirs. We believe that these texts provide first-person experiences and, as such, that they can offer valuable insights that will broaden our horizons regarding the history of popular music. In other words, we are interested in how the women rockers whose memoirs are included in this volume narrate their lives to the public and what type of knowledge this narrative provides for our understanding of culture and history.

Instead of reading the experiences merely as "historical facts," or naturalizing them, we believe that they need to be understood through their constructed nature.[9] This is especially the case with memoirs, where it is necessary to consider both the context in which they are published, and how experience is narrated in them. Memoirs are, moreover, often creative, at times combining reality and fiction, while as constructed pieces of one's life story, they are essentially selective. Written in the present about the past, memoirs offer carefully chosen elements of the writer's life to present to the public, so that—since remembering is an active act—many present factors may

---

[8] See, e.g., Lucy O'Brien, *She Bop: The Definitive History of Women in Popular Music* I (London: Penguin, 1995) and II (London: Continuum, 2002); Helen Reddington, *The Lost Women of Rock Music: Female Musicians of the Punk Era* (London: Equinox, 2007); Sheila Whiteley, *Women and Popular Music: Sexuality, Identity and Subjectivity* (London: Routledge, 2000); Sheila Whiteley, ed., *Sexing the Groove. Popular Music and Gender* (London: Routledge, 1997).

[9] See, e.g., Joan W. Scott, "Experience," in *Women, Autobiography, Theory*, ed. Sidonie Smith and Julia Watson (Madison: University of Wisconsin Press, 1998), 69.

influence the way that memories are presented on the page. It is important, too, to acknowledge both the performative aspect of acts of autobiographical memory and the use of affective memories to generate engaging experiences for the audience.

According to G. Thomas Couser, we are living in the age of memoir to such an extent that it has already eclipsed autobiography.[10] But what is exactly the difference between the two? The answer to this is far from clear-cut, and as Sidonie Smith and Julia Watson state, both memoir and autobiography are included under the concept "life-writing,"[11] an umbrella term for many different types of narrative, including memoirs and autobiographies. Since the concept of a memoir is historically associated with famous people recounting their lives to the public, we believe that the term is well-suited to the title of this volume.[12] Nevertheless, in this book we often use the term "autobiography" as an alternative to "memoir," since both terms highlight life-writing.

Interest in memoirs does not end with the general public, for as of late, attention to musical memoirs has also been growing in the academic sphere. The pioneering work *Music, Memory, and Memoir* analyzes memoirs by artists from a wide range of music genres, such as punk, indie, and dance, and examines the nature of memory and the role of music in this process of remembering.[13] The book's multidisciplinary approach includes a wide range of contributors consisting of academics, critics and musicians.[14] As the book's editors Robert Edgar, Fraser Mann, and Helen Pleasance state, the articles included explore the relationship between music, memory, and written memoir, with an emphasis on examining "the role that storytelling has in revisiting musical experience and how this functions in structuring personal and broader cultural memory."[15] The writers of the present volume share the same interest, but with a special focus on women-identified musicians, paying attention not only to what they have to say about music, but about life in general. Despite the differences between them, women rockers have faced

---

[10] G. Thomas Couser, *Memoir: An Introduction* (Oxford: Oxford University Press, 2011), 3.
[11] Sidonie Smith and Julia Watson, *Reading Autobiography: A Guide for Interpreting Life Narratives*, 2nd ed. (Madison: University of Wisconsin Press, 2010), 4.
[12] Ibid., *Reading Autobiography*, 3–4.
[13] Robert Edgar, Fraser Mann, and Helen Pleasance, eds., *Music, Memory and Memoir* (London: Bloomsbury Academic, 2019).
[14] The collection includes two articles on women: Fraser Mann, "Portrait of an Artist as an Indie Star: Kristin Hersh and the Memoir of Process," and Janine Bradbury, "Grace Jones: Cyborg Memoirist," in *Music, Memory and Memoir*, ed. Robert Edgar, Fraser Mann, and Helen Pleasance (London: Bloomsbury Academic, 2019), 39–51, 65–80.
[15] Edgar et al., *Music, Memory and Memoir*, 2–3.

similar, gender-related issues when seeking to enter the male-dominated music industries, as well as in patriarchal society at large. The interplay of their memoirs with cultural, social, and economic factors cannot be lightly dismissed.

Oliver Lovesey's recent *Popular Music Autobiography. The Revolution in Life-Writing by 1960s' Musicians and their Descendants* addresses the rising number and quality of life-writing texts by musicians associated specifically with the 1960s and their inheritors.[16] The book examines several popular music artists (among them Patti Smith and Cosey Fanni Tutti, also present in this volume), offering an major insight into the phenomenon of music and life-writing.[17] As Lovesey states, "recent critical interest in life writing, particularly since the 21st-century memoir boom, has largely overlooked the growth in autobiographies by artists of popular music."[18] Both life-writing researchers and music scholars have historically dismissed music autobiographies, which have been considered "merely manifestations of sub-cultural ephemera related to an inferior, amateur art associated with a disembodied cultural tradition, and popular music itself has not always been taken seriously."[19] Discussions on the value of popular music itself have been the subject of books such as *Art into Pop* (1987) by Simon Frith and Howard Horne, *Studying Popular Music* (1990) by Richard Middleton, and *Performing Rites* (1996) by Simon Frith, to name just three. But the artistic value of music memoir seems uncertain. Aware of this, Laura Watson reminds us that this may be because musicians are often first-time literary authors. (But Watson also reminds us that memoirs are also artistic outputs, and that musicians who wrote their own lyrics are not, in fact, new to writing.)[20]

Such concerns with value are not new in the history of art, returning us as they do to issues of high and low culture, cultural hierarchies, and to what does, and does not, deserve critical attention. In Mary Karr's words, "Memoir done right is an art, a made thing. It's not just raw reportage flung splat on the

---

[16] Oliver Lovesey, *Popular Music Autobiography. The Revolution in Life-Writing by 1960s' Musicians and their Descendants* (London: Bloomsbury Academic, 2021).

[17] For a similar interest in musical autobiographies, see also the special issue by Daniel Stein and Martin Butler, "Musical Autobiographies: An Introduction," *Popular Music & Society* 38, no. 2 (2015): 115–121. However, unlike Lovesey, Stein and Butler do not study any women, and their focus is exclusively on US musical autobiographies.

[18] Lovesey, *Popular Music Autobiography*, 2.

[19] Ibid., 12.

[20] Laura Watson, "Reading Lyrics, Hearing Prose: Morrissey's *Autobiography*," in *Music, Memory and Memoir*, ed. Robert Edgar, Fraser Mann, and Helen Pleasance (London: Bloomsbury Academic, 2019), 121.

page. . . . From the second you choose one event over another, you're shaping the past meaning."[21] Memoirs by women rockers may vary greatly from more artistic pieces to reportage, but all can shape our understanding of the past. So that in this collection, we do not make value judgments about whether some memoirs are more "artistic" than others. Our interest rather falls on the question of *how* these musicians narrate their lives in their memoirs, and what their main aim is. In other words, we focus on what they do, and what they seek to do, with their narratives.

Sidonie Smith and Julia Watson's edited collections, *Women, Autobiography, Theory* (1998) and *Interfaces: Women, Autobiography, Image, Performance* (2003), offer a well-appointed toolbox on the theory of autobiographical writing and gender, one to which our book, with its specific interest in the memoirs of female-identified rock musicians, responds.[22] We wish to establish a dialogue with these discussions and themes, and to acknowledge the feminist and intersectional perspective of the memoirs we analyze. Such recognition is not new to life-writing studies, as Craig Howes reminds us, since it was the impetus of feminist theory itself, as well as the establishment of cultural studies and "the well-worn 'race, class, and gender' trilogy of shared concerns," that provided the discourse and theoretical frame through which to study life-writing.[23]

The memoirs analyzed here must be understood not only as life-writing, but also in the context of celebrity culture, taking into account the capitalist markets and the financial motivations of both the musicians who write memoirs and the various publishing companies that profit from them. This emphasis has been analyzed in volumes such as Julie Rak's *Boom! Manufacturing Memoir for the Popular Market* (2013), where Rak analyzes the history of the memoir genre and its current popularity, especially in the United States. Sandra Mayer and Julie Novak's *Life Writing and Celebrity: Exploring Intersections* (2019) covers the theme more broadly, taking in a wide selection of disciplines and approaches; their subject matter consists, for example, of TV documentaries, journalism, and biography. Women's life-writing in the context of celebrity culture can be found in Katja

---

[21] Mary Karr, *The Art of Memoir* (New York: HarperPerennial, 2015), xvii.
[22] The former book is a comprehensive guide to the field of women's autobiography in general, including important insights to the theoretical discussions on women's life-writing since the 1960s. The focus of the latter is rather on the connection between image and text.
[23] IABA Students and New Scholars Network, "Interview with Professor Craig Howes. Looking Back, Looking Forward: Discussing the History and Future of the Field with Craig Howes." Accessed March 20, 2022. https://iabasns.wordpress.com/2019/05/08/reflections-on-life-narrative-studies-past-present-and-future-an-interview-with-craig-howes/.

Lee's *Limelight: Canadian Women and the Rise of Celebrity Autobiography* (2020), where the author ranges wide, from Shania Twain to L. M. Montgomery, with a consideration of the historically specific conditions in which fame is experienced and represented. Meanwhile, Hannah Yelin's *Celebrity Memoir: From Ghostwriting to Gender Politics* (2020) explores the role of ghostwriters in life-writing, including both traditional genres and less traditional ones such as YouTube or TV documentaries. The author discusses the genre of the female celebrity memoir by paying special attention to how it provides an understanding of celebrity culture in general and female celebrities in particular. We believe that this book on women in rock's memoirs will make a valuable addition to this list, leading to further understanding of life narrative production in the sphere of celebrity studies.

Women in Rock Memoirs

Artists associated specifically with the rock genre seem to dominate the current trend for woman musicians' memoirs. It is important to highlight that we are interested in the narratives written by women who are/were active participants in the rock world, but this does not mean we are interested only in the music memoir. There is, in our opinion, a difference between *a music memoir written by a woman*, and a *woman musician's memoir*: several memoirs featured in this volume do not deal specifically with music, and hence cannot be considered music memoirs. This is the case with Patti Smith's latest two books, *M Train* (2015) and *The Year of the Monkey* (2019), or Viv Albertine's *To Throw Away Unopened* (2018).

We understand the term "rock" in a very flexible and nuanced way, as an umbrella term that includes different types of music genres. Many musicians whose memoirs feature here are perhaps better identified in terms such as "punk," "pop," or "indie." Hence, rather than considering rock to be simply music, we understand it to have a broader cultural significance, drawing in aspects beyond the actual music—values, aesthetics, styles, visuals, and other entities with whom the musicians interact, such as industries and audiences. Rock as a cultural concept, has, of course, been highlighted by many researchers.[24] Fabian Holt argues that incorporating culture into a discussion

---

[24] See, e.g., Peter Wicke, *Rock Music: Culture, Aesthetics and Sociology*, trans. Rachel Fogg (Cambridge: Cambridge University Press, 1990); Lawrence Grossberg, *We Gotta Get Out of*

of musical genres also "stresses the social and historical dimensions that are ignored when categories are defined only in relation to the music itself."[25] Similarly, Lawrence Grossberg considers that there is no essence in rock, since "As a historical event, rock itself has a history which cannot be reduced to the history of its sonic register."[26] Thus, we also consider that rock is constantly being debated outside of the actual music, and therefore, what we understand by rock is affected by cultural and historical factors and products, including memoirs as well.[27]

Indeed, memoirs are linked to history and time, affecting what is written in them and how they are written, also in regarding the concept of rock. It is important to examine how the authors of these memoirs use their own words to explain rock—which is often defined in terms of what it is not, as can be seen in its relationship to other genres such as pop, and in concepts such as authenticity.[28] Thus, what is important in this volume is to address the relationship between rock, traditionally considered to be masculine terrain, and gender.

The use of the term "women in rock" is necessary, as Norma Coates points out, because "Refusing the title of women in rock only reinforces the naturalization of the unspoken 'men in rock.'"[29] Although in an ideal world such categorizations as "women in rock" would not need to be made, refusing to use the term also conceals many historical gender-based problems and inequalities. There are many distinctions to be taken into account when we speak of women in general, meaning differences of ethnicity, class, and other cultural factors, but women do share some similar challenges and dangers, precisely because they are identified under the term "women."

In *Revenge of the She Punks: A Feminist Music History from Poly Styrene to Pussy Riot* (2019), Vivien Goldman quotes Chimamanda Ngozi Adichie: "Of

---

This Place: Popular Conservatism and Postmodern Culture (New York: Routledge, 1992); Sheila Whiteley, *The Space between the Notes: Rock and the Counter-culture* (New York: Routledge, 1992); Claude Chastagner, *De la culture rock* (Paris: PUF, 2011); and John C. Hadjuck, *Music Wars: Money Politics and Race in the Construction of Rock and Roll Culture 1940–1960* (Lanham, MD: Lexington Books, 2018).

[25] Fabian Holt, *Genre in Popular Music* (Chicago: University of Chicago Press, 2007), 19.
[26] Grossberg, *We Gotta Get Out of This Place*, 131.
[27] See, e.g., Pekka M. Kolehmainen, *Rock, Freedom, and Ideologies of "Americanness"* (Turku: University of Turku, 2021), 36–37.
[28] See, e.g., Marion Leonard, *Gender in the Music Industry: Rock, Discourse and Girl Power* (London: Ashgate Publishing, 2007).
[29] Norma Coates, "(R)evolution Now? Rock and the Political Potential of Gender," in *Sexing the Groove. Popular Music and Gender*, ed. Sheila Whiteley (London: Routledge, 1997), 62.

course, I am a human being, but there are particular things that happen to me because I am a woman."[30] The position of women in music history has its own idiosyncratic characteristics.

As Gerri Hirshey reminds us, much has changed for women in the music scene since the beginning of the twentieth century. One century later, women now own copyrights, record companies, and destinies.[31] However, despite these social and economic changes, as Hirshey says, there are still constants in their lives: the fact that if you want to be a rock woman, you have to leave the place that has been designed for you:

> Talk to them, immerse yourself in their biographies, memoirs, interviews and songs and you'll hear a couple of insistent refrains:
> Gotta sing.
> Gotta go.[32]

Women undeniably face more difficulties than do men if they want a career in the musical world, and this sentiment is expressed by every memoir written by women in rock. When Hirshey refers to leaving the house, she is speaking not only literally, but metaphorically: women do have to leave the house, to abandon the idea of domesticity that has too long been associated with them. Women who left their house to become rock musicians had to forge a new path and, in many cases, to undertake an epic journey. In Hirshey's words, "It's about the long struggle for ownership and entitlement, about earning the right and the desire to come back in off that road and claim a home of one's own."[33] They narrate this epic journey and the many obstacles that they found along the way, obstacles found not only in the music industry but in patriarchal society in general.

Indeed, most of the memoirs written by women who took part in the rock scene narrate their authors' memories through the lens of such suffering and resilience. However, in most of the memoirs analyzed in this volume, the public exhibition of vulnerability is often mitigated with humor. Controversial issues such as gender-based violence, rape, unwanted pregnancies, abortion, bipolar disorder, eating disorders, cancer, and divorce

---

[30] Vivien Goldman, *Revenge of the She Punks: A Feminist Music History from Poly Styrene to Pussy Riot* (Austin: University of Texas Press, 2019), 7.
[31] Gerri Hirshey, *We Gotta Get Out of This Place: The True, Tough Story of Women in Rock* (New York: Grove Press, 2001), 3.
[32] Ibid., 3
[33] Ibid., 15.

are discussed, exposing intimate details of the lives of the protagonists, foregrounding both the vulnerability and the resilience of those who have been recognized as models of strong women and combative artists. Gender-based violence, for instance, seems to be a central element in many of the memoirs written by women. Many of them (such as those by Chrissie Hynde, Viv Albertine, Debbie Harry, among others) narrate episodes of sexual abuse, including rape, and other traumatic events. There are violent fathers in the memoirs of Viv Albertine and Astrid Joutseno as well as in that of Alice Bag. In all these cases, the narrator presents the father as a figure whose violent behavior determines the rebellious attitude of the authors and would-be artists, as well as their interest in a non-normative lifestyle and in feminist consciousness.

Their memoirs make readers aware of the difficulties they had to overcome, not only as artists but as women living in a patriarchal world. We believe, then, that this collection forms a valuable contribution to the vindication of the role of women in rock music, as well as being a valuable document for the exploration of the dynamics of the musical memoir as a genre.

In this volume, we emphasize an intersectional understanding of the subject.[34] Besides gender, we also seek to consider how other elements shape the musicians' experiences and influence the remembrance and narration of their lives in memoirs. Many other factors besides gender influence the possibilities of acting and narrating, such as class, race, and sexuality.

However, the lack of narratives by rock women of color is noticeable. As opposed to genres such as blues or jazz, where women of color are dominant, rock has been a predominantly white Anglo genre, at least commercially. Although there have undoubtedly been women rock artists with differing ethnicities and traditions, little has been written by/on them as yet—but this is slowly changing, as more women of color write about their experience in rock and scholars start to rescue figures who were not adequately acknowledged in their time.[35]

---

[34] The concept of intersectional feminism was coined by Kimberlé Crenshaw and it has become very influential since then. Kimberlé Crenshaw, "Demarginalizing the Intersection of Race and Sex: A Black Feminist Critique of Antidiscrimination Doctrine, Feminist Theory and Antiracist Politics," *University of Chicago Legal Forum* 1, Article 8 (1989). Accessed October 13, 2022. http://chicagounbound.uchicago.edu/uclf/vol1989/iss1/8.

[35] See, e.g., Michelle Cruz Gonzáles, *The Spitboy Rule: Tales of a Xicana in a Female Punk Band* (Oakland, CA: PN, 2016); and Skin (Deborah Dyer) with Lucy O'Brien, *It Takes Blood and Guts* (London: Simon & Schuster 2021).

Moreover, although we share a common idea that feminism is the radical idea that men and women are the same, as Angela Davis said, it is undeniable that there are different currents in feminism. As said above, one reason why women in rock's memoirs have been booming over the last ten years is the #MeToo movement, which has offered women new possibilities for discussing their experiences in the music industry and raised more interest from the audience in their lives and writing. The relationship of these authors to the feminist movement is not, however, straightforward, several having refused in the past to be considered feminists at all, and having had a conflictive relationship with some versions of feminism.

For instance, many punk rock musicians rejected the feminist label because they associated it with an organized political movement, opting for a more individual approach to feminism rather than collective practice. To take Patti Smith, who was such a role model for women in rock, the fact that she retired to Detroit to raise her children was taken as an act of treason to feminist values. According to Lucy O'Brien: "It seemed all her adolescent angst had been expressed and spent, that the warrior had retreated."[36] This controversy was clear in the discussion on feminism in the special number "Women in Rock," published by the *New Musical Express* on October 11, 1980, in which members of the Slits, Raincoats, and the Au Pairs participated and accused Smith of being anti-feminist. However, the resistance to being labeled as feminist has noticeably changed, and a majority of the authors of the memoirs considered here nowadays acknowledge that they have no objection to being considered feminists.

Thematic Axes of the Book

The volume is divided into three parts, according to the overall themes of the different chapters: Part I. Memory, Trauma, and Writing; Part II. Authenticity, Sexuality, and Sexism; and Part III. Aging, Performance, and the Image. This division allows us to focus on themes and perspectives through which the memoirs can be analyzed, although, inevitably, these themes sometimes overlap.

The first part tackles the issue of how memory is represented in the memoirs. As memory is always selective, it is essential to consider which

---

[36] O'Brien, *She Bop II*, 117.

stories in a memoir are told and which are silenced: in other words, how one's life story is constructed through remembering. Also, since most of the memoirs analyzed here are by well-known artists and targeted at a particular audience, certain themes are emphasized over others. For example, a focus on the author's personal life, rather than details about music-making, is often considered to sell more books. Then, again, it is important to consider questions of how these authors write about other people (family, friends, lovers, etc.): what do these representations tell the readers about the authors? Does there exist an ethical way to write about other people?

The chapters included in this section deal with personal memories and traumas, difficult family or emotional relationships, and with how these traumas are expressed—in the case, for instance, of composers such as Alice Bag, Kim Gordon, and Christina Rosenvinge—not only in the writing of their memoirs, but also in their lyrics. Careful attention is paid to the authors' explanations of how they became rock artists, that is, how they narrate what drove them to music. We find in these texts the narrative of how memory tackles traumatic events and how writing about one's life and music—becoming a musician and writing songs—helps to come to terms with the past. The theme of dealing with traumas in remembering and writing a memoir echoes in all chapters of the book in different ways, but the topic is especially emphasized in the first part.

Based in Finland, Astrid Joutseno is not only an academic, but also a musician who performs under the name Astrid Swan. In the first chapter, she writes about her own memoir, positioning it next to that of a pioneer in the music scene, Dory Previn. Joutseno examines the relationship between childhood trauma narratives and the lack of music-related stories by introducing the concept of "the musical in-between." By contrasting these two writers from different periods, she demonstrates that the traditions of songwriting and life-writing share a long cross-cultural history.

In the second chapter, Cristina Garrigós connects the narration of gender-based violence in Alice Bag's house to her punk attitude. Close attention is paid to the Chicana identity of the author as it connects to her memories of growing up in East Los Angeles at a key moment for the Chicano movement. Bag addresses how trauma inside her, derived from witnessing her father's violence toward her mother, relates to a rebellious spirit which is reflected in her music.

The next chapter, by Ángel Chaparro, explores Kim Gordon's memoir by focusing on how writing the book allowed Gordon to become aware of herself as a musician, a woman, a mother, and a band member. Her book thus becomes a way of questioning and exploring her life, and of coming to terms with her contradictions and desires as a woman musician.

The final chapter of the first section is by Marika Ahonen, who examines memory, truth, and narrative ethics in the memoir of Spanish singer-songwriter Christina Rosenvinge, a long-standing figure in music in Spain who has worked in the industry since the 1980s. In Rosenvinge's book, memories are inextricably associated with the creation of music. Ahonen focuses on the narration of remembering and its relation to songwriting, which both connect ultimately to the questions of survival and finally, to ethical issues as well.

Part II of the volume includes chapters that address the issue of authenticity, sexuality, and sexism in women's rock memoirs, often tied together due to rock's association with sex. As music is not only about music and musical skills, authenticity can be constructed through many platforms—concerts, interviews, images, music videos, and, of course, in books such as memoirs. Authenticity is especially important in the rock-oriented world, and owing to various gender-related notions, recognition for their authenticity has been challenging to achieve for women artists. For example, traditionally the focus of interviewers (usually male) has been more on the looks and personal life of the musician than on their actual profession, music. This lack of credibility can also be seen through the rock history, since women have rarely been included in official histories of the genre. Recognition from your audience, whether that means fans, critics, or other musicians, is essential for becoming an artist with credibility.

The theme of sexuality is closely related to that of authenticity, especially in rock. In line with the legendary "Sex, Drugs, and Rock & Roll" catchphrase, it is a truism to say that rock music is associated with sex, and these memoirs often explore women's sexuality in relation their own understanding and expression it. The idea of sex, explicit in the catchphrase, means very different things for males and females in rock; for women, sex can also be identified with danger, as is the case of many episodes of sexual abuse narrated in the memoirs. The issue of sexism is central here, since these women condemn the sexist discrimination that they received both in the music scene and in their personal lives.

The second part opens with Karen Fournier's chapter about transgender punks in the United States, in which she critically examines punk's willingness to embrace difference in the 1970s—a willingness that, however, she argues had its limits. Fournier examines the memoirs of Jayne County and Laura Jane Grace, who write about their similar experiences concerning gender stereotyping and transphobia, in and outside of the punk scene. The article brings new important historical insight—a herstory of transgender punks—to the table, while simultaneously demonstrating the societal limitations placed on transgender performers at different historical moments in the United States.

Margaret Henderson's chapter continues the theme of punk by focusing on the concept of authenticity in the memoir of Debbie Harry, also placing Harry in relation to women musicians in general. Henderson shows how the ideology of authenticity has strongly gendered implications, in which male-dominated rock is contrasted to more feminine pop. Henderson explores how in Harry's memoir, the notions of authenticity are played out and negotiated in the context of punk and new wave, and she demonstrates that self-reflexive manipulation of rock and pop codes plays a major role.

Wayne Heisler Jr.'s chapter examines how Pat Benatar, Kathy Valentine, and Cyndi Lauper frame their memoirs by establishing their gender and feminist consciousness. He explores their relationship with the 1980s music industry, focusing on its sexism in relation to image and music. The three artists are very different, but they all encountered sexism in an industry that tried to influence their appearance and careers. Heisler discusses how these authors use their memoirs as a vehicle for condemning this sexism and communicating their opinion of the patriarchal system underlying it.

In her chapter, Beatriz A. Medeiros examines how Amanda Palmer's memoir explores the issue of performing authenticity. Amanda Palmer is an alternative rock musician from the United States who gained visibility following her successful Kickstarter campaign in 2012: her memoir follows the theme of the campaign of "helping out" with motivational self-help elements. Medeiros explores the debate around the performance of authenticity, and the negotiations that can be observed in Palmer's book, as a strategy for connecting with her public. Medeiros believes that this strategy involves, for example, the performance of intimacy in Palmer's memoir, to persuade her audience of her authenticity.

The last chapter in this section, by Amy McCarthy, discusses Patti Smith's memoirs. The author uses the recurrent appearance of the cowboy figure in Smith's three memoirs to date, *Just Kids*, *M Train*, and *The Year of the Monkey*, to subvert patriarchal heteronormativity. McCarthy states that by adopting the mythical figure of the cowboy, a very masculine symbol, and appropriating it, Smith is claiming authority inside male-dominated spaces, both in her art and in those whom she classifies as her role models, therefore queering a masculine space.

Part III tackles three central issues in women's rock memoirs: aging, performance, and the image. All the memoirs included in this volume are written from the perspective of mature women who are looking back and reflecting on their current age and their younger selves. (This narrative distance is evident in the titles of the many memoirs that use the word "girl" rather than "woman.") At a time when Aging Studies are becoming increasingly significant, it is fascinating to consider how these women look at this question from the perspective of their maturity. Abigail Gardner, whose chapter closes the book, has carried out key research into this crucial topic in her books *Rock On: Women, Aging and Popular Music* (2015), *Ageing and Contemporary Female Musicians* (2019), and *Aging and Popular Music in Europe*, with Ros Jenner (2019); her work is essential to an understanding of the question of age in the memoirs.

Attention is also paid to how the authors reflect about their performances and images, and how these configure how they are presented to the audience, beyond music and words. The authors interrogate the memoirs, in order to explore the performative function of the narratives, as well as to offer reflections on the public display of their voices and images. The concept of "performance" is crucial in studies of rock culture, as is the image, and to analyze these two concepts, an exploration of the use of photographs in memoir is very revealing.[37]

As Nancy Pedri says, "Like other forms of life writing, memoir sets out to communicate truthfully through self-representation an identity and a life."[38] In this sense, the use of images in memoirs becomes an intrinsic part of this self-representation. When selecting the photographs to be included in an autobiography, the author is exercising control over the image that she wants to portray of herself. Thus, even if this image has been produced by someone else, the photography is placed in conjunction with autobiographical texts, thereby unpacking, in Linda Rugg's words, "the issue of reference in all its complexity."[39] Most of the memoirs include pictures of the authors

---

[37] See, e.g., Jacqueline Warwick and Allison Adrian, eds., *Voicing Girlhood in Popular Music: Performance, Authority, Authenticity* (London: Routledge, 2016).

[38] Nancy Pedri, "Cartooning Ex-Posing Photography in Graphic Memoirs," *Literature and Aesthetics* 22, no. 2 (2012): 248.

[39] Linda Haverty Rugg, *Picturing Ourselves: Photography and Autobiography* (Chicago: University of Chicago Press, 1997), 2.

at different periods of their lives, of their parents, houses, friends, as well as of concerts, and snapshots of the music scene, which attest to the testimonial use of photography as contributing to the re-creation of an era. These memoirs make the readers aware of the difficulties their writers had to overcome, not only as artists but as women in a patriarchal world, and so by recounting their personal experiences, these author/artists offer a particular vision and version of their personal and professional evolution. In sharing their private photograph albums with the audience and making the private public, these authors seek complicity with the readers, ensuring that it is they who are now in control.

In the first chapter of this section, Jacqueline Dickin investigates memoirs by two members of the Runaways, lead singer Cherie Currie and guitarist Lita Ford. Dickin argues that these memoirs are more than simply a peep behind the stardom of the Runaways, as they also offer engagement with the more intimate details of Currie's and Ford's lives. Moreover, reading the two memoirs comparatively, Dickin demonstrates how they rewrite the masculine rock tradition through the lens not of glamour, but of survival. This way, they reveal not only an industry rooted in misogyny but expose those structures in the industry that produce particular "rock chick" subjectivities.

Next, Satoko Naito examines Grace Jones's memoir, addressing questions of agency and authority in the performance of the self. Naito considers how Jones's memoir resists and rewrites the narrative that identifies her primarily as a model and muse, as compared with other, more influential artists. This is examined especially in relation to designer Jean-Paul Goude's memoir, in which he claims to have the creative authorship of Jones's image. His authority is undermined in Jones's memoir, as she claims ownership over her identity and demands to be recognized, above all else, as human.

Silvia Hernández Hellín explores the non-testimonial use of photography. As against the regular use of photos to represent family, friends, or moments related to the music scene, Hernández Hellín analyses the use of photography in Patti Smith's, Viv Albertine's, and Liz Phair's memoirs, all of which incorporate images that do not conform to the long-standing celebrity memoir practice of displaying career-related portraits of an author and their life. Instead, they illustrate their narratives with pictures taken by themselves of people, objects, or places that are relevant to their story. In doing so, these three women raise questions about the boundaries between fact and fiction, the faultiness of memory, and the need to contextualize photographs, all the while seeking to maintain control over their image. The images serve thus as memory tools, selected to represent or convey a metaphor or a message associated with the text.

The final chapter of the book is by Abigail Gardner, the leading authority on studies of aging and popular culture from a gender perspective. Her piece on Cosey Fanni Tutti's memoir analyses the importance of place in aging and memoir. Gardner explores the use of an older literary voice, from a different time and place, to reflect on the transgressive aspects of Cosey Fanni Tutti's youth, seeing in her narrative a certain acceptance of the younger woman she was, but also a tension between her and the mature one that is writing. This chapter is a fitting one with which to close our volume, as this tension between the rebellious and transgressive character of the young artists and the serenity and reflection of the mature writers is common to all the memoirs discussed.

The essays included in this collection are written by authors from Australia, Brazil, Canada, Finland, Spain, the United Kingdom, and the United States. This underlines the internationalization that we think that the topic deserves. We believe that it would be a major step were this volume to encourage women in the global music industry to write their own life stories, and researchers to carry out their work beyond the Anglo-American frame. Academically, the scholars come from subject areas as varied as Literary Studies, Cultural History, Gender Studies, Communication, Popular Culture Studies, Music, and Media Studies, and as such, their perspectives and emphasis also vary widely. By thus bringing together scholars from different fields to analyze memoirs in an interdisciplinary manner, we invite readers everywhere to study memoirs, as well as other life-writing texts, in order to help us to better understand both the history of music and the narrative strategies used to represent individual and cultural memories, and to vindicate the voices of women in rock, both as musicians and as authors.

We hope that our book may help us reach a better future understanding of today's possibilities and challenges for women in music; hopefully, it will be followed by further studies that will broaden and develop our themes and research.

We would like to thank the authors, without whom this book would not have been possible. Thank you also to our publisher and reviewers, for their enlightening comments throughout the process of completing the book, and to our families and friends who have always encouraged us to read and listen to the voices of women in rock.

Bibliography

Albertine, Viv. *Clothes, Clothes, Clothes. Music, Music, Music. Boys, Boys, Boys.* New York: St. Martin's Press, 2014.

Bag, Alice. *Violence Girl: East L.A. Rage to Hollywood Stage. A Chicana Punk Story.* Port Townsend, WA: Feral House, 2011.

Brownstein, Carrie. *Hunger Makes Me a Modern Girl.* New York: Riverhead Books, 2016.

Chastagner, Claude. *De la culture rock.* Paris: PUF, 2011.

Coates, Norma. "(R)evolution Now? Rock and the Political Potential of Gender." In *Sexing the Groove. Popular Music and Gender*, edited by Sheila Whiteley, 50–64. London: Routledge, 1997.

County, Jayne. *Man Enough to Be a Woman: The Autobiography of Jayne County.* London: Serpent's Tail, 2021.

Couser, G. Thomas. *Memoir: An Introduction.* Oxford: Oxford University Press, 2011.

Crenshaw, Kimberlé. "Demarginalizing the Intersection of Race and Sex: A Black Feminist Critique of Antidiscrimination Doctrine, Feminist Theory and Antiracist Politics," *University of Chicago Legal Forum* 1, Article 8 (1989).

Currie, Cherie. *Neon Angel: Memoir of a Runaway.* New York: It Books, 2011.

Edgar, Robert, Fraser Mann, and Helen Pleasance, eds. *Music, Memory and Memoir.* London: Bloomsbury Academic, 2019.

Ford, Lita. *Living Like a Runaway.* New York: Dey Street, 2015.

Frith, Simon. *Performing Rites: On the Value of Popular Music.* Cambridge, MA: Harvard University Press, 1996.

Frith, Simon. *Taking Popular Music Seriously: Selected Essays.* London: Ashgate, 2017.

Frith, Simon, and Howard Horne. *Art into Pop.* London: Methuen Young Books, 1987.

Gaar, Gillian G. *She's a Rebel: The History of Women in Rock and Roll.* New York: Seal, 2002.

Goldman, Vivien. *Revenge of the She Punks: A Feminist Music History from Poly Styrene to Pussy Riot.* Austin: University of Texas Press, 2019.

Gonzáles, Michelle Cruz. *The Spitboy Rule: Tales of a Xicana in a Punk Rock Band.* Oakland, CA: PM Press, 2016.

Gordon, Kim. *Girl in a Band.* New York: Dey Street, 2015.

Grossberg, Lawrence. *We Gotta Get Out of This Place: Popular Conservatism and Postmodern Culture.* New York: Routledge, 1992.

Hadjuck, John C. *Music Wars: Money Politics and Race in the Construction of Rock and Roll Culture 1940–1960.* Lanham, MD: Lexington Books, 2018.

Harry, Debbie. *Face It.* London: HarperCollins, 2019.

Havraneck, Carrie. *Women Icons of Popular Music: The Rebels, Rockers, and Renegades.* Westport, CT: Greenwood Press, 2008.

Hirshey, Gerri. *We Gotta Get Out of This Place: The True, Tough Story of Women in Rock.* New York: Grove Press, 2001.

Holiday, Billie, with William Dufty. *Lady Sings the Blues.* New York: Doubleday, 1956.

Holt, Fabian. *Genre in Popular Music.* Chicago: University of Chicago Press, 2007.

Hynde, Chrissie. *Reckless: My Life as a Pretender.* London: Ebury Press, 2015.

Karr, Mary. *The Art of Memoir.* New York: Harper Perennial, 2015.

Kolehmainen, Pekka M. *Rock, Freedom, and Ideologies of "Americanness."* Turku, Finland: University of Turku, 2021.

Lankford, Ronald D., Jr. *Women Singer-Songwriters in Rock: A Populist Rebellion in the 1990s.* Toronto: Scarecrow Press, 2010.

Lee, Katja. *Limelight: Canadian Women and the Rise of Celebrity Autobiography*. Waterloo, ON: Wilfrid Laurier University Press, 2020.

Leonard, Marion: *Gender in the Music Industry: Rock, Discourse and Girl Power*. London: Ashgate Publishing, 2007.

Lovesey, Oliver. *Popular Music Autobiography. The Revolution in Life-Writing by 1960s' Musicians and Their Descendants*. London: Bloomsbury Academic, 2021.

Lunch, Lydia. *Paradoxia: A Predator's Diary*. New York: Akashic Books, 1997.

Lynn, Loretta, with George Vecsey. *Coal's Miner Daughter*. New York: Da Capo Press, 1976.

Mayer, Sandra, and Julie Novak, eds. *Life Writing and Celebrity: Exploring Intersections*. London: Routledge, 2019.

Middleton, Richard. *Studying Popular Music*. Maidenhead, Berkshire, UK: Open University Press, 1990.

O'Brien, Lucy. *She Bop: The Definitive History of Women in Popular Music*. 2nd ed. London: Penguin, 1995.

O'Brien, Lucy. *She Bop II: The Definitive History of Women in Rock, Pop and Soul*. 2nd ed. London: Continuum, 2002.

O'Brien, Lucy. "The Woman Punk Made Me." In *Punk Rock, So What?: The Cultural Legacy of Punk*, edited by Roger Sabin, 186–198. London: Routledge, 1999.

Pedri, Nancy. "Cartooning Ex-Posing Photography in Graphic Memoirs." *Literature and Aesthetics* 22, no. 2 (2012): 248–266.

Phair, Liz. *Horror Stories: A Memoir*. New York: Random House, 2019.

Rak, Julie. *Boom! Manufacturing Memoir for the Popular Market*. Waterloo, ON: Wilfried Laurier University Press, 2013.

Reddington, Helen. *The Lost Women of Rock Music: Female Musicians of the Punk Era*. London: Equinox. 2007.

Romano, Sally Mann. *The Band's with Me: Tour 1964–1975*. San Francisco: Big Gorilla Books, 2018.

Rugg, Linda Haverty. *Picturing Ourselves: Photography and Autobiography*. Chicago: University of Chicago Press, 1997.

Scott, Joan W. "Experience." In *Women, Autobiography, Theory*, edited by Sidonie Smith and Julia Watson, 57–71. Madison: University of Wisconsin Press, 1998.

Simone, Nina, with Stephen Cleary. *I Put a Spell on You*. New York: Pantheon, 1992.

Skin (Deborah Dyer) with Lucy O'Brien. *It Takes Blood and Guts*. London: Simon & Schuster, 2021.

Slick, Grace. *Somebody to Love: A Rock and Roll Memoir*. New York: Grand Central Publishing, 1999.

Smith, Patti. *Just Kids*. New York: Bloomsbury, 2011.

Smith, Patti. *M Train*. New York: Bloomsbury, 2016.

Smith, Patti. *Year of the Monkey*. New York: Bloomsbury, 2020.

Smith, Sidonie, and Julia Watson. *Reading Autobiography: A Guide for Interpreting Life Narratives*. 2nd ed. Minneapolis: University of Minnesota Press, 2010.

Smith, Sidonie, and Julia Watson, eds. *Interfaces: Women, Autobiography, Image, Performance*. Ann Arbor: University of Michigan Press, 2003.

Smith, Sidonie, and Julia Watson, eds. *Women, Autobiography, Theory: A Reader*. Madison: University of Wisconsin Press, 1998.

Stein, Daniel, and Martin Butler. "Musical Autobiographies: An Introduction." *Popular Music & Society* 38 (2015): 115–121.

Tutti, Cosey Fanni. *Art, Sex, Music*. London: Faber & Faber, 2017.

Valentine, Kathy. *All I Ever Wanted: A Rock 'n' Roll Memoir*. Austin: University of Texas Press, 2020.

Warwick, Jacqueline, and Allison Adrian, eds. *Voicing Girlhood in Popular Music: Performance, Authority, Authenticity*. London: Routledge, 2016.

Watson, Laura. "Reading Lyrics, Hearing Prose: Morrissey's *Autobiography*." In *Music, Memory and Memoir*, edited by Robert Edgar, Fraser Mann, and Helen Pleasance, 119–132. London: Bloomsbury Academic, 2019.

Whiteley, Sheila. *The Space between the Notes: Rock and the Counter-Culture*. New York: Routledge, 1992.

Whiteley, Sheila. *Women and Popular Music: Sexuality, Identity and Subjectivity*. London: Routledge 2000.

Whiteley, Sheila, ed. *Sexing the Groove. Popular Music and Gender*. London: Routledge, 1997.

Wicke, Peter. *Rock Music: Culture, Aesthetics and Sociology*. Translated by Rachel Fogg. Cambridge: Cambridge University Press, 1990.

Yelin, Hannah: *Celebrity Memoir: From Ghostwriting to Gender Politics*. London: Palgrave, 2020.

PART I
MEMORY, TRAUMA, AND WRITING

1
Childhood Trauma and the Musical In-Between in Memoirs by Astrid Swan and Dory Previn

Astrid Joutseno

Introduction

Certain slant of sunlight on July evenings sends my body back to the moment when my mother and I escaped our home. Something shattered for good. I had a run-away rabbit's heart. We ran past the garden plots in front of the apartment buildings. Blue cornflowers shot out of the ground there. I halted my running to buckle up my shoes. That much I dared. We ran to a bus stop farther from home. It was particularly sad to be running away from my father. To leave him for good. Cornflowers bowed their goodbyes.[1]

This passage from *My Last Book* describes a traumatic childhood moment. In this chapter, I will examine my memoir, while also referring to an earlier songwriter memoir, Dory Previn's *Midnight Baby: An Autobiography* (1976).[2] In both artist narratives childhood plays a significant role.

My Last Book explores becoming a songwriter in the 1990s and 2000s surrounded by family encouragement, albeit lacking professional support. The book discusses the contexts of my experience, constructing relations between seemingly unrelated and fragmentary pieces. In writing about my life, the investigation into *how* to tell my unfinished story as a woman, as a creative artist, and later, as an ill person,[3] becomes important. Still, stories

---

[1] Astrid Swan, *Viimeinen kirjani: kirjoituksia elämästä* (Helsinki: Nemo 2019), 13. I will refer to the book in English as *My Last Book*. All translations from *My Last Book* are my own.
[2] Dory Previn, *Midnight Baby: An Autobiography* (New York: Macmillan, 1976).
[3] I was diagnosed with breast cancer in 2014 and have been living with metastatic breast cancer since 2017.

about making music or songwriting are patently nonexistent in the memoir. Hanna Meretoja interprets *My Last Book* as an example of "metanarrative autofiction,"[4] writing: "Swan's book contributes to a narrative in-between in which it is possible to share experiences of fundamental vulnerability without being paralyzed by shame and feelings of inadequacy."[5] In this chapter I introduce the concept of a *musical-in-between*, developed from my reading of the memoirs and from Meretoja's concept of the narrative-in-between.[6] With the *musical in-between*, I show how narratives around being and becoming a songwriter can be wide-ranging in both subject matter and temporality. What at first looks like absence may be a method of creating a more meaningful presence in the in-between spaces—in this case, the narrative of becoming a songwriter. Dory Previn's memoirs are early examples of women's rock biographies. *Midnight Baby* is an example of a near-lost-life narrative. I present it in relation to, and compare its style with, my own rock autobiography. While my memoir braids together separate narrative strands, Previn's is of one childhood. Addressing the following questions, I focus on childhood depictions and (un)acknowledged silences:

A) How do childhood trauma narratives function in the memoirs and how does narration change the trauma by contextualizing it as part of a story of a songwriter?

B) How can the absence/light presence of musical narratives be interpreted with the concept of a *musical-in-between*?

I will perform a close reading of extracts from both memoirs, drawing from feminist life-writing studies:[7] narrative studies,[8] the study of trauma, and the cultural history of women in music.

---

[4] Hanna Meretoja, "Metanarrative Autofiction: Critical Engagement with Cultural Narrative Models," in *The Autofictional: Approaches, Affordances, Forms*, ed. Alexandra Effe and Hannie Lawlor (London: Palgrave Macmillan, 2022), 121–140.

[5] Meretoja, "Metanarrative Autofiction," 136.

[6] Meretoja, *The Ethics of Storytelling: Narrative Hermeneutics, History, and the Possible* (New York: Oxford University Press, 2018); Meretoja, "Metanarrative Autofiction."

[7] Sidonie Smith and Julia Watson, *Reading Autobiography: A Guide for Interpreting Life Narratives* (Minneapolis: University of Minnesota Press, 2010); Julie Rak, *Boom! Manufacturing Memoir for the Popular Market* (Waterloo, ON: Wilfrid Laurier University Press, 2013).

[8] Meretoja, *The Ethics of Storytelling*; Hanna Meretoja and Colin Davis, eds., *Storytelling and Ethics: Literature, Visual Arts and the Power of Narrative* (New York: Routledge, 2018).

Approaching Women's Songwriter Memoirs and Trauma

To theorize women songwriters in the twentieth and early twenty-first centuries, I lean on feminist intersectionality.[9] I understand the social and cultural positions of women (artists) as result of intersecting influences, and not a matter of choice/excellence. I use the terms "life-writing," "autofiction," and "memoir" following these definitions: life-writing is a capacious term often used in feminist studies of autobiographically linked material. Memoir and autofiction might also be defined as life-writing. Life-writing studies were developed to be distinct from autobiography studies, which until the 1980s were a masculinist tradition focusing on the so-called master narratives and the worthy life stories of men.[10] Autofiction blurs the boundaries between the literary distinctions separating fiction and life-writing. It addresses questions of selfhood, narrative, and experience. Autofiction usually assumes a close relationship between the author and main character. Effe and Lawlor suggest that autofiction has to do with "self and fiction"; for them, it is hybridity and experimenting, distinct from life-writing.[11] Effe and Lawlor suggest that the term *autofictional* better serves to address autofiction as a strategy, a mode, or a practice.[12] Hanna Meretoja has suggested that *My Last Book* is metanarrative autofiction.[13] In my view, Dory Previn's memoir is also autofictional. Finally, as I understand it, memoir is a term for the published book-form entity that consists of autobiographical/autofictional elements.

Bearing witness to experiences that exceed understanding is central to both memoirs. Injurious experience in the family setting—violence and prolonged insecurity—turns to literary narrative in the memoirs. Trauma lingers. In literary studies, trauma is identified as post-structuralist or phenomenologist-hermeneutic, with poststructuralist understandings presenting trauma as single-event ruptures that are nearly impossible to translate into language. Phenomenologist-hermeneutic definitions consider trauma as experience on a spectrum.[14] For example, Meretoja has focused on

---

[9] Patricia Hill Collins and Sirma Bilge, *Intersectionality* (Cambridge: Polity Press, 2016).
[10] Valérie Baisnée-Keay et al., *Text and Image in Women's Life Writing: Picturing the Female Self*, Palgrave Studies in Life Writing (Cham: Springer International, 2022); Marlene Kadar and Sidonie Smith, "Marlene Kadar Interview with Sidonie Smith," *A/b Auto/Biography Studies* 33, no. 3 (2019): 523–531.
[11] Alexandra Effe and Hannie Lawlor, eds., *The Autofictional: Approaches, Affordances, Forms* (London: Palgrave Macmillan, 2022), 2.
[12] Effe and Lawlor, *The Autofictional*, 3–4.
[13] Meretoja, "Metanarrative Autofiction."
[14] Hanna Meretoja, "Philosophies of Trauma," in *The Routledge Companion to Literature and Trauma*, ed. Colin Davis and Hanna Meretoja (London: Routledge, 2020), 24–29.

everyday trauma, such as family violence or structural racism, which contribute to life stories where what is traumatic is also a fundamental part of the narrator's life experience.[15] I engage with trauma as such a lingering force.[16] In my reading, I suggest that the *musical in-between* is related to the temporal arrangement of both trauma and life narrative. In the memoirs, the inexpressible is not trauma, but the metanarratives of creativity.

As both researcher and author of one memoir, I am unconventionally situated. I relate in multiple ways to the subject matter via threads that can be unraveled according to feminist research ethics of situatedness. Donna Haraway has emphasized acknowledging situated research positions rather than obscuring them.[17] Following her, I think it ethical to make my relating to the research material part of coming to knowledge. Situating generates the possibility of knowledge that would be unattainable from elsewhere.[18] I become a critical auto-ethnographer, explicating products and processes of art and science that implicate myself as a producer of art.[19] With this method, I contextualize not only by referring to Dory Previn's writing, but also by describing and analyzing my own process and its consequences. My experience is part of the analysis.

Dory Previn and *Midnight Baby*

Dory Previn (1925–2012) published two memoirs: *Midnight Baby: An Autobiography* (1976) and *Bogtrotter: An Autobiography with Lyrics* (1980). Previn first found success working as a songwriter for Hollywood films.[20]

---

[15] Meretoja, "Philosophies of Trauma," 27.

[16] I recognize that mine isn't a wide understanding of trauma. Robert Eaglestone has said that for too long, trauma studies has focused on Western definitions and forced a universalist approach that has not considered where trauma narration is or how it functions outside of "Western modernity." See Robert Eaglestone, "Forms of Ordering: Trauma, Narrative and Ethics," in *Storytelling and Ethics: Literature, Visual Arts and the Power of Narrative*, ed. Hanna Meretoja and Colin Davis (New York: Routledge, 2018), 56.

[17] Donna Haraway, "The Cyborg Manifesto," in *Manifestly Haraway* (Minneapolis: University of Minnesota Press, 2016), 5–90; Haraway, "It Matters What Stories Tell Stories; It Matters Whose Stories Tell Stories." *A/b Auto/Biography Studies* 34, no. 3 (2019): 565–575.

[18] Haraway, "Situated Knowledges: The Science Question in Feminism and the Privilege of Partial Perspective," *Feminist Studies* 14, no. 3 (1988): 575–599; Haraway, "The Cyborg Manifesto."

[19] Stacy Holman Jones, "Creative Selves/Creative Cultures: Critical Autoethnography, Performance, and Pedagogy," in *Creative Selves/Creative Cultures: Critical Autoethnography, Performance and Pedagogy*, ed. Stacy Holman Jones and Marc Pruyn (Cham: Palgrave Macmillan, 2018), 3–20.

[20] Colin Larkin, "Previn, Dory," in *The Encyclopedia of Popular Music*, ed. Colin Larkin, Vol. 4 (New York: Oxford University Press, 2006).

Between 1958 and 2002, Previn released nine albums, her active singer/songwriter phase beginning in 1970 and her first three albums becoming critical successes. Previn's songs are influenced by cabaret, chanson, and the folk singer-songwriter aesthetics of the 1970s. Her material, described as "scarily blunt,"[21] leans on witty narratives, which pull the listener in through surprising, colorful, and shocking stories of disappointment across such disparate themes as romantic love, incest, and mental health. Previn's life story is filled with trauma and a string of mental health issues, but also successes and decades of writing and publishing. However, during the 1980s Previn fell into relative obscurity, and her legacy awaits reappraisal.

Midnight Baby begins with the adult author's breakdown. The remainder of the book is told from the perspective of childhood. Previn narrates a childhood during the Great Depression in New Jersey, defined by an unpredictable World War I veteran father and an alcoholic mother.[22] Short chapters are interspersed with poems. The narratives tell of a shared dream that the daughter will become a star. As a child, Previn participated in competitions dancing and singing; she also took part in musical theater and was a chorus line member.[23] The narrative voice lacks emotion, much context, or any explanation, with scenes unfolding one after the other. Reading *Midnight Baby*, as Anaïs Nin warns on the back sleeve, is often "overwhelming."

My Last Book: Essays on Living by Astrid Swan

My Last Book was published in Finland in 2019. The book consists of seven chapters, weaving together disparate times, locations, and feelings to form a map of affectively associative connections. An award-winning songwriter who had released six albums, I wrote the book following a diagnosis of metastatic breast cancer at the age of thirty-five. *My Last Book* approaches life narrative as a mode of literary creation. I ask who can tell their story, and how does a personal narrative ethically implicate others? Hanna Meretoja has described *My Last Book* as "genre-defying": "Swan's experimental narrative challenges linear narrativity and plays with the permeable border between fictionality and nonfictionality."[24]

---

[21] See Stephen Holden, "A Nod to the Path a Singer Paved, with Stories of Pain Laid Bare," *New York Times*, December 18, 2014.
[22] Previn, *Midnight Baby*, 58–61.
[23] Larkin, "Previn, Dory."
[24] Meretoja, "Metanarrative Autofiction," 133.

Insecure childhood is the background for the unfolding of the chapters. The memoir juxtaposes childhood experiences with adult life and ponderings about why a memoir is being written amid life, at the "wrong time." I am an unwilling memoirist. Under the subheading "Bird's Nest, I write: "Imagine a family at home in flames, and then living in the ruins as if no one noticed the blackened edges of the porcelain cups or how the bed has turned to cinders. Imagine a nest full of broken pieces; eggshell and dead bodies which a mother bird still hatches. So much sadness. Sadness hiding in organs and muscles."[25] This description reveals an emotional landscape through a metaphor. On the one hand, this presentation protects the writer (and audience) from re-traumatization by offering no specifics; on the other, it refuses to draw a direct correlation between experience, memory, and narrative. In a review of the memoir, musicologist Susanna Välimäki reads it from the perspectives of musicianship and gender, describing the author of *My Last Book* as belonging to the canon of Finnish women composers who have extended their creativity into multiple fields.[26] According to Välimäki, the memoir applies the theory of life writing to autofictional writing. Välimäki also relates the memoir to my academic research: the search for an ethics of care that can be found in both artistic and academic work.[27]

Traumatic Childhood in the Artist Narrative

Dory Previn's memoir opens with the rushing in of a repressed memory on an airplane. She ends up being treated for a breakdown.[28] In *Midnight Baby* the father directs violence and controlling behavior toward his family[29]; he is plagued by the belief that neither of his children are his, which leads him to imprison the whole family in the dining room.[30] Previn explains that for years, this memory was inaccessible to her. The book ends with this poem: "from then on/we were a family/we even had some fun/the boards/on the dining room door/came down/and daddy put away his gun and/i forgot

---

[25] Swan, *Viimeinen kirjani*, 26–27.
[26] Susanna Välimäki, "Musisoivien ja kirjoittavien naisten elämät, ylisukupolviset verkostot ja huolenpidon etiikka," *Musiikin suunta*, 2021, http://musiikinsuunta.fi/2021/05/08/musisoivien-ja-kirjoittavien-naisten-elamat-ylisukupolviset-verkostot-ja-huolenpidon-etiikka/.
[27] See Astrid Joutseno, "Becoming D/Other: Life as a Transmuting Device," *A/b Auto/Biography Studies* 35, no. 1 (2020): 81–96.
[28] Previn, *Midnight Baby*, 1–10.
[29] Ibid., e.g., 166–167, 188–190.
[30] Ibid., 234–245.

it happened/like something i'd been dreaming/till eighteen odd years later/ when I suddenly woke up/screaming."[31] Her story is hung on the thread of (not)remembering. There is a sense that every wish will be upended by further disappointment. The shared dream of stardom of the father and daughter is replaced by isolation. And although as the poem suggests, life did go on, the trauma reoccurred impacting the author's life narratives.

In *My Last Book*, trauma is a ghost appearing and vanishing. Trauma gushes and trickles between the lines, escaping the thread and emerging in fragments. Photograph-like memories appeared as I wrote, yet most of them never surfaced to the page as language. There is a gap between memory and narrative. Hanna Meretoja has noted that the way experience is defined has implications for how trauma can be theorized.[32] She advocates an understanding of experience "as pervaded by both the past and the future, as something we go through as embodied beings, as only partly accessible to consciousness, and as something that is constantly reinterpreted."[33] *My Last Book* approaches traumatic memory as reinterpretation. In Meretoja's narrative hermeneutics, stories function as "vehicles of change," because like trauma, the act of narration implements changes in what she lists as "pregiven categories, values, identity."[34] Narration, therefore, is a constructive element, and never merely a method of mediation.[35] What both memoirs share are their episodic, descriptive, and ruptured narrative styles. Instead of a linear timeline they transmit emotion without attempting to prove historical exactness.

In both memoirs the depicted violations have remained undetected by authorities—sometimes also unrecognized by victims themselves. Experiences of violence are woven into the everyday; events remain protected by silence and are belittled within the families.[36] Trauma narratives and interpretations are open-ended.[37] The passage at the start of this chapter describes how I ran away from home to escape the violence of my father[38]; but it doesn't reveal why, or what was happening. Instead, I describe the intense moment of escape, showing how the wish of the narrator-child is never to

---

[31] Ibid., [sic] 246.
[32] Meretoja, *The Ethics of Storytelling*, 113–114.
[33] Ibid., 218, 114.
[34] Ibid., 115.
[35] Smith and Watson, *Reading Autobiography*.
[36] E.g., Swan, *Viimeinen kirjani*, 39, 48–54; Previn, *Midnight Baby*, 166–167.
[37] Meretoja, "Philosophies of Trauma."
[38] Swan, *Viimeinen kirjani*, 13–14.

return, to be safe and free from fear. The passage ends with the adult-author commenting that this was just a one-night escape and that in the morning the mother-daughter pair returned home. In other words, these were everyday conditions rather than a single rupture.[39] The possibility of violence is merely a context in which life and creativity occur.

How, then, does narration of childhood trauma change when it is interpreted in the context of creativity? Saidiya Hartman has developed a method of "close narration" to imagine and narrate the lives of Black women in New York City in the early twentieth century. In *Wayward Lives, Beautiful Experiments*, Hartman fills in the gaps in counter-narrated lives for which there exist only criminal records and sparse photographic evidence. Hartman tells life stories of non-conformist women and traces their influence on culture,[40] an approach that shows just how much interpretation matters. These women were only accessible to her through archives that presented them as unworthy criminals, and yet Hartman portrayed their complexity, suffering, and beauty. At one point, describing the life of Mabel in a chorus line, Hartman writes: "On the dance floor it was clear that existence was not only a struggle, but a beautiful experiment too. . . . How was it possible to thrive under assault?"[41] Hartman notes the existence of extreme struggle due to structural racism alongside the dreaming, and seeing a better future for oneself. The memoirs I examine are not comparable to Hartman's book. Reading her, I have learned to notice the coexistence of struggle and a sustaining dream. In both memoirs a counter-remembering and counternarrative construction takes place. For example, the kinds of obstacles that Previn narrates are life-threatening, yet a dream shared with her abusive father (of music and dance) is interpreted in the knowledge that the author is a professional songwriter. The dream is a root.

I return once more to the first excerpt from *My Last Book* introduced at the start of this chapter. It describes how evening light reactivates a memory. Alongside the trauma of the undescribed violent altercation, I present the blue cornflowers and a sense of freedom as well as an alignment with my mother who, in the act of escape, momentarily appears to inhabit the same reality. This example demonstrates how the trauma memory and its narrative description, decades later, exist in an "interpretive continuum"[42] and

---

[39] Meretoja, "Philosophies of Trauma," 34.
[40] Saidiya Hartman, *Wayward Lives, Beautiful Experiments: Intimate Histories of Riotous Black Girls, Troublesome Women, and Queer Radicals* (New York: W. W. Norton, 2019).
[41] Ibid., 307.
[42] Meretoja, *The Ethics of Storytelling*, 54.

how beauty permeates the description. Marianne Liljeström has noted that remembering is a process that includes two acts: repetition and the visual memories or memory images that come to dominate or remain via repeated recalling.[43] Remembering is always dependent on the causal process of making memories and recalling them, which as a narrative process can also be an aesthetic one.[44] Memory relates to experience. Meretoja notes that experience and narrative are created in an interpretative continuum. Experience is always preconditioned by cultural and social parameters and via temporal definitions, or what she calls a "socially embedded process of reinterpreting experiences."[45] There is no "pure" experience that can be mediated, but living and telling occur simultaneously.[46] Narrative and experience exist in tension. Both require (re)interpretation. Meretoja describes the interpretive structure as "double hermeneutic," which means that there is the layer of interpreting experience and also creating a narrative interpretation.[47] What becomes interesting is the relationship between the two. In *My Last Book* the tension between narrative and experience is under examination, as is the coexistence of beauty and harm. In both memoirs temporality is non-linear. In a preface Previn tells that she writes to a girl who has, quite suddenly, appeared; this girl is her childhood self (*Midnight Baby*, ix–x). I begin my memoir by presenting moments from differing points of time, giving my age as the subtitle of each textual fragment. Non-linear and inventive literary styles can act as strategies that reposition the traumatic and connect it with creative work. Life stories are constantly reinterpreted. They can be made out of "radical ruptures and disconnectedness."[48] My memoir creates new meaning by relating beauty to the narrative arrangement of trauma. The telling becomes a story onto which I project myself, which then shapes *how* I remember and interpret.[49]

---

[43] Marianne Liljeström, "Ajallisuuden, ajoitusten ja ajattelun silmukoita," *Sukupuolentutkimus* 1 (2021): 39–40.

[44] Mia Hannula, "Towards an Intercultural Aesthetics: Shaping the Memory of Political Violence, and Historical Trauma in Eija-Liisa Ahtila's Artwork Where Is Where?," in *Storytelling and Ethics: Literature, Visual Arts and the Power of Narrative*, ed. Hanna Meretoja and Colin Davis (New York: Routledge, 2018), 245.

[45] Meretoja, *The Ethics of Storytelling*, 56–57.

[46] Ibid., 58. This view is supported by work on the interdependence of material subjectivity in Karen Barad, *Meeting the Universe Halfway: Quantum Physics and the Entanglement of Matter and Meaning* (Durham, NC: Duke University Press, 2007).

[47] Meretoja, *The Ethics of Storytelling*, 61.

[48] Ibid., 64.

[49] Eaglestone, "Forms of Ordering," 61.

Hospitals, Fathers, and the *Musical In-Between*

In both memoirs, childhood narratives do not function merely as recollections but are offered in relation to the development of their respective author-artists. Therefore, they are more than autobiography, and indeed for Previn, childhood is the basis for the entire book. For example, the relationship between childhood and being a creative adult is evident in the story about attempting to become a child star in musical theater.[50] In my interpretation, survival, living on, and dealing with trauma are intertwined with the creative process and the construction of narrative. In *My Last Book*, the lack of details about practicing, performing, songwriting, recording, and learning suggests that there are other constructive narratives to consider. These narratives are, for example, the disappearance of my great-aunt, the pianist Astrid Joutseno[51] from the family story, generational family silences,[52] my relationship to literature by women,[53] and my experiences of being mothered and mothering.[54] These narratives join together and break into silences, forming what I term *a musical in-between*.

A *musical in-between* in a songwriter memoir describes what gives meaning to the musical creativity and activity of the author. These memoirs achieve this by circling around the subject and telling constructive stories, while not directly addressing songwriting. The term echoes Meretoja's "narrative in-between," by which she describes the dialogic functioning of narratives; that they are not merely tools of self-understanding but form "new communities and modes of relationality"[55] because meaning in narratives is constructed in dialogue with normative narratives, for example. Thus, in-between-ness is formed between different stories and storytelling subjects both in what is narrated and in what is left out.

In a *musical in-between*, the creative process is present in the confluence of narrative strands around what is absent or scarcely referred to (music as activity, creation, human interaction). What appears as absence can also be a presence: existing in between narratives or the spaces that they create. A *musical in-between* is a dialogue between the explicit—the stories that appear—and the in-between. My extension of Meretoja's concept builds on the

---

[50] Previn, *Midnight Baby*, e.g., 14–24.
[51] Swan, *Viimeinen kirjani*, 101–103.
[52] Ibid., 55–63.
[53] Ibid., 201–219.
[54] Ibid., 166–222.
[55] Meretoja, *The Ethics of Storytelling*, 117.

dialogical foundation of stories[56] by bringing up the intra-narrative dialogue of fragments and absences. Here I note that the *musical in-between* exists in explicit narratives too: *My Last Book* directly addresses my musicianship at times. In the chapter titled "The Artist,"[57] for example, I discuss the music business I entered in the late 1990s. In one of the chapter's subsections, "Methods," I review my experience of not belonging within the contexts of classical music, being a woman songwriter, and lacking a sense of belonging to the Finnish pop tradition, working on my craft while dreaming of international stardom and experiencing professional disappointments.[58] In the rest of "The Artist," I describe making alternative pop in English in Finland. The fact that my memoir does indeed tell such narratives strengthens the sense of the *musical in-between*. It directs toward an interpretation that understands other narratives, such as the trauma stories as related to becoming a songwriter.

Like trauma, music is difficult to capture in writing. It is not only a question of senses and audio waves. One might suggest that music is absent from these memoirs, but this would be a failure in recognizing the presence of a narrative in-between. These other-than-narratives are in this case the *musical in-betweens*, full of possibility for expressing a lived experience via different senses or invited into the memoirs via that which has been told (around the untold).

Both *Midnight Baby* and *My Last Book* address paternal illness and describe the experiences of having hospitalized parents; the theme of loss comes in many forms to children of mentally unstable adults. Although neither memoir ever directly names loss, it is viscerally felt in the scenes that describe paternal hospitalizations. There is the loss of the domestic family structure, even if that was chaotic to begin with. The child also loses her sense of being cared for, because although just one parent is gone, both are absent. Mothers are left to take care of the household alone, expending their energies on survival, worrying, and grieving.

In *Midnight Baby*, Previn describes visiting her father at the veterans hospital. It turns out that children must wait outside. She waits in the garden with her aunt. This reminds her of picnicking. She is handed a mint, which mingles with her bitter experience of waving to her embarrassing-looking

---

[56] Ibid., 258–259, 265, 278.
[57] Swan, *Viimeinen kirjani*, 98–134.
[58] Ibid., 104–114.

pajamaed father, who appears on a balcony: "I looked up. He was standing on the balcony. One hand was hanging on to the ugly metal fence. Gray flannel bathrobe. No cord. Pajamas in the daytime. He was waving with the hand that wasn't holding on. I wasn't waving back."[59] The mint sticks to her throat, distracting her from her acute feelings: "Life-Saver, please. I put it in my mouth. Wintergreen. Winterbrown, maybe. Or Winter-black. Summergreen, of course. But winter-green? Never."[60] The adult-narrator holds her explanative role at bay, depicting details that hightlight her emotional bewilderment. The child is simultaneously missing her father and ashamed by him. This passage exemplifies how Previn conveys the vividness of her childish presence even as the language in use twinkles with her professional work as a lyricist.

In *My Last Book*, my father's hospitalizations shadow the narrative both in passages where I do not explicate his absence[61] and where I describe visiting the hospital. Upon writing my memoir, I often ended up telling the story around the trauma. Fragments of trauma experience appeared separately in the text. For example, I described myself at home one Christmas Eve morning with my mother, waking up and asking to open my presents:

> The kitchen is dark. The hallway is dark. Christmas is here and it is way too early in the morning. From her sleep mother has barked at me that I can open my presents already, but she is going to sleep. It feels like an eternity before I can show her what I got. My father's absence is both a relief and a stifling blanket thrown over Christmas. I cannot forgive mother's earlier tone. I am lost somewhere. I am an invisible little hopeless girl.[62]

This was a morning when my father was in the hospital. I woke up alone spending the rest of the day at my aunt's house together with other maternal relatives. What I describe is the hollow feeling of worry and disappointment, loneliness, and bafflement that eat at the expected feelings of giddy excitement related to Christmas celebration. Grief overshadows the festivities while my mother is absent too—she wants to sleep. Twenty pages later, I continue:

---

[59] Previn, *Midnight Baby*, 131
[60] Ibid., 130
[61] Swan, *Viimeinen kirjani*, e.g., the passage titled 5 on page 16.
[62] Ibid., 16.

> There is a closed ward at the hospital and an elevator that makes me anxious and where I end up with my mother and a few loonies. My father has admitted himself. He has taken a taxi to the hospital. I should know this, but for once I have slept through the catastrophe. I am taking a card to him. He lies in a bed. Next to him on another bed lies another man sleeping. They are both scary to me. Everywhere smells disgusting.[63]

The passage recounts that this isn't my only visit to the hospital, and that I quietly wish for my father to never return home. I end with a description of how a dance performance I am in becomes a joke my father will tell for years to come; in that joke there is an expression of vulnerability, pride, and love that if told otherwise could be too much to bear.[64] It is not important that the reader unite these scenes. They illustrate how childhood experiences resonate in adulthood and how interpretations of the memories are made. These narratives may have nothing to do with the historical events, yet they are central to constructing my life story.

In the act of narration, both *My Last Book* and *Midnight Baby* construct the *musical in-between* while at the same time storing memories and not representing the authors as victims alone. In this sense I see my memoir as a part of the construction of an ethics of care, which I have outlined elsewhere.[65] The memoirs offer bursts of resistance to the normative narrative of family violence that is told after the fact or forever silenced. The narrative usually has clear victims and a perpetrator. But in presenting family violence and its generational impact, these memoirs avoid blame in examining the gray areas of attachment. They describe the difficulty of family narratives that do not end with the butter knife of a clean break. Childhood is retold throughout life; it is also a beautiful story, open to one's "narrative imagination," which may, as Meretoja has noted, "engender multiple interpretations over a life time."[66] In these memoirs, the *musical in-between* invites readers to listen/imagine otherwise, which might mean putting on albums or songs, watching videos, interviews, or looking at an image. (It can also occur as gaps and ruptures, incoherencies.) Meretoja's definition of trauma, and its relation to experience as only partly consciously accessible and constantly

---

[63] Ibid., 36.
[64] Ibid., 37.
[65] Joutseno, "Becoming D/Other"; Joutseno, *Life Writing from Birth to Death: How M/Others Know* (Helsinki, 2021).
[66] Meretoja, *The Ethics of Storytelling*, 20–21.

reinterpreted, helps to conceptualize the *musical in-between*. If stories are "vehicles of change," as Meretoja puts it,[67] then songwriting is one such instrument of change and the *musical in-between* functions with the narrative elements of the memoirs constructing a depiction of songwriting and of change.

Conclusions

Memoirs, like songs, are not written in vacuums. They appear in a dialogue against what others have published or never articulated. To write one's story, a path is signposted by those who came before. For women songwriters in popular music, obvious foremothers have been few and far between. My encouragement came from poets, novelists, and the few songwriters from the twentieth century who had written about their lives and creative efforts[68] in journals, diaries, memoirs, and autofictional novels. It was not a large pool on which to draw.[69] As a young artist, my peer support came from a diary: *The Journals of Sylvia Plath*.[70] Plath's journal was a window into an artist's development, her struggles between conformity and rebellion against societal norms. Plath showed the teenage-me that women could use their voices ambitiously and artistically.[71] Heather Clark's biography confirms the singular importance of Plath's journals for seeing how women have come up against, and are formed by structural arrangements;[72] I imagine, for example, that Patti Smith's love for Plath is linked to the fact that at the latter's death in 1963, the trails of women artists were few and far between.[73] Dory Previn, meanwhile, addresses a lineage of creative women in her second memoir *Bogtrotter*,[74] writing: "Most creative women commit bloodless suicide. Sappho, Virginia Woolf, Sylvia Plath, Anne Sexton, all suicides. Emily

---

[67] Ibid., 114.
[68] Smith and Watson, *Reading Autobiography*.
[69] Although I now recognize that there is an increasing number of creative women writing about their lives: see Patti Smith, *Just Kids* (New York: HarperCollins, 2010); Shawn Colvin, *Diamond in the Rough* (New York: William Morrow, 2012); Judy Collins, *Sweet Judy Blue Eyes: My Life in Music* (New York: Three Rivers Press, 2011); Rickie Lee Jones, *Last Chance Texaco: Chronicles of a Troubadour* (London: Grove Press, 2021).
[70] Plath, *The Journals of Sylvia Plath 1950–1962*, edited by Karen V. Kukil (London: Faber & Faber, 2000).
[71] Astrid Joutseno, "'The Impractical Vagabond Wife and Mother': Constructing a Woman Artist in the Journals of Sylvia Plath 1950–1962" (master's thesis, University of Helsinki, 2009).
[72] Clark, *Red Comet: The Short Life and Blazing Art of Sylvia Plath* (London: Jonathan Cape, 2020).
[73] Patti Smith, *M Train* (London: Bloomsbury, 2015).
[74] Dory Previn, *Bogtrotter: An Autobiography with Lyrics* (New York: Doubleday, 1980).

Dickinson, the Brontës, victims of death by self-entombment."[75] For Previn too, the lineage of women artists mattered. Previn ends by saying: "Only men die for something, God and country, honor, the team. Men die for each other. Women die for themselves."[76] I bring up this passage to show that Previn too wrote into the canon of women. By mentioning women artists' deaths, she addresses the common interpretations of their life stories. Even in death they struggled to become part of shared narratives.

Childhood doesn't end; it lingers, filtering everything that comes after and changes (in) time. Childhoods are always reinterpreted, sometimes re-remembered. Previn's and my own childhood descriptions are motivated by how they relate to the construction of a songwriter and the narrative of the self. In *Midnight Baby*, childhood narrative and poems create an intertwined structure. This is a method of highlighting artistic practice in the vicinity of trauma. Previn presents the narratives of her ailment and her self-prescribed medicine, the experience as story and what can be made of/with it. In *My Last Book*, trauma and artistic process appear in fragments of how childhood memories are entwined with witnessing beauty and, furthermore, with having the wish and encouragement of others to express myself.

Constructing narrative about suffering has become central to my survival. In my memoir I write about falling ill with cancer and then making music and writing with the awareness of my impending death. The absence in both memoirs of descriptions of a life in music can better be understood with the concept of a *musical in-between*. In their narratives of childhood, both reach for a method of turning tragedy into art. This is not in itself a valuable process, but it may better shine light on the artistic process than the registration of exact dates, studios, recording engineers, or other such staples of rock biographies. Herein lies the strength of life-writing. It succeeds in painting an emotional landscape that is both the soil and the seed for one kind of truth: a song.

Bibliography

Baisnée-Keay, Valérie, Corinne Bigot, Nicoleta Alexoae-Zagni, Stéphanie Genty, and Claire Bazin, eds. *Text and Image in Women's Life Writing: Picturing the Female Self*. Palgrave Studies in Life Writing. Cham: Springer International, 2022.

---

[75] Ibid., 80–81.
[76] Ibid., 81.

Barad, Karen. *Meeting the Universe Halfway: Quantum Physics and the Entanglement of Matter and Meaning*. Durham, NC: Duke University Press, 2007.

Clark, Heather. *Red Comet: The Short Life and Blazing Art of Sylvia Plath*. London: Jonathan Cape, 2020.

Collins, Judy. *Sweet Judy Blue Eyes: My Life in Music*. New York: Three Rivers Press, 2011.

Collins, Patricia Hill, and Sirma Bilge. *Intersectionality*. Cambridge: Polity Press, 2016.

Colvin, Shawn. *Diamond in the Rough*. New York: William Morrow, 2012.

Eaglestone, Robert. "Forms of Ordering: Trauma, Narrative and Ethics." In *Storytelling and Ethics: Literature, Visual Arts and the Power of Narrative*, edited by Hanna Meretoja and Colin Davis, 55–67. New York: Routledge, 2018.

Effe, Alexandra, and Hannie Lawlor, eds. *The Autofictional: Approaches, Affordances, Forms*. London: Palgrave Macmillan, 2022. https://link.springer.com/content/pdf/10.1007%2F978-3-030-78440-9.pdf.

Gaar, Gillian G. *She's a Rebel: The History of Women in Rock & Roll*. Seattle: Seal Press, 1992.

Hannula, Mia. "Towards an Intercultural Aesthetics: Shaping the Memory of Political Violence, and Historical Trauma in Eija-Liisa Ahtila's Artwork Where Is Where?" In *Storytelling and Ethics: Literature, Visual Arts and the Power of Narrative*, edited by Hanna Meretoja and Colin Davis, 237–252. New York: Routledge, 2018.

Haraway, Donna J. "The Cyborg Manifesto." In *Manifestly Haraway*, 5–90. Minneapolis: University of Minnesota Press, 2016.

Haraway, Donna J. "It Matters What Stories Tell Stories; It Matters Whose Stories Tell Stories." *A/b Auto/Biography Studies* 34, no. 3 (2019): 565–575.

Haraway, Donna J. "Situated Knowledges: The Science Question in Feminism and the Privilege of Partial Perspective." *Feminist Studies* 14, no. 3 (1988): 575–599.

Hartman, Saidiya. *Wayward Lives, Beautiful Experiments: Intimate Histories of Riotous Black Girls, Troublesome Women, and Queer Radicals*. New York: W. W. Norton, 2019.

Hill, Rosemary Lucy, Daisy Richards, and Heather Savigny. "Normalising Sexualised Violence in Popular Culture: Eroding, Erasing and Controlling Women in Rock Music." *Feminist Media Studies* 1, no. 1 (2021): 1–17.

Holden, Stephen. "A Nod to the Path a Singer Paved, with Stories of Pain Laid Bare." *New York Times*, December 18, 2014. https://www.nytimes.com/2014/12/19/arts/music/dory-previn-as-portrayed-by-kate-dimbleby.html?searchResultPosition=1.

Holman Jones, Stacy. "Creative Selves/Creative Cultures: Critical Autoethnography, Performance, and Pedagogy." In *Creative Selves/Creative Cultures: Critical Autoethnography, Performance and Pedagogy*, edited by Stacy Holman Jones and Marc Pruyn, 3–20. Cham: Palgrave Macmillan, 2018.

Jones, Rickie Lee. *Last Chance Texaco: Chronicles of a Troubadour*. London: Grove Press, 2021.

Joutseno, Astrid. "Becoming D/Other: Life as a Transmuting Device." *A/b Auto/Biography Studies* 35, no. 1 (2020): 81–96.

Joutseno, Astrid. "'The Impractical Vagabond Wife and Mother': Constructing a Woman Artist in the Journals of Sylvia Plath 1950–1962." Master's thesis, University of Helsinki, 2009.

Joutseno, Astrid. *Life Writing from Birth to Death: How M/Others Know*. Helsinki, University of Helsinki, 2021. http://urn.fi/URN:ISBN:978-951-51-7459-8.

Kadar, Marlene, and Sidonie Smith. "Marlene Kadar Interview with Sidonie Smith." *A/b Auto/Biography Studies* 33, no. 3 (2019): 523–531.

Larkin, Colin. "Previn, Dory." In *The Encyclopedia of Popular Music*, edited by Colin Larkin, Vol. 4. New York: Oxford University Press, 2006. https://www-oxfordreference-com.ezproxy.utu.fi/display/10.1093/acref/9780195313734.001.0001/acref-9780195313734-e-48309?rskey=T8Nb1c&result=21662.

Larsen, Gretchen. "'It's a Man's Man's Man's World': Music Groupies and the Othering of Women in the World of Rock." *Organization* (London, England) 24, no. 3 (2017): 397–417.

Liljeström, Marianne. "Ajallisuuden, ajoitusten ja ajattelun silmukoita." *Sukupuolentutkimus* 1 (2021): 39–45.

Meretoja, Hanna. *The Ethics of Storytelling: Narrative Hermeneutics, History, and the Possible*. New York: Oxford University Press, 2018.

Meretoja, Hanna. "Metanarrative Autofiction: Critical Engagement with Cultural Narrative Models." In *The Autofictional: Approaches, Affordances, Forms*, edited by Alexandra Effe and Hannie Lawlor, 121–140. London: Palgrave Macmillan, 2022.

Meretoja, Hanna. "Philosophies of Trauma." In *The Routledge Companion to Literature and Trauma*, edited by Colin Davis and Hanna Meretoja, 23–35. London: Routledge, 2020.

Meretoja, Hanna, and Colin Davis, eds. *Storytelling and Ethics: Literature, Visual Arts and the Power of Narrative*. New York: Routledge, 2018.

O'Brien, Lucy. *She Bop II: The Definitive History of Women in Rock, Pop, and Soul*. London: Continuum, 2002.

Plath, Sylvia. *The Journals of Sylvia Plath 1950–1962*. Edited by Karen V. Kukil. London: Faber & Faber, 2000.

Previn, Dory. *Bogtrotter: An Autobiography with Lyrics*. New York: Doubleday, 1980.

Previn, Dory. *Midnight Baby: An Autobiography*. New York: Macmillan, 1976.

Rak, Julie. *Boom! Manufacturing Memoir for the Popular Market*. Waterloo, ON: Wilfrid Laurier University Press, 2013.

Reddington, Helen. *Lost Women of Rock Music: Female Musicians of the Punk Era*. London: Equinox, 2012.

Smith, Patti. *Just Kids*. New York: HarperCollins, 2010.

Smith, Patti. *M Train*. London: Bloomsbury, 2015.

Smith, Sidonie, and Julia Watson. "Autobiographical Acts." In *Reading Autobiography: A Guide for Interpreting Life Narratives*, edited by Sidonie Smith and Julia Watson, 63–104. Minneapolis: University of Minnesota Press, 2010.

Smith, Sidonie, and Julia Watson. *Reading Autobiography: A Guide for Interpreting Life Narratives*. 2nd ed. Minneapolis: University of Minnesota Press, 2010.

Swan, Astrid. *Viimeinen kirjani: kirjoituksia elämästä*. Helsinki: Nemo, 2019.

Välimäki, Susanna. "Musisoivien ja kirjoittavien naisten elämät, ylisukupolviset verkostot Ja huolenpidon etiikka." *Musiikin Suunta*, 2021. http://musiikinsuunta.fi/2021/05/08/musisoivien-ja-kirjoittavien-naisten-elamat-ylisukupolviset-verkostot-ja-huolenpidon-etiikka/.

2
The Monster in the House

Gender-Based Violence and Punk in Alice Bag's *Violence Girl: East L.A. Rage to Hollywood Stage. A Chicana Punk Story*[*]

Cristina Garrigós

Violence Girl

In Alice Bag's song "He's So Sorry" (2016), one woman tries to help another, encouraging her to leave her abusive partner: "You better get out! (Better get away, better get away!) / Get out now / Just because he's sorry doesn't mean he's gonna change / Just because you love him doesn't mean you've gotta stay."[1] As Bag has acknowledged, the song is based on the experience of a friend who was the victim of abuse by her boyfriend, a situation Bag could relate to after undergoing something similar in her childhood home:

> "He's So Sorry" is a song of both urgency and agency. Nobody should risk their life waiting for an abuser to change their ways. I grew up around domestic violence, so when a good friend of mine asked me for help and advice, I recognized that she was in an abusive situation. Our conversations inspired this song. When I was growing up, my father would frequently beat my mother. I would often go to school wondering if my mother would still be alive when I got home.[2]

Gender-based violence is a key concern for the Chicana punk musician. Bag's memoir, *Violence Girl: East L.A. Rage to Hollywood Stage. A Chicana*

---

[*] The research for this chapter is part of the project "(Un)Housing: Dwellings, Materiality, and the Self in American Literature," Spanish Ministry of Education, Culture, and Sports. PL: Rodrigo Andrés y Cristina Alsina (University of Barcelona) 2021–2025, PID2020-115172GB-I00.

[1] "He Is So Sorry" is included in Alice Bag's debut solo album, *Alice Bag*, released on Don Giovanni Records in 2016. Her second album, *Blueprint*, was also released on Don Giovanni in 2018.

[2] Gabriela Tully, "Alice Bag—'He's So Sorry' Video," *Stereogum*, June 7, 2016.

Punk Story (2011) addresses this issue by describing her father's violent nature and how he beat her mother in front of the young Alicia, who was powerless to prevent it. Even though her father was never aggressive with her, as she explains in her writing, the violence that she witnessed at home became an important part of her growing up, and she channeled it through the ethos of punk. This chapter discusses how, by writing her memoir, Bag explores gender-based domestic violence; it reflects on the effect that this violence had on her life as a woman and artist, and on the development of her identity as Chicana, punk musician, and feminist.

Lourdes Torres explains the rise of autobiographical fiction by Latina writers, specifically Chicanas, such as Cherríe Moraga, Aurora Levins, Rosario Morales, and Gloria Anzaldúa, as ways to subvert Anglo and Latino patriarchal definitions of culture, to create a cultural genealogy, and to theorize a politics from which to forge the survival of Latinas and other women of color.[3] "Violence Girl" is the title of Bag's memoir, as well as of a blog, a webpage, and her first 7" album (Artifix, 2011). The title highlights both her gender and the impact of her father's aggressivity during her childhood. Bag writes as a mature woman in her fifties, but the "girl" in the title invokes the girl who was a witness of the violence, and by reviving this girl through memories, she addresses the issues that shaped her life, with the violence that Bag witnessed during her formative years building up into the anger that she will later show on stage. The picture of herself on the cover, fiercely singing as her lips bleed, illustrates the violence inside her, violence that Bag seeks to articulate by explaining its origins to the readers. Meanwhile, the subtitle of the book is a declaration of her role as part of a minority ethnic group, the Chicanxs, and punk. When asked in an interview about the choice of these words in the title, Bag stated:

> I think all three words reflect the way I relate to the world. Punk is rebellion, it's the part of me that claims ownership of my life and feels empowered to shape my future. Chicana is the part of me that refuses to be erased in terms of history and culture, it comes from living in a country where the dominant class filters its values through a white and Eurocentric lens and is constantly seeking to negate the histories and contributions of people of color.

---

[3] Lourdes Torres, "The Construction of the Self in U.S. Latina Autobiographies," in *Women, Autobiography, Theory*, ed. Sidonie Smith and Julia Watson (Madison: University of Wisconsin Press, 1998), 276.

I identify as a woman and as a feminist because I believe in equality. Punk has the power both to destroy and create, so being a Chicana punk means I use my creativity to destroy the white patriarchal system and create something more inclusive.[4]

The impulse to destroy in order to create, which is in the spirit of punk, is clear in the importance that Bag gives to the role of violence in her life. The book opens with a chapter titled "Violence" in which she describes herself on stage with The Bags, wildly singing her song "Violence Girl" ("She's taken too much of the domesticated world / she's tearing it to pieces / she's a violence girl"). While dancing and singing, Bag grabs the glasses of a punk in the audience who was giving her the middle finger, smashing them. The mature narrator, who is Alice, looks back on this scene and tries to understand what made her act that way: "How did I come to unleash the wrath of Kali upon the world of punk? The answer to that question lies way back into my childhood and perhaps even before that because the seeds of Violence Girl were sown way before I was ever born."[5]

The Therapeutic Effect of Writing

As Soraya Alonso and Ángel Chaparro point out, the idea of writing a memoir came to Bag after the success of her blog, which led her to realize that there was an interest in her life and that there were issues from her past that she had not dealt with.[6] Not being a professional writer did not deter Bag from writing, as she applied the same DIY philosophy of punk to the writing of the memoir as she had to playing in a band with no musical training. As she explains, "People need to understand that they don't have to be the best writer to write, and it's the same sort of attitude that I had when I decided to be in a punk band. . . . I've always felt that I don't have to master a particular instrument to make it say what I want it to say. It's the same with writing. It doesn't have to meet any superior standard, it just has to be good enough for

---

[4] This is an excerpt of an interview that the author of this chapter conducted with her in English. The translation into Spanish of the interview was published in Cristina Garrigós, Nuria Triana, and Paula Guerra, *God Save the Queens!: Pioneras del Punk* (Barcelona: 66rpm, 2019), 18–30.

[5] Alice Bag, *Violence Girl: East L.A. Rage to Hollywood Stage. A Chicana Punk Story* (Port Townsend, WA: Feral House, 2011), 8.

[6] Soraya Alonso and Ángel Chaparro, "Punk Pioneers: Chicana Alice Bag as a Case in Point," *Lectora* 23 (2017): 94–95.

you."[7] Bag may lack writing experience, but she does have experience as an educator.[8] She knows how to communicate to the audience and has a message to deliver: she wants people to learn from her experience.

Alice Bag was born Alicia Armendariz[9] in 1959 in Los Angeles, the daughter of two Mexicans, Manuel and Candelaria. Both were born there, but Manuel always identified himself as Mexican, while Candelaria, or Candy, as she preferred to be called, considered herself Mexican American, having moved to the United States as a small child. The narration of their first encounter on a bus in Mexico foreshadows their relationship, as her future father is described as "sweaty and covered with dust and dirt from a day of construction," whereas her mother is a "very fashionably dressed lady."[10] Bag presents him as a rough, unpolished man who was affectionate toward his only daughter but abusive to his wife. The titles of the chapters are very explicit: "The Pit Bull Takes a Bride," "Daddy's Knock-out Punch," "Caveman," "The Wrestler," etc. The episode titled "Daddy Dearest" starts with the sentence "My father was a monster."[11] Bag continues:

> By that, I mean that everything I know about the deep, dark, ugly side of mankind, I learned from my father. He was like a dark sensei, passing on his knowledge through transmission to an acolyte—me. It's not that he actually did evil things imaginable, but that he tapped into the energy which makes humans capable of committing any atrocity. Some people believe that the archetype, idea or shared experience of divinity is contained within each of us. I believe that its polar opposite—the capacity for evil—is also carried within us all, like a latent gene.[12]

---

[7] Alice Bag, "It Just Has to Be Good Enough for You," *Diary of a Bad Housewife* (blog), April 18, 2015, accessed March 25, 2022, http://alicebag.blogspot.com/.

[8] Alice Bag's second book, *Pipe Bomb for the Soul* (Los Angeles: Alice Bag, 2015), is based on the diaries that she wrote while she was teaching in Nicaragua. She has worked as teacher at several schools and at the Chicxs Rockerxs in South East of Los Angeles, a rock camp that "envisions a transformative movement by communities of color where trans and gender-expansive youth, girls, and women of all ages are leaders in artistic creation, decision-making and socially conscious change" (https://www.crsela.org/).

[9] Although her birth name is Alicia Armendariz, and after her marriage she becomes Alicia Velasquez, in this chapter, I refer to her as Alice Bag because that is how she signs her memoirs.

[10] Bag, *Violence Girl*, 9.

[11] Ibid., 19

[12] Ibid., 19.

Violence can be perpetrated and experienced in many ways.[13] Gender-based violence is a "manifestation of historically unequal power relations between women and men, which have led to domination over, and discrimination against, women by men and to the prevention of the full advancement of women."[14] According to Laura O'Toole, Jessica Shiffman, and Rosemary Sullivan, "gender violence is any interpersonal, organizational, or politically oriented violation perpetrated against people due to their sex, gender identity, sexual orientation, or location in the hierarchy of male-dominated social systems such as families, military organizations, or the labor force."[15] In Bag's case, her male-dominated household is ruled by her father with her mother's passive acquiescence. Writing the memoir thus becomes, for the author, therapeutic; her narration becomes a way to come to terms with traumatic episodes in her past and with the fact that, as a young girl, she could do little to help her mother.

For instance, in the chapter titled "Caveman," Bag describes an episode of domestic violence when her mother flees the house, followed by her angry husband. Alice tries to stop her father, but she is unable to: "He walked on, unbuckling his belt. I tried again to hold him back but he pushed me away effortlessly, now gripping the folded belt with the metal buckle and prong dangling menacing by his side."[16] He reaches her mother and beats her with the belt in the neighbor's yard. When he is done, he grabs her by the hair and drags her down the street "in a public display of caveman might."[17] Young Alice witnessed the police arriving and handcuffing him; however, her mother "once again" refused to cooperate and did not press charges. Bag closes the chapter by saying that her father returned home that evening and that in the morning, everything would go back to normal.

The normalization of gender-based domestic violence among the Latinx population is an issue that gives pause. As Yoko Sugihara and Judith Ann Warner explain, the traditional stereotype "represents Mexican men as machos who are dominant and demand total obedience and submission from women and children while behaving in an independent manner

---

[13] Nancy Lombard, ed. *The Routledge Handbook of Gender Violence* (Abingdon: Routledge, 2018), 2.
[14] Council of Europe, 2011, 1, quoted in ibid.
[15] Laura O'Toole, Jessica Shiffman, and Rosemary Sullivan, *Gender Violence: An Interdisciplinary Perspective* (New York: New York University Press, 2020), xiii.
[16] Bag, *Violence Girl*, 32.
[17] Ibid.

that shows complete disrespect for them."[18] However, this stereotype also carries positive traits, since loyalty and the family are important to men. "Therefore, being macho has contradictory gender role implications: being dominant and using violence to obtain compliance as well as being loyal and loving with family and children."[19] For Gloria Anzaldúa, the Chicanx author, whereas being macho formerly meant being strong enough to protect and support a family and show love, the oppression, poverty, and low self-esteem of Mexican men have created in them doubts about their ability to protect and feed their families, so that this machismo becomes, according to Anzaldúa, the result of hierarchical male dominance. Oppressed by the Anglos, the Chicano suffers from excessive humility and self-effacement, shame of self, and self-deprecation: "The loss of sense of dignity and respect in the macho breeds a false machismo which leads him to put down women and even brutalize them."[20] In other words, the economic, social, and cultural oppression of Mexicans or Chicanos by Anglos has contributed to the frustration, and sense of inadequacy, that they project on their wives and children, perpetuating violence on them.

A Chicana Punk

Bag defines herself as Chicana. The term "Chicano," which had been used derogatorily to allude to the Mexican Americans who worked as *braceros*, was reconverted into a symbol of pride in the 1960s,[21] and the awakening of her Chicana consciousness is explained in the chapter "Chicano Power!" where she explains how, on August 29, 1970, she attended, along with her father, the famous Chicano Moratorium march in East LA to protest about the war in Vietnam. There, she is impressed by the women among the Brown

---

[18] Matthew C. Guttman, *The Meanings of Macho: Being a Man in Mexico City* (Berkeley: University of California Press, 1996), and Alfredo Mirande, *Hombres y Machos: Masculinity and Latino Culture* (Boulder, CO: Westview Press, 1997), quoted in Yoko Sugihara and Judith Ann Warner, "Dominance and Domestic Abuse among Mexican Americans: Gender Differences in the Etiology of Violence in Intimate Relationships," *Journal of Family Violence* 17, no. 4 (December 2002): 320.

[19] Sugihara and Warner, "Dominance and Domestic Abuse," 320.

[20] Gloria Anzaldúa, *Borderlands/La frontera* (San Francisco: Aunt Lute, 1987; repr. 2012), 105.

[21] Although it was the result of decades of struggle, the 1960s saw the emergence of the Chicano *movimiento*. The Chicanas vindicated stereotypes such as that of La Malinche and focused on the restructuring of gender-oppressive institutions such as the family and the Catholic Church. Amaia Ibarraran-Bigalondo, *Mexican American Women, Dress, and Gender* (London: Routledge, 2019), 63.

Berets, wearing their military outfits.[22] As the mature narrator points out, this event was empowering for Bag, leading her to realize that she was part of a minority group, the Chicanos. Bag further realizes that those with power are not always there to protect the people who need them: she narrates an incident where a bottle being thrown at the protesters ended up in a police charge. Bag now sees the policemen through different eyes:

> Throughout my early childhood, policemen had been the knights in shining armor who had rescued my mother from my father's vicious attacks. In my eyes, they had always lived up to their motto, "To Protect and Serve." That day, I saw my knights like the other people in my life: Their capacity for good was matched by their capacity for evil. It almost seemed like diametrically opposed impulses had to exist for the world to make sense. My own world was coalescing into a ball of love and hate, trust and treachery.[23]

This episode marks Alice's awakening to the fact that the police are unfriendly toward a minority like the Chicanxs (or the black population), a reflection reinforced later in the book, when she refers to the police charge against punks at a concert at the Elks Lodge on February 9, 1979.[24] In describing the police brutality toward those who were innocently attending the concert, she remembers the Chicano Moratorium, "where what had started out as a peaceful march had turned ugly in a matter of seconds."[25] As Bag writes:

> The violence was definitely provoked by the LAPD riot squad. There was no need to use force against the people who were peacefully waiting to watch a concert. There was no opportunity for concert goers to escape the attack. You had to walk or run down the stairs to make it to the exit as the riot squad walked up those same stairs, shoulder to shoulder with their batons swinging. I'm not sure what provoked the attack but, in my experience, systems of control are fearful of anything new or challenging and in 1979, punk was both.[26]

---

[22] The Brown Berets (1966–1973) was an organization focused on the education of people of Chicano and Latino origin. They were organized like the African American Black Panthers (ibid., 67).
[23] Bag, *Violence Girl*, 70.
[24] The show included bands such as X, the Alleycats, the Plugz, the Zeros, and the Go-Go's.
[25] Bag, *Violence Girl*, 304.
[26] Bag, interview by Cristina Garrigós, in Garrigós et al., *God Save the Queens!*, 25. Translated from the English by the author.

For Bag, both punks and Chicanxs are minority groups, victims of the violence of hegemonic forces, just as women are victims of the brutality of men.[27]

East LA, the Latino neighborhood where Bag grew up, underwent an enormous transformation in the 1960s, with the construction of the postmetropolis[28] bringing with it the destruction of formerly inhabited spaces to make for the freeways. This newly mobilized city was designed by Anglo politicians, engineers, and urban planners who had little respect for the houses and memories of ethnic communities: in the East part of Los Angeles, a neighborhood of predominantly Mexican origin, more than 50,000 houses were torn down between 1933 and 1980.[29] In *Mi raza primero!* Ernesto Chávez explains that East LA residents protested that the construction of the freeways would eliminate large residential and commercial areas of Boyle Heights and Hollenbeck Heights, neighborhoods that were mostly Mexican American.[30] This Chicano-directed urban violence is also remembered in Bag's memoir.[31] The chapter titled "A Near Escape" starts with Bag's mother awakening her because there was an earthquake, while Alice dreams that the bulldozers are coming to demolish her house:

> I watched our little house bouncing up and down whining like a colicky baby on its mother's knee. Standing there between the bedroom and the living room, I saw a huge crack spread diagonally across the wall. Photographs, knickknacks and dishes crashed to the floor. . . . I felt as I was looking out through someone else's eyes, shielded by a calm sense of disbelief at the destruction, unperturbed by my mother's distress as our home literally fell to pieces around us.[32]

---

[27] Bag tackles this issue in her song "White Justice" (2016), where she denounces white justice of being an oxymoron. She also addresses sexual abuse in "No Means No" (*Alice Bag*, 2016).

[28] The term "postmetropolis" is used by Edward Soja to refer to Los Angeles. Edward W. Soja, *Postmetropolis. Critical Studies in Cities and Regions* (Malden, MA: Wiley-Blackwell, 2000).

[29] Norman Klein, *The History of Forgetting: Los Angeles and the Erasure of Memory* (New York: Verso, 2008).

[30] Ernesto Chávez, *Mi raza primero! [My People First!]* (Berkeley: University of California Press, 2002), 26.

[31] Beside Norman Klein, the destruction of the houses of the Chicano community is discussed by Roberto Acuña in *A Community under Siege: A Chronicle of Chicanos East of the Los Angeles River, 1945–1975* (Los Angeles: Chicano Studies Research Center, UCLA, 1984), and Mary Pat Brady, *Extinct Lands, Temporal Geographies: Chicana Literature and the Urgency of Space* (Durham, NC: Duke University Press, 2002), among other scholars.

[32] Bag, *Violence Girl*, 71.

Although this turns out to be merely a nightmare, the threat of the destruction of the house is paralleled with the damaged marriage of her parents. Bag's portrait of her father is not, however, entirely negative, and she admits to having many things in common with him:

> I identified more with my father than with my mom. I, too, enjoyed reading incessantly, and I was comfortable being alone most of the time. At our Bonnie Beach house, we had a proper dining table, and although we rarely ate meals together, when we did, my dad and I just ignored each other and read our books while eating.... My mother never ate with me and my dad; she was always busy warming up tortillas or doing something else in the kitchen.[33]

Her mother is described as sweet and caring, but as someone who takes on a space that had traditionally been reserved for women and does not want to subvert it. She is associated with the kitchen and the sewing machine. Unlike the protagonist of Sandra Cisneros's short story "Woman Hollering Creek," about a Mexican woman in Texas who suffers abuse by her husband and leaves him with the help of two women, her mother does not dare to break the cycle of violence and denounce her father.[34] Like many women, she does not believe that she would be able to survive alone, and that her daughter needs a father. However, as Bag later explains, this abusive situation provokes a sense of frustration in Alice:

> My mother would tell me that she stayed with my father for my sake because I needed to have a mother and a father. It was a different time and a different set of values. As a child, I hated my father for beating my mother and I felt anger and frustration at my mother's inability to leave. My mother WAS NOT to blame for the abuse—that is unequivocal—but she did fail to recognize that she had the power to leave the situation. She was tethered by the fear that she wouldn't be able to survive financially and by what I imagine was societal and familial pressure to stay in a dysfunctional marriage.[35]

Bag's mother is the victim of a system where women have no agency. As a Chicana in the 1960s whose feminist consciousness remains unawakened,

---

[33] Ibid., 97.
[34] Sandra Cisneros, *Woman's Hollering Creek and Other Stories* (New York: Random House, 1991).
[35] Tully, "Alice Bag," 2016.

she adopts the position of the suffering mother.[36] The author portrays her father as a brute, but she also recognizes that her mother's codependency does not allow her to leave him: "Now that I was getting older, I started to see how my mom's actions played into the cycle of violence they were both trapped in."[37] Candelaria's inability to act "even to defend her own life... sent my anger rising to the surface,"[38] and it is not until Manuel's health deteriorates that she manages to gain confidence in herself as a woman. As Vivien Goldman remarks, "in the final years, as her father's health weakened, the marriage grew stronger: a codependent by-product of the sort of social structure and relationship that Bag whips on 'Babylonian Gorgon.'"[39]

Punk and Violence

The song "Babylonian Gorgon," like "Violence Girl," was written by Craig Lee about Bag, who onstage was recognized for her fierceness, as Brendan Mullen remarks when he says that he had "never seen a woman so angry"; Bibbe Hansen, meanwhile, describes Bag as an "Avenging Goddess."[40] When asked about this, Alice Bag acknowledges that:

> The part of me that inspired those descriptions was born of rage. It was an emotion that had been barely contained until I stepped onstage with The Bags. The origin of that rage is the abuse that I experienced growing up; abuse that was directed at my mother but which was experienced by anyone who witnessed the violent physical attacks she suffered at the hands of my father. There was self-loathing due to the feeling of impotence that went along with being unable to stop the attacks. Violence Girl, Babylonian Gorgon, Avenging Goddess—none of those were deliberate creations, nor are they a stage persona. They are all incarnations of my very real rage and fury.[41]

---

[36] This position fits the Mexican stereotype of machismo and marianismo, that is, of male dominance and female submission.
[37] Bag, *Violence Girl*, 71.
[38] Ibid., 72.
[39] Vivien Goldman, *The Revenge of the She Punks: A Feminist Music History from Poly Styrene to Pussy Riot* (Austin: University of Texas Press, 2019), 118.
[40] Bag, *Violence Girl*, 308.
[41] Bag, interview by Cristina Garrigós, in Garrigós et al., *God Save the Queens!*, 29. Translation into English by the author.

In punk, which is characterized by the exhibition of vehement, intense, and powerful emotions, as well as the release of primitive passions, Bag's rage and fury found the perfect vehicle to express those feelings. Punk has been associated with hate from the Sex Pistols' third gig, on November 7, 1975, when Johnny Rotten sang wearing a T-shirt with the words "I hate Pink Floyd" on it. The peace and love of the hippy movement were replaced by anger. As Joe Strummer explained in an interview with Caroline Coon: "The hippie movement failed. The hippies around now just represent apathy. There's a million reasons why the thing failed. But I'm not interested in why. Because the only thing we've got to live with is that it failed." And, as Coon explains, "then Strummer stood up slowly, relishing the drama, and turned his back on me to reveal, written across the shoulders of his gunmetal-grey boiler-suit, the peace and love negative: HATE AND WAR."[42]

Punk presented itself as the negative of the hippy movement; not constructive, but destructive. However, in its destructive angst, this movement created a synergy, especially among women. Punk gave women the opportunity to be rebellious, to face their fears, to not be apologetic. For Lucy O'Brien, punk values are about identification with the disadvantaged, the dispossessed, the subcultural, and as such, they offer women permission to explore gender boundaries, to investigate their own power, anger, aggression—and even nastiness.[43]

Such anger and nastiness are, of course, part of the punk ethos. As Helen Reddington remarks, the names of the punk bands themselves sound menacing: Stranglers, Sex Pistols, Clash, Slits, Dictators, Avengers, Germs, Dead Kennedys, etc.[44] In this context, many women found in punk the chance to release the anger derived from experiencing situations of abuse. For Reddington, "Violence and abuse have always been part of women's lives; punk turned fear of violence inside out and encouraged expressions of female assertiveness both on- and offstage, potentially making women objects of fear rather than objects of desire."[45] Hence the idea of an avenging goddess, or Gorgon, who can be furious and release this emotion in an artistic

---

[42] Caroline Coon, "The Summer of Hate," *The Independent*, August 5, 1995.
[43] Lucy O'Brien. *She Bop: The Definitive History of Women in Rock, Pop, and Soul* (London: Penguin, 1995), 65.
[44] Helen Reddington, "Danger, Anger, and Noise: The Women Punks of the Late 1970s and Their Music," in *The Oxford Handbook of Punk Rock*, ed. George McKay and Gina Arnold. Online Publication, August 2020. Accessed March 25, 2022, 3.
[45] Ibid.

context, is not alien to the punk scene, as it might have been in other musical genres. For Alice Bag,

> I don't know if punk created new models for women. More than anything, I think women felt like they could be themselves. Punk had its own standard of beauty that had nothing to do with what was promoted as the standard on television or in fashion magazines. This was well before punk fashion became a commodity that could be purchased at any mall, but it was about more than clothing. Punk women were not demure or soft-spoken as society had trained them to be; they did not feel the need to be led by a man. Punk women did not seek to be valued for their sexuality alone, and though there was plenty of sex in the L.A. punk scene, women were no longer relegated to the role of muse or groupie, and this was a revolutionary change. Punk allowed women to be complete human beings who could celebrate their own creative and/or sexual urges.[46]

Bag's first group, Femme Fatale, was an all-girl high school group; her decision to be in a band came after reading *Punk* magazine: "I was back to school reading and stuffing chips into my mouth. I devoured the magazine just like the chips, and promptly called Marlene to tell her about it. The magazine featured new bands like the Ramones, Television, and Patti Smith. I immediately subscribed and sought out the music they were writing about."[47] Bag's curiosity was confirmed when she saw Patti Smith at the Roxy Theater in January 1976, with Smith's performance style and physical appearance transforming the way Bag thought about female performances. She recognized in Smith a power that came from raw sexual androgyny: "She came on stage, a skinny, make-up-less wisp of a girl, and before my astonished eyes and ears, she transformed herself into a superhuman androgynous, sensuous, venomous, writhing shaman, spewing words like poison darts that pierced and destroyed my stereotypes. She held me enthralled with the magical power of a rock deity."[48] As Pierre Bourdieu remarks, patriarchal society has dominated women symbolically by making them follow supposedly feminine models, depriving them of masculine (hence, powerful) traits, and imposing a submissive model in behavior and looks.[49] Like Smith, Bag

---

[46] Bag, in Garrigós et al., *God Save the Queens!*, 26. Translated into English by the author.
[47] Bag, *Violence Girl*, 136.
[48] Ibid.
[49] Pierre Bourdieu, *Masculine Domination*, trans. Richard Nice (Redwood City, CA: Stanford University Press, 2002), 27–29.

was interested in challenging the characteristics traditionally associated with women as feminine and submissive. She wanted to subvert the stereotypes by adopting an attitude on stage that would be perceived by some as being too masculine, too aggressive and violent, "too in your face for a girl."[50]

As Reddington remarks, "Women punk singers displayed in their delivery and subject matter a sense of agency that had hitherto been missing from women's pop music. Their vocal styles, where volume and expression were to the forefront, were designed to disrupt and convey aggression."[51] In Bag's case, much of this aggression derived from her childhood trauma as the daughter of a woman who was the victim of gender-based abuse, and a Chicana.

Determined to be a rock star, Bag narrates how she became involved in the early punk scene in Los Angeles; although it was not with Femme Fatale, but with the Bags that she became best known. The Bags were one of the bands included in Penelope Spheeris's documentary *The Decline of Western Civilization* (1981),[52] which focuses on the destructive aspect of punk. For Bag, "Destruction is as much a part of punk as creation because violence and anger can be the catalyst for action and action can bring about change. Creative individuals and creative communities can derive inspiration and drive change from both negative and positive elements in their lives."[53]

It is with the Bags that the singer finally found the punk attitude that allowed her to channel her anger; following their breakup, she played in other bands, including one called Castration Squad, made up of four women with a feminist agenda and a defiant attitude. However, living a nonstop party lifestyle at the Canterbury apartments in Hollywood, a place that Bag calls "L.A. punks' messy little crib,"[54] together with a toxic relationship, where she saw herself reproducing the violent pattern in her parents' marriage, led her to self-harming.[55]

When Bag realized that she was projecting her anger and frustration onto herself, she decided to return to her parents' home in East LA, a return to her origins. Although her father had been violent with his mother in the past, his attitude had now changed, and now he was supportive of Bag: "In retrospect,

---

[50] Bag, *Violence Girl*, 221.
[51] Reddington, "Danger, Anger, and Noise,"14.
[52] The film features punk bands from Los Angeles that were playing in 1979 and 1980, such as Black Flag, X, the Germs, Circle Jerks, Catholic Discipline, Fear, and the Bags.
[53] Bag, in Garrigós et al., *God Save the Queens!*, 30. Translated into English by the author.
[54] Bag, *Violence Girl*, 233.
[55] Ibid., 284.

having a caring and supportive mother and father to provide a safety net spelled the difference between survival and disaster when I felt I was slipping off the tightrope."[56] Going back to live with her family helped her come to terms with her own aggressiveness and to regain control of her life.

Years later, when her father was about to die, Bag forgave him, although he never recognized what he did to his mother. Her mother told her, "Make peace with yourself, Alicia. Let God deal with your father."[57] The memoir opens with a reference to the violence in her and closes with her father's death, and how she found her calling working as a teacher for children, many of them undocumented migrants like her father. It is unquestionable that the figure of the father is central to Bag's memoir, as it is in her life, and also that he is a very contradictory figure; so the book becomes a reflection on how her father's violent behavior traumatized her, and how, after having learned to channel the violence and anger in her, she wants to recount her experience.

Earlier in the book, Bag recognizes the duality of her feelings toward her father:

> I learned to understand the concept of duality at an early age.... I realized that I both loved and hated my father, that a rudo—a villain—could also be a good guy. It was as much a part of Mexican culture as eating a sweet apple with salt and chili or celebrating the bleak inevitably of death by making brightly colored sugar skulls with your name on them.... I ... was a daughter of duality, caught up in a wrestling match between love and hate that was only in the first round.[58]

Love is rarely associated with the punk discourse. Alice Bag's memoir is full of violence, but to a great extent, it is also a book in which she expresses her love for her father. By making him a representative of the stereotypical Mexican macho man, she is admitting the duality between violence and affection that creates a conflict in her. She hated him because she loved him, and she could not accept the monster that he was. By writing about the violence in her house, and remembering him, Bag comes to understand the origins of both her anger and her own internal contradictions as a Chicana punk woman.

---

[56] Ibid., 301.
[57] Ibid., 357.
[58] Ibid., 50.

Bibliography

Acuña, Rodolfo. *A Community under Siege: A Chronicle of Chicanos East of the Los Angeles River, 1945–1975*. Los Angeles: Chicano Studies Research Center Publ., UCLA, 1984.

Alonso, Soraya, and Ángel Chaparro. "Punk Pioneers: Chicana Alice Bag as a Case in Point." *Lectora* 23 (2017): 83–97.

Anzaldúa, Gloria. *Borderlands/La frontera*. San Francisco: Aunt Lute, 1987; repr. 2012.

Bag, Alice. *Violence Girl: East L.A. Rage to Hollywood Stage. A Chicana Punk Story*. Port Townsend, WA: Feral House, 2011.

Bag, Alice. *Pipe Bomb for the* Soul. Los Angeles: Alice Bag, 2015.

Bag, Alice. "It Just Has to Be Good Enough for You." *Diary of a Bad Housewife* (blog), April 18, 2015. Accessed March 25, 2022. http://alicebag.blogspot.com/.

Bourdieu, Philip. *Masculine Domination*. Translated by Richard Nice. Redwood City, CA: Stanford University Press, 2002.

Brady, Mary Pat. *Extinct Lands, Temporal Geographies: Chicana Literature and the Urgency of Space*. Durham, NC: Duke University Press, 2002.

Chávez, Ernesto. *Mi raza primero! [My People First!]*. Berkeley: University of California Press, 2002.

Cisneros, Sandra. *Woman's Hollering Creek and Other Stories*. New York: Random House, 1991.

Coon, Caroline. "The Summer of Hate." *The Independent*. August, 5, 1995.

Garrigós, Cristina, Nuria Triana, and Paula Guerra. *God Save the Queens! Pioneras del Punk*. Barcelona: 66rpm, 2019.

Goldman, Vivien. *The Revenge of the She Punks: A Feminist Music History from Poly Styrene to Pussy Riot*. Austin: University of Texas Press, 2019.

Guttman, Matthew C. *The Meanings of Macho: Being a Man in Mexico City*. Berkeley: University of California Press, 1996.

Ibarraran-Bigalondo, Amaia. *Mexican American Women, Dress, and Gender*. London: Routledge, 2019.

Klein, Norman. *The History of Forgetting: Los Angeles and the Erasure of Memory*. New York: Verso, 2008.

Lombard, Nancy, ed. *The Routledge Handbook of Gender Violence*. London: Routledge, 2018.

Mirande, Alfredo. *Hombres y Machos: Masculinity and Latino Culture*, Boulder, CO: Westview Press, 1997.

O'Brien, Lucy. *She Bop: The Definitive History of Women in Rock, Pop, and Soul*. London: Penguin, 1995.

O'Toole, Laura, Jessica Shiffman, and Rosemary Sullivan, eds. *Gender Violence: An Interdisciplinary Perspective*. New York: New York University Press, 2020.

Reddington, Helen. "Danger, Anger, and Noise: The Women Punks of the Late 1970s and Their Music." In *The Oxford Handbook of Punk Rock*, edited by George McKay and Gina Arnold. Online Publication Date: August 2020, Accessed March 25, 2022. doi: 10.1093/oxfordhb/9780190859565.013.5.

Reddington, Helen. *The Lost Women of Rock Music: Female Musicians of the Punk Era*. Lancaster: Equinox, 2007.

Smith, Sidonie, and Julia Watson, eds. *Women, Autobiography, Theory*. Madison: University of Wisconsin Press, 1998.

Soja, Edward W. *Postmetropolis. Critical Studies in Cities and Regions*. Malden, MA: Wiley-Blackwell, 2000.

Sugihara, Yoko, and Judith Ann Warner. "Dominance and Domestic Abuse among Mexican Americans: Gender Differences in the Etiology of Violence in Intimate Relationships." *Journal of Family Violence* 17, no. 4 (2002): 315–340.

Torres, Lourdes. "The Construction of the Self in U.S. Latina Autobiographies." In *Women, Autobiography, Theory*, edited by Sidonie Smith and Julia Watson, 276–287. Madison: University of Wisconsin Press, 1998.

Tully, Gabriela (2016), "Alice Bag—'He's So Sorry' Video." Stereogum, June 7, 2016. http://www.stereogum.com/1881432/alice-bag-hes-so-sorry-video/mp3s/.

3
Memory and Writing in Kim Gordon's *Girl in a Band*

Ángel Chaparro Sainz[*]

Introduction: Identity, Gender, and Music

In 2012, a journalist asked Kim Gordon about Pussy Riot and the feminist movement in Russia, at a moment when this feminist punk rock band and performance art collective was gaining international notoriety following the detention and trial of three of their members.[1] Gordon replied: "Women make natural anarchists and revolutionaries because they've always been second-class citizens and had to claw their way up."[2] Years later, when asked by Jenn Pelly in another interview if she had ever had to fight for her ideas, Gordon replied with abstract but powerful imagery: "There's some unseen wall of faceless men that I have to climb over."[3] Gordon has stated that she is "kind of a sloppy feminist."[4] In that same interview, she explains in detail what she means by that: "Any ideology makes me a little nervous because there's some point where it doesn't allow for the complexity of things. I think feminism is

---

[*] I am indebted to the Spanish Ministry of Education, Culture, and Sports (PGC2018-094659-B-C21), FEDER, and the Basque Government (IT1026-16) for funding the research carried out for this essay.

[1] The original video of the interview can be found at the YouTube video platform via the Exploded View MEF channel. However, the item in the reference list comes from a publication in *Open Culture* in which, under the title "Fear of a Female Planet: Kim Gordon (Sonic Youth) on Why Russia and the US Need a Pussy Riot," they talk about the aforementioned video conversation. Kim Gordon, "Fear of a Female Planet: Kim Gordon (Sonic Youth) on Why Russia and the US Need a Pussy Riot," *Exploded View*, *Open Culture*, September 12, 2012, https://www.openculture.com/2012/09/kim_gordon_on_why_russia_and_the_us_need_a_pussy_riot.html.

[2] Ibid.

[3] Jenn Pelly, "Kim Gordon: 'There's a Wall of Faceless Men I Have to Climb Over,'" *The Guardian*, October 10, 2019, https://www.theguardian.com/music/2019/oct/04/kim-gordon-theres-a-wall-of-faceless-men-i-have-to-climb-over.

[4] Barbara O'Dair, "Kim Gordon: The Godmother of Grunge on Feminism in Rock," *Rolling Stone* 773, November 13, 1997, https://www.rollingstone.com/music/music-news/kim-gordon-the-godmother-of-grunge-on-feminism-in-rock-184535/,.

really interesting historically. It is a term for me that does belong in the '70s."[5] Her feminist position has been acknowledged by others too: "Gordon has also been known as an unapologetic critic of male hegemony, making fierce yet nondidactic feminist statements with diverse talents such as Lydia Lunch, Public Enemy's Chuck D and Bikini Kill's Kathleen Hanna."[6]

In tune with these statements, in *Girl in a Band: A Memoir*, Gordon's autobiography, gender issues are handled uncomplicatedly: "Every woman knows what I'm talking about when I say girls grow up with a desire to please, to cede their power to other people."[7] Gordon's book is a multilayered examination of identity that takes place in a liminal space of transition, where identity is approached not as something established and narrated, but as a source for self-revelation, a quest for meaning, and the promise of definition. As Gordon herself says: "When Sonic Youth toured England, journalists took to asking me a single question over and over: 'What's it like to be a girl in a band?' I'd never really thought about that, to be honest."[8] In *Girl in a Band*, the question[9] is never answered straightforwardly, but, in the process of writing it, Kim Gordon's journey into her personal memory reveals a complex process in which her developing identity takes shape. In this chapter, I examine how Gordon's identity is investigated in an autobiography in which her awareness of herself as a musician interacts with her being a woman, a mother, and a band member.

The Girl and the Band Gordon was born in Rochester, New York, but she was raised in Los Angeles. She graduated from Los Angeles's Otis College of Art and Design and moved to New York City in the early 1980s. After thirty years of pursuing a career in both art and music, she published her memoir, *Girl in a Band*, in 2015, to positive critical reception from the likes of the *New York Times*, *Guardian*, the *NME*, *Kirkus Review*, and *Rolling Stone*. It was chosen by *Observer* as one of the Best Music Books of 2015,[10] and among the fifty greatest Rock Memoirs of All Time by *Rolling*

---

[5] Ibid.
[6] Ibid.
[7] Kim Gordon, *Girl in a Band: A Memoir* (New York: Dey Street Books, 2015), 132.
[8] Ibid., 150.
[9] These circumstances are not unique. Pauline Murray, lead singer of the band Penetration, for instance, admits that people used to ask her how it felt to be a woman in a band: "'What's it like to be a woman in rock?' I never considered myself to be a woman in rock. I just thought I was part of the band. But when you look back it seems quite revolutionary, the way that the women were behaving. Females in the bands were breaking down stereotypes. Lots of these things get overlooked." John Robb, *Punk Rock. An Oral History* (London: Ebury Press, 2006), 386.
[10] Brad Cohan, "The Best Music of 2015," *The Observer*, December 17, 2015, https://observer.com/2015/12/the-best-music-books-of-2015/.

Stone.[11] In 2016, Gordon's memoir was also included among the 100 Greatest Music Books of All Time by Billboard.[12] The title's use of common nouns certainly invokes the idea of an anonymous girl and a nameless band, suggesting possible universal or paradigmatic readings of the text. However, any understanding of the book's reception must certainly fall on the woman on the cover. And also on her band—Sonic Youth.

Sonic Youth was formed in downtown New York around 1981. The band was originally founded with Thurston Moore on guitar and vocals; Kim Gordon on bass, guitars, and vocals; and Lee Ranaldo on guitar and vocals. Around 1984, Steve Shelley joined on drums; Jim O'Rourke, a well-known musician and producer, would join the band in the late 1990s on guitar and keyboards; and, finally, Mark Ibold took over on bass in around 2006. At the start they were linked with independent record companies such as Enigma, SST Records, and Homestead, but, in the 1990s, the band signed with Geffen, a major record label—a highly controversial move, as they themselves have testified. In *Girl in a Band*, Gordon recalls this moment: "we felt confident that our band had been together long enough to ensure that if for some reason the major deal didn't work out, we'd survive."[13]

Seventeen studio albums are mentioned on Sonic Youth's official website, from *Sonic Youth* in 1982 to *The Eternal* in 2009. *Goo* (1992) was included among the best 100 albums from the 1990s by *Pitchfork*; *Evol* (1986) was placed by *Pitchfork* at fifty-first among the best 200 albums of the 1980s; and *Daydream Nation* (1987) ranked seventh in the same classification. This last album is considered a milestone, even though the band laments the fact that, in certain circles, their impact is reduced to this narrow period: "For a lot of people, we're an '80s band. *Daydream Nation* is the record people hold up. That's what happens with everything."[14] The band has a broader discography, including a good number of compilations, live records, singles, and bootlegs. Sonic Youth's lengthy history confirms Craig Mathieson's statement that "The phrase 'body of work' doesn't feel physically substantial enough for their back catalogue."[15]

---

[11] Rob Sheffield, "The 50 Greatest Rock Memoirs of All Time," *Rolling Stone*, December 19, 2020, https://www.rollingstone.com/music/music-lists/books-greatest-rock-memoirs-of-all-time-161198/.

[12] At https://www.billboard.com/music/features/music-books-100-greatest-ever-7511014/.

[13] Gordon, *Girl*, 163.

[14] Olivier Zahm, "Kim Gordon," *Purple Magazine*, F/W, 14 (2010), https://purple.fr/magazine/fw-2010-issue-14/kim-gordon/.

[15] Craig Mathieson, "Sonic Youth," *The Age* 5 (June 2009): 10, https://www.theage.com.au.

From their early days, Sonic Youth have been associated with a recognizable, guitar-based sound: "They put out records that are non-stop guitar, but almost completely devoid of any 6-strings cliché."[16] Gordon herself, in the book, concedes that they were a group that relied "on the interplay of the guitars"[17] and that interplay was characterized by the use of unorthodox tunings. This innovation was an opportunity for creative improvement: "Not only did the radical approach make Sonic Youth sound like no other band; it also provided a bottomless wellspring of compositional ideas."[18] Michael Azerrad sources this fact in a practical detail: "With Sonic Youth, the approach to tuning stemmed partly from lack of technique—it's easy to get cool sounds out of an open-turned guitar—and lack of funds. They could only afford cheap guitars, and cheap guitars sounded like cheap guitars."[19] Gordon herself corroborated this idea: "At first we had really cheap guitars that didn't sound good in regular tuning, but sounded better in stranger tunings. It wasn't about having a pristine sound or being perfect. Our sound was an uglier kind of one."[20] The use of different objects, like drumsticks, to play guitars, together with the changes in song structure, the use of overdrive, or unorthodox scordatura patterns, became the trademarks of a band—one that has been continuously thought of key to understanding the indie or alternative music scene in the 1980s and 1990s—usually categorized as playing noise rock. In fact, their popularity through these two decades derived from the fact that they were reaching out to a wider audience: "One indication of how diverse the non-mainstream pop scene could be Sonic Youth, which began as a hardcore punk band but began to expand its range toward both mainstream pop and the 'downtown' avant-gardism of the minimalist and performance artists."[21]

After a twenty-eight-year career, one might expect their résumé, as Mathieson explains, to be complex and varied: "Sonic Youth no longer have a historic narrative, instead there's a succession of guitar-driven epochs rising and falling one after the other: American hardcore and skeletal minimalism, pop culture confrontation and muscular indie anthems, tectonic drones and

---

[16] Matt Blackett, "Sonic Youth," *Guitar Player*, *Guitar Player* 38, no. 9 (2004): 46.
[17] Gordon, *Girl*, 169.
[18] Michael Azerrad, *Our Band Could Be Your Life: Scenes from the American Indie Underground 1981–1992* (Boston: Little, Brown, 2012), 243.
[19] Ibid., 243–244.
[20] Zahm, "Kim Gordon."
[21] Richard Crawford and Larry Hamberlin, *An Introduction to America's Music* (New York: W. W. Norton, 2018), 499.

barbed wire soundscapes."[22] Steve Chick also highlights the band's complexity: "Sonic Youth are large; they contain multitudes. They have chased inspiration in myriad directions, trawled the sonic subterranean and flirted with the mainstream (only for as long as it suited them)."[23] The ending of the band was abrupt and unexpected for many of their fans;[24] indeed, years later there was hope that Gordon's memoir would shed light on some still unanswered questions.

Bonding in a Band

Gordon's own personal story is woven into this complex history: "On bass and guitar, Gordon was always what made Sonic Youth punk: the inspired reach of her speak-sung vocals, her declaration that 'women make natural anarchists.' "[25] Her being a member of a band is key to understanding how Gordon explores her identity and life experience; it is also interesting to explore how she examines the desire that came before that involvement. When revealing that she had for a long time been interested in joining a band, Gordon already hints at certain gender undertones:

> Guys playing music. I *loved* music. I wanted to push up close to whatever it was men felt when they were together onstage—to try to ink in that invisible thing. It wasn't sexual, but it wasn't unsexual either. Distance mattered in male friendships. One to one, men often had little to say to one another. They found some closeness by focusing on a third thing that wasn't them: music, video games, golf, women. Male friendships were triangular in shape, and that allowed two men some version of intimacy. In retrospect, that's why I joined a band, so I could be inside that male dynamic, not staring in through a closed window but looking out.[26]

---

[22] Mathieson, "Sonic Youth," 10.
[23] Steve Chick, *Psychic Confusion: The Sonic Youth Story* (London: Omnibus, 2009).
[24] The breakup of Kim Gordon and Thurston Moore affected the band that the two had founded. As might be expected, this is a major theme in any potential reading of this memoir: "The couple everyone believed was golden and normal and eternally intact, who gave young musicians hope they could outlast a crazy rock-and-roll world, was now just another cliché of middle-aged relationship failure—a male midlife crisis, another woman, a double life." Gordon, *Girl*, 3.
[25] Pelly, "Kim Gordon."
[26] Gordon, *Girl*, 102–103.

An often-quoted short piece that Gordon wrote for *Real Life* magazine reveals this fascination with male bonding. In "Trash Drugs and Male Bonding,"[27] she reviews a concert by Rhys Chatham. The piece is a creative exercise in close listening, with Gordon paying careful attention to chords, beats, sections, and tunings, all technical aspects, that do not however hamper her observation of the more social aspects of the music. Male bonding is not only addressed straightforwardly in the title, but also constantly referenced throughout the text.

It is when Gordon achieves her desire to become a woman in a band that she seems to become aware of how her self-definition is also articulated by her playing a part in a collective: "Sonic Youth had always been a democracy, but we all had our roles, too."[28] David Browne has noted how Sonic Youth's internal affiliations were a defining component: "From the start, the group dynamic had been complicated. Compared to many bands, they were a true democracy."[29] *Girl in a Band* makes it clear that being in Sonic Youth had shaped how Gordon would understand herself: "The band gave us all new identities, thrilling but protected. None of us were alone anymore."[30] In the context of this understanding of the band as a sort of a family that, as she says, "almost defines the word *dysfunction*,"[31] Gordon is conscious of her individuality, which is shaped by the fact that she is in a relationship with Moore: "I'd been careful not to come across as the female half of a 'power couple.'"[32] The couple that founded the band was still running it: "And yet the fact that Moore and Gordon were a couple, as well as the genesis of the band, was hard to avoid."[33] This reveals a personal awareness that helps Gordon identify a specific role for herself: "for a long time, I didn't want to be seen as being in a relationship. I wanted to be seen as an individual. I thought that was important."[34] Gordon did somehow find a place for herself: "I became an ambassador, a diplomat."[35] In fact, she also surveys how this balance later

---

[27] The original piece was first published in *Real Life* magazine in 1980. However, for the writing of this article I read a republished version that can be found in Miriam Katzeff, Thomas Lawson, and Susan Morgan, eds. *Real Life Magazine: Selected Writings and Projects, 1979-1994* (New York: Primary Information, 2006).

[28] Gordon, *Girl*, 3.

[29] David Browne, *Goodbye 20th Century: A Biography of Sonic Youth* (Boston: Da Capo Press, 2009), 353.

[30] Gordon, *Girl*, 136.

[31] Ibid., 136.

[32] Ibid., 242.

[33] Browne, *Goodbye 20th Century*, 353.

[34] Zahm, "Kim Gordon."

[35] Gordon, *Girl*, 242.

changes: "After I became a mother, I stepped back a lot, recognizing I couldn't be involved in every decision involving the band, that I lacked the energy, and in some cases even the interest."[36]

The Woman on Stage

Gordon displays a strong awareness of how she is projecting a certain external vision: she is keenly conscious of the visible role that she performs on stage, of her visual authority within the band. In fact, she is further developing the presence and strength of certain gendered expectations and conventions that have marked rock and roll. Gordon explains how from the very beginning she was very aware of this visual projection: "When Sonic Youth started out, I really made an effort to punk myself out, to lose any and all associations with my middle-class West L.A. appearance and femininity."[37] She has always been aware of her public image: "People become objects through their public image. There is a fascination with seeing a girl/woman playing an electric guitar, like holding a shotgun. It's a power stance, but it also feels empowering—inverting the idea of what's supposed to be."[38] Her musical career in Sonic Youth will make her be more sensitive to this process: "The increased media attention, and seeing more photos of myself, and of Sonic Youth as a band, had me more self-conscious."[39] However, she always embraces paradox, relating how she tried to maintain a certain freedom that restrained her from a full self-consciousness: "I'd spent my entire life never doing what was easy, never doing what was expected. I had no idea what image I projected onstage or off, but I was willing to let myself be unknown forever. Self-consciousness was the beginning of creative death to me."[40]

In performance, gender roles are enacted with the same discursive applicability that we perceived in other spheres of our lives. Rock and roll is affected by gendered standards that promote women as subjects of the male gaze: "Rock has always served as a harbinger of contemporary sexual and social boundaries, but this type of hollow hedonism merely reflected the

---

[36] Ibid., 242–243.
[37] Ibid., 128.
[38] Kim Gordon, "Afterword," in *No Icon* (New York: Rizzoli International, 2020), 269.
[39] Gordon, *Girl*, 161.
[40] Ibid., 150.

social confines of beauty for women in rock—submissive, white, thin, and existing mainly for men's physical satisfaction."[41] Lucy O'Brien has stated that female artists have been historically fixed within "the role of decorative-front women."[42] In her book, Gordon expresses a perhaps more intimate and emotional understanding of how identity can be performed on stage, combining different nuances. She discusses her experience when performing as an opportunity for letting herself go and flowing with the music: "Rock music as a gestural dance of sexualized electricity uses image as another instrument, a seduction of sorts, the unspoken promise to take us somewhere we've never been."[43] She goes on to elucidate how she has perceived progress from when she started performing and how the experience has shaped her understanding of the personal and emotional part that it entails: "When I first began playing onstage, I was pretty self-conscious. I was just trying to hold my own with the bass guitar, hoping the strings wouldn't snap, that the audience would have a good experience."[44]

Gordon's reflection does touch upon gendered views when she says that "I wasn't conscious of being a woman, and over the years I can honestly say I almost never think of 'girliness' unless I'm wearing high heels, and then I'm more likely to feel like a transvestite."[45] This elevated feeling of freedom and individual transcendence seems to be related to her experience of performing as an opportunity for escapism: "I feel a sense of space with edges around it, a glow of self-confident, joyful sexiness. It feels bodiless, too, all weightless grace with no effort required. The need to be a woman out in front never entered my mind at all until we signed with Geffen."[46] When Sonic Youth signed for Geffen Records, Gordon experienced that external vision that seemed to operate a certain gendered division: "It was then that we learned that for high-end music labels, the music matters, but a lot comes down to how the girl looks. The girl anchors the stage, sucks in the male gaze, and, depending on who she is, throws her own gaze back out into the audience."[47] That male gaze that determines the definition of the feminine is also operational in music: "Since our music can be weird and dissonant, having

---

[41] Maria Raha, *Cinderella's Big Score: Women of the Punk and Indie Underground* (Cypress, CA: Seal Press, 2005), 111.
[42] Lucy O'Brien, *She Bop: The Definitive History of Women in Popular Music* (London: Jawbone Press, 2012), 12.
[43] Gordon, "Afterword."
[44] Gordon, *Girl*, 125.
[45] Ibid., 125.
[46] Ibid., 125.
[47] Ibid., 4.

me center stage also makes it that much easier to sell the band. *Look, it's a girl, she's wearing a dress, and she's with those guys, so things must be okay.*"[48]

Becoming a Mother

Another important element in my analysis is motherhood. Motherhood is key to the articulation of a further stage in Gordon's self-exploration: "Coco Hayley Gordon Moore, born July 1, 1994. Yes, she changed our lives, and no one is more important to me. But the band played on."[49] In that transition, Gordon's paradigm is significantly modified; she evolved from being the girl in the band to the mother in the band: "Having a baby also created a huge identity crisis inside of me. It didn't help that during press interviews, journalists always said, 'What's it like to be a rock-and-roll mom?' just as over the last decades they couldn't help asking, 'What's it like to be a girl in a band?'"[50] Gordon explains in the book that she found it difficult to provide a good answer: "It's a question I could never answer to my, or anyone else's, satisfaction without giving one of those 'Like any woman balancing a family and a job . . .' answers—the most boring one I could think of, which only seems appropriate."[51] Motherhood did alter her role in Sonic Youth, but she shows confidence and ease with this new withdrawal, which indeed she seems to approve, in part because music is invoked as an opportunity for agreement and consensus: "I trusted Thurston to make good decisions. In response, he would always present the available options to me and for the most part I concurred with him. I was just more selective about what I cared about."[52] At home, music works as a source of harmony: "the music connected us, taking the place of words, and we ended up in agreement about those things."[53]

According to Lucy O'Brien, women hit the professional glass ceiling because motherhood continues to be thought of as mainly their duty, with the result that some women feel guilty when separating from their children to rehearse or perform.[54] In other words, "Marriage and motherhood were

---

[48] Ibid., 4.
[49] Ibid., 201.
[50] Ibid., 221.
[51] Ibid., 238.
[52] Ibid., 243.
[53] Ibid., 219.
[54] O'Brien, *She Bop*, 95.

considered incompatible with the image of rockin' country girl."[55] In Gordon's memoir, expectations and roles do also appear on the horizon: "Traveling to California with a two-month-old baby was another 'new mom' thing to have to worry about; dripping breast milk during a video shoot is not very rock!"[56] The source for part of that discriminating standardization derives from practical hindrances that can be then used as excuses or one-sided justifications. Gordon pragmatically explains that the main problem with motherhood in rock and roll was operational: "The hardest part of being a mother in a band had to do with logistics."[57] "Scheduling is our biggest nightmare," confessed Gordon in an interview.[58] She is referring to the banal elements of touring: "Packing, unpacking, rushing to catch planes, boarding a van to the hotel and then to sound check."[59] She also mentions personal hygiene and elimination needs: "Then there were the dressing rooms and bathrooms. Every female musician who has ever toured has a mental history ingrained of what the tour was like, based on the dressing rooms backstage and the dingy bathrooms."[60]

Such a functional and/or pragmatic perspective always comes accompanied by other reflections, in which authority and gender are discussed from a personal perspective that rejects moral judgments but offers universal assumptions. Time is also mentioned when she is asked about how her daughter had changed her work plans: "I don't know; I have less time, but on the other hand I often feel more relaxed about certain things. You know what your priorities are, what your battles are."[61]

Motherhood had altered Gordon's role in the band as well as the balance in her marriage; she admits this with detachment and without remorse, expressing with expansive significance how she and Moore would find in music an opportunity for release. In the same way that music has also been a source of relief in other circumstances: "All the hours and years since then inside vans, on buses, in airplanes and airports, in recording studios and lousy dressing rooms and motels and hotels were possible only because of the music that sustained that life."[62] Those musical references elevate the

---

[55] Sheila Whiteley, *Women and Popular Music: Sexuality, Identity and Subjectivity* (Oxford: Routledge, 2000), 122.
[56] Gordon, *Girl*, 202.
[57] Ibid., 232.
[58] Zahm, "Kim Gordon."
[59] Gordon, *Girl*, 232.
[60] Ibid., 233.
[61] O'Dair, "Kim Gordon."
[62] Gordon, *Girl*, 10.

potential interpretation of her examination of motherhood, one that Gordon links meaningfully with her own personal identity: "Having a baby also created a huge identity crisis inside of me."[63]

However, in the domestic sphere, that identity crisis is also articulated as a couple's issue, since parenthood has modified their intimacy and routine: "it made me feel like I was the only one in control, the only one looking out for us as a family, the lighthouse keeper."[64] Gordon does not accuse Moore of doing anything wrong as a father—"Thurston immediately took to fatherhood. He was a natural, in fact"[65]—but she acknowledges the lack of balance in the sharing of responsibility: "Like most new moms, I found that no matter how just and shared you expect the experience to be, or how equal the man thinks parenting should be. It isn't. Most child-raising falls on women's shoulders."[66] Somehow, that imbalance is, for Gordon, generic and she links this to the female body: "that desire to make the crying stop not only to comfort your baby but for your own body's sake."[67]

In conclusion, as she confesses, her role had been modified and a process of renovation and adjustment was on its way: "I wasn't always comfortable in that role, but I had little choice. I had to do what was right for our family."[68] As it is told in the book, her domestic role is definitely tested: "Coco once repeated to me something a friend's mother had said to her, that the reason I couldn't do anything—by which I assumed she meant domestic things like crafts, sewing, or baking—was because I was a musician."[69] She is astonished when she realizes how other people perceives her: "Even when you're in the public eye, you never understand how you come across to other people."[70] Whether there is remorse, disappointment, criticism, or sadness, the point is that her resolution resolves it: "I never wanted to be a housewife. I never wanted to be anything other than who I was."[71] That "who I was" evokes that construction of identity as the sum of different parts that she is balancing in her writing.

---

[63] Ibid., 221.
[64] Ibid., 221
[65] Ibid., 220.
[66] Ibid., 220.
[67] Ibid., 220.
[68] Ibid., 221.
[69] Ibid., 233.
[70] Ibid., 241.
[71] Ibid., 234.

Legacy, Heritage, Tradition

In the book, that resolution is designated as partially originated from an bequeathed vitality. One way to observe this (and some other aspects that I have explored in this chapter) is through an analysis of Sonic Youth's lyrics, even though, in her memoir, Gordon confesses that the writing of lyrics in Sonic Youth was very arbitrarily done: "Critics would point out how meaningful the lyrics were, not realizing how randomly they came about in the first place."[72] However, there is still space for a significant interpretation of those lyrics, and a feminist approach seems pertaining, since different views on gender emerge in some lyrics.[73] For instance, in "Brave Men Run," Gordon evokes the memory "of the pioneer women in my mother's family slogging their way out to California through Panama, and my grandmother being a single parent during the Depression with no real income."[74] She explains later that she had heard stories about the strength of these women: "My great-grandmother who sold sewing patterns up and down the West Coast in the 1800s. My grandmother, traveling all over with a brood of five kids, finally landing in Kansas during the Great Depression. Stoic, enduring, no questions, no complaints."[75] Legacy, heritage. The bonding between women is not merely an isolated subject of one particular lyric, however; it is a recurrent theme in the book. That bonding is visible in Gordon's artistic involvement. For instance, when she explores her vocal performance, finding inspiration in previous female examples: "When the band first started, I went for a vocal approach that was rhythmic and spoken, but sometimes unleashed."[76] She expands on her explanation by providing a deeper analysis of how women have been limited by gendered musical expectations: "In general, though, women aren't really allowed to be kick-ass";[77] and she extends this conclusion to other realms of culture and life: "Culturally we don't allow women to be as free as they would like, because that is frightening. We either shun those women or deem them crazy."[78] She ends her analysis by

---

[72] Ibid., 123.
[73] Other examples can be found in songs such as "Contre Le Sexisme," "Shaking Hell," "Swimsuit Issue," or "Little Trouble Girl," for instance. Regarding the last one, in the book, Gordon states: "'Little Trouble Girl' is about wanting to be seen for who you really are, being able to express those parts of yourself that aren't 'good girl' but that are just as real and true." Ibid., 203.
[74] Ibid., 4.
[75] Ibid., 141.
[76] Ibid., 127.
[77] Ibid., 127.
[78] Ibid., 127.

mentioning some specific names, among them Janis Joplin, Billie Holiday, and Kathleen Hanna.[79]

These names reveal a specific musical need that Gordon tackles in her memoir: that women had not enjoyed a solid tradition in which they could embed their attempts to become involved in rock. And such a tradition is necessary if female musicians are to be a part of the music scene: "Other women needed a catalyst—and seeing other women play live made performing seem easy enough to try."[80] The lack of support and validation that comes from the invisibility suffered by women as potential role models may lead those who seek a rock career to the conclusion that female marginalization is the norm: "Without knowledge that other girls have successfully transgressed the gendered barriers of rock musicianship, aspiring female rock performers likely feel isolated and unsupported in their practices, often losing interest after only a short while."[81] Gordon has explained how she found inspiration and support in those examples from before and now: "People like PJ Harvey and Patti Smith have done it, but as with all true rock chicks, they are more than an image of the sum of their parts."[82] In another interview, she sets another example: "There are a lot of bands, including punk bands, with women in them. I was inspired by bands like The Slits."[83] In that same interview, she insists on the importance of Pussy Galore.[84] Both in *Girl in a Band*, and in other interviews, she expands on this topic, focusing on female musicians such as Madonna or Karen Carpenter. For the latter, she wrote "Tunic (Song for Karen)" (*Goo*, 1990), a song she thoroughly explores in the book; regarding Madonna, she says: "I think that she changed the way that people write about women in rock."[85]

In referring to particular women who might become the models that would establish a female foundation in rock and roll, Gordon also mentions Lydia Lunch, Debbie Harry, and the Raincoats: "I found the British band the Raincoats both cool and inspirational. They were an all-girl post-punk band, playing noncommercial music—rhythmic and off-kilter. They came across as ordinary people playing extraordinary music. They didn't use typical

---

[79] Ibid., 127.
[80] Helen Reddington, *The Lost Women of Rock Music: Female Musicians of the Punk Era* (Sheffield: Equinox, 2012), 27.
[81] Mary Kearney, *Gender and Rock* (Oxford: Oxford University Press, 2017), 115.
[82] Kim Gordon, "The Perfect Rock Chick," *The Guardian*, June 3, 2001.
[83] Zahm, "Kim Gordon."
[84] Julie Carfitz, also in Pussy Galore, worked with Gordon in the project Free Kitten.
[85] O'Dair, "Kim Gordon."

instrumentation, either."[86] This last declaration works as a perfect illustration of how Gordon envisions her identity within the realm of womanhood. In fact, Gordon's performing in Sonic Youth and her artistic career, whether for its outsider's eye or for the subplot of her lyrics, reveals one fresh model, under construction in the book, which articulates the complexity and richness of female participation in punk and rock and roll music.

An Open Ending: Conclusions

Susan McClary has denoted how music operates as a vital tool for the formation of individual identities: "Along with another influential media such as film, music teaches us how to experience our own emotions, our own desires, and even (especially in dance) our own bodies. For better or for worse, it socializes us."[87] In surveying Gordon's memoir, I felt obliged to focus on the issue of identity and self-representation. However, identity in this memoir is not something that is apparently consolidated and then confirmed by retrospective telling. It is rather epitomized in the aspirational desire for questioning and exploration. In the classic notion, memoirs are related to concepts such as preservation, unity, completion, and authority: "identity as self-contained unit that can be efficiently wrapped in language."[88] On the contrary, Gordon's autobiographical exercise divulges a sense of identity that coincides with James Olney's understanding of selfhood: "by its very nature, the self is (like the autobiography that records and creates it) open-ended and incomplete: it is always in process or, more precisely, is itself a process."[89]

In *Girl in a Band*, then, facts are not delivered from a safe distance. Gordon's survey of the most important events in her life is arranged as a composition of discovery and searching, one that is closely linked to her determination and confidence. Gordon's memoir, from my point of view, reveals an emotional attempt at self-definition. Gordon has confessed that "I'm a relatively shy person, but I love being challenged and putting myself in positions that are scary."[90] She traces a personal journey, one in which dichotomies are

---

[86] Gordon, *Girl*, 150.
[87] Susan McClary, *Feminine Endings* (Minneapolis: University of Minnesota Press, 1991), 53.
[88] Kathleen Boardman and Gioia Woods, *Western Subjects: Autobiographical Writing in the North American West* (Salt Lake City: University of Utah Press, 2004), 17.
[89] James Olney, *Autobiography: Essays Theoretical and Critical* (Princeton, NJ: Princeton University Press, 1980), 25.
[90] O'Dair, "Kim Gordon."

erased and connection is exercised. Her determination to pursue an artistic and musical career is always laced with candid confessions of uncertainty and shrewdness, a sense of unpretentiousness and self-consciousness that does not impair her resolution to persevere. Her identity is established in a liminal territory that seems far-reaching, "scary" but still rich in personal fulfillment.

This memoir significantly ends with a guess: "I know, it sounds like I'm someone else entirely now, and I guess I am."[91] Gordon is in a car, and she has to take a plane; her journey, then, will not end here. Because it thus ends with a new beginning, perhaps this is the best possible ending for a memoir whose first chapter was entitled "The End."

Bibliography

Azerrad, Michael. *Our Band Could Be Your Life: Scenes from the American Indie Underground 1981–1991*. Boston: Little, Brown, 2012.

Blackett, Matt. "Sonic Youth." *Guitar Player* 38, no. 9 (2004): 46–162.

Boardman, Kathleen A., and Gioia Woods, eds. *Western Subjects: Autobiographical Writing in the North American West*. Salt Lake City: University of Utah Press, 2004.

Browne, David. *Goodbye 20th Century: A Biography of Sonic Youth*. Boston: Da Capo, 2009.

Chick, Steve. *Psychic Confusion: The Sonic Youth Story*. London: Omnibus, 2009.

Cohan, Brad. "The Best Music Books of 2015." *Observer*, December 17, 2015. https://observer.com/2015/12/the-best-music-books-of-2015/.

Crawford, Richard, and Larry Hamberlin. *An Introduction to America's Music*. New York: W. W. Norton, 2018.

Gordon, Kim. "Afterword." In *Kim Gordon: No Icon*, 259. New York: Rizzoli International, 2020.

Gordon, Kim. "Fear of a Female Planet: Kim Gordon (Sonic Youth) on Why Russia and the US Need a Pussy Riot." *Open Culture*, September 12, 2012. https://www.openculture.com/2012/09/kim_gordon_on_why_russia_and_the_us_need_a_pussy_riot.html.

Gordon, Kim. *Girl in a Band: A Memoir*. New York: Dey Street Books, 2015.

Gordon, Kim. "The Perfect Rock Chick." *The Guardian*, June 3, 2001. https://www.theguardian.com/theobserver/2001/jun/03/life1.lifemagazine3.

Gordon, Kim. "Trash Drugs and Male Bonding." In *Real Life Magazine: Selected Writings and Projects 1979–1984*, edited by Miriam Katzeff, Thomas Lawson, and Susan Morgan, 46. New York: Primary Information, 2006.

Kearney, Mary C. *Gender and Rock*. Oxford: Oxford University Press, 2017.

Mathieson, Craig. "Sonic Youth." *The Age*, June 5, 2009, 10. https://www.theage.com.au.

McClary, Susan. *Feminine Endings*. Minneapolis: University of Minnesota Press, 1991.

---

[91] Gordon, *Girl*, 273.

O'Brien, Lucy. *She Bop: The Definitive History of Women in Popular Music.* London: Jawbone Press, 2012.

O'Dair, Barbara. "Kim Gordon: The Godmother of Grunge on Feminism in Rock." *Rolling Stone* 773, November 13, 1997. https://www.rollingstone.com/music/music-news/kim-gordon-the-godmother-of-grunge-on-feminism-in-rock-184535/.

Olney, James, ed. *Autobiography: Essays Theoretical and Critical.* Princeton, NJ: Princeton University Press, 1980.

Pelly, Jenn. "Kim Gordon: 'There's a Wall of Faceless Men I Have to Climb Over,'" *The Guardian*, October 10, 2019. https://www.theguardian.com/music/2019/oct/04/kim-gordon-theres-a-wall-of-faceless-men-i-have-to-climb-over.

Raha, Maria. *Cinderella's Big Score. Women of the Punk and Indie Underground.* Cypress, CA: Seal Press, 2005.

Reddington, Helen. *The Lost Women of Rock Music. Female Musicians of the Punk Era.* Sheffield: Equinox, 2012.

Robb, John. *Punk Rock. An Oral History.* London: Ebury Press, 2006.

Sheffield, Rob. "The 50 Greatest Rock Memoirs of All Time: Awesome Rock & Roll Reads, from Keith Richards and Patti Smith to Slash and Nikki Sixx." *Rolling Stone*, December 19, 2020. https://www.rollingstone.com/music/music-lists/books-greatest-rock-memoirs-of-all-time-161198/.

Whiteley, Sheila. *Women and Popular Music. Sexuality, Identity, and Subjectivity.* Oxford: Routledge, 2000.

Zahm, Olivier. "Kim Gordon." *Purple Magazine F/W* 14 (2010). https://purple.fr/magazine/fw-2010-issue-14/kim-gordon/.

4
Memory, Truth, and Narrative Ethics in Christina Rosenvinge's *Debut*

Marika Ahonen

You will forget the thousands of mornings from your childhood with exquisitely squeezed orange juice made by mom and you will remember only one, the one when you had the fantastic idea of putting the fork in the socket and felt for the first time the fierce lash of electricity. Hundreds of comforting breakfasts with butter rolls and unconditional love will vanish beyond repair. There will only remain the 220-volt jolt that ran through your little sugared body under the ironed uniform, although, in reality, it happened only once. And the function of the memory is not to keep you happy, even though you live through many decades without getting electrocuted. It's not a perfect machine.[1]

This is how Spanish singer-songwriter Christina Rosenvinge contemplates the nature of her memory in her autobiographical work, *Debut: Cuadernos y canciones* (*Debut: Notebooks and Songs*). As the lines indicate, Rosenvinge does not consider memory to be trustworthy, a notion that casts a light over her book in its entirety. We are not to expect, in other words, a full summary of Rosenvinge's life, but a selected compilation of fragmentary memories. Similarly, as Rosenvinge's quote suggests, it is easier to remember "the electrocutions" rather than the peaceful moments of everyday life, with Rosenvinge's notion of memory thus linking it to trauma.

Despite the emphasis on memory's fragmented nature and its connection to trauma, memory in *Debut* is also closely tied to the theme of songwriting, as Rosenvinge states: "I do not know why among the few everyday images that my memory keeps intact are those in which a song appeared."[2]

---

[1] Christina Rosenvinge, *Debut: Cuadernos y canciones* (Barcelona: Literatura Random House 2019). 9. All the translations from Spanish to English by Marika Ahonen.
[2] Ibid., 10.

Rosenvinge wonders why she recalls so vividly the emergence of a particular song, connecting the meaning of songwriting to her survival: "Why has my brain decided that it's worthwhile preserving so many details of those innocuous scenes, in which I'm almost always alone, and not others connected to life moments of much greater importance? How is music interwoven with my survival as an animal?"[3] Here Rosenvinge associates the memories (electrocutions) specifically to her songwriting. As cultural historian Anna Green argues, to understand a particular history and its culture is to understand how one experiences and locates oneself in a certain place and time. This brings with it the further question of what gives meaning to one's actions, and what are the possibilities in a certain time and place of acting in a certain way.[4] In my interpretation, Rosenvinge relates the meaning of songwriting to her entire existence: it is a way of dealing with traumas and hence of surviving. Playing with the concept of "truth" can thus be thought of as a technique that facilitates discussion of the painful issues from which the songs often emerge.

In this chapter, I examine the themes of memory, truth, and narrative ethics in Rosenvinge's book. More specifically, I reflect upon the ethical possibilities of storytelling as conceived in her memoir, focusing on the issue through the lens of narrative ethics, in that ultimately, memory and songwriting connect to questions of survival. This approach seeks to understand how narratives take shape and are repeated under different forms, thus imbuing us with the capacity to transform our previous understanding.[5] Narrative ethics is thus connected to the concept of *possible*, drawing from literary historian Hanna Meretoja's *Ethics of Storytelling Narrative Hermeneutics, History, and the Possible*, in which the author emphasizes that interpretation is not so much about unveiling deep meanings of narratives, but rather about understanding how narratives, in their performative nature, negotiate the possibilities of acting out.[6] Meretoja also reminds us that "possible selves are not only cognitive, but also have a strong existential-ethical dimension: they provide visions of what kind of life one could and would like to live."[7] So that

---

[3] Ibid., 10.
[4] Anna Green, *Cultural History* (New York: Palgrave Macmillan 2008), 4.
[5] For an analysis of narrative ethics in Rosenvinge's songwriting, see Marika Ahonen, "Sirens, Narrative Ethics, and Christina Rosenvinge's 'Mi vida bajo el agua,'" *Cultural History* 12, no. 1 (April 2023): 120–138.
[6] Hanna Meretoja, *Ethics of Storytelling: Narrative Hermeneutics, History, and the Possible* (New York: Oxford University Press 2018), 10.
[7] Ibid., 48.

although memoirs are indeed about the past, they are written in the present, while gesturing toward the future: and Rosenvinge's memoir is no exception.

Rosenvinge's Journey in Music

Rosenvinge has a lengthy history in music: though she works mainly in Spain, she also does so in the United States and has toured in Latin America. Works such as her memoir therefore offer intriguing source material for a study of singer-songwriters in both the transnational and the Spanish contexts. In their article on singer-songwriters in Spain, Fernán del Val and Stuart Green state that women artists have typically been prevented from entering the field since male artists have traditionally been valued more highly. New research, they argue, is needed to recognize and examine the work of singer-songwriters such as Rosenvinge, so as to consider the ways in which women challenge and transform the figure of the singer-songwriter.[8] To reach an understanding of what Rosenvinge's memoir can offer us, then, it is also important to understand her personal story and how it intertwines with the wider music world.

Rosenvinge was born when Spain was living under the National Catholic regime of Francisco Franco. Rosenvinge's parents had moved to Spain from Denmark in the 1950s, and Christina was the youngest of four siblings. According to Rosenvinge, her father was an admirer of Franco, which can be seen in her family dynamics also: her mother was a homemaker, and Rosenvinge was raised to become a good spouse for her future husband. Rosenvinge used music to rebel against this role from an early age, by writing lyrics that took an oppositional stance on women's role in society, a position that has always been characteristic of Rosenvinge's work.[9]

To date, Rosenvinge has made nineteen albums: the first seven with different groups, and the rest as a solo artist. She cannot easily be categorized,

---

[8] Fernán del Val and Stuart Green, "Transitions of the *Cantautor*: Aesthetics, Politics and Authenticity in Spanish Popular Music from the Late Franco Dictatorship to the Present Day," in *The Singer-Songwriter in Europe: Paradigms, Politics and Place*, ed. Isabelle Marc and Stuart Green (New York: Routledge 2016), 176.

[9] Christina Rosenvinge, interviews by Marika Ahonen, Madrid: December 4, 2018; June 20, 2019; November 8, 2021. I have interviewed Rosenvinge three times for a doctoral dissertation that I am currently working on—*Memory, Music, and Narrative Ethics: Christina Rosenvinge as a Transnational Storyteller*. The interviews I have conducted can be used for future research as I will place them in the History, Culture and Arts research archive (Faculty of Humanities, University of Turku).

as she has performed in many different genres down the years: punk, rock, pop, indie, and so on. Music genres are not fixed but overlap, and are essentially cultural and historical, attached to a certain place and time, so in this chapter when I discuss musical genres, I do not consider them primarily in a musicological sense, but rather culturally, by using the concept of *genre* as an analytical tool. Music genres, with their aesthetics, styles, and values, can be articulated in many ways: through the themes of the music, the appearance of the visual material, the ways of using voice and lyrics, and also, importantly, through other people: musicians, industries, and audiences. As Fabian Holt states, "genre is not only 'in the music,' but also in the minds and bodies of particular groups of people who share certain conventions. These conventions are created in relation to particular musical texts and artists and the contexts in which they are performed and experienced."[10]

Rosenvinge started out with punk in Madrid, at the beginning of the 1980s. In this period, punk offered a new aesthetics for members of a younger generation seeking to differentiate themselves from both their parents and Franco's regime. Following Franco's death in 1975, a cultural movement emerged in Spain known as La Movida Madrileña ("The Madrid Scene"): Rosenvinge was a part of this movement and, at the age of fifteen, wrote her first punk-style song for her first band, Ella y Los Neumáticos.[11] Punk in Spain thus developed in a post-Franco atmosphere of liberation from the old regime's moral values,[12] with music offering Rosenvinge a way to rebel.

After the punk band, Rosenvinge, along with guitarist Álex de la Nuez and bassist Massimo Rossi, started to work in more pop-oriented music. Their group Magia Blanca (White Magic) published a maxi-single in 1985, which was also the trio's last. After Magia Blanca, Rosenvinge formed with Álex de la Nuez a duo, Álex & Christina (1989), who had a hit single ¡Chas! y aparezco a tu lado ("Chaz and I show up at your side").[13] Both punk and pop then offered new models of behavior and of having fun. Rosenvinge emerged early on as a writer of the lyrics, often playing with the notions of a "good" and a "bad" woman: for example, women's traditional roles are rejected when Rosenvinge performs in the music video of "El souvenir" as a bored

---

[10] Fabian Holt, *Genre in Popular Music* (Chicago: University of Chicago Press 2007), 2.
[11] Jordi Bianciotto, "Flor rara," in *Un caso sin resolver* (Madrid: Warner Music Spain, 2011), 11.
[12] Mark Allinson, "Alaska: Star of Stage and Screen and Optimistic Punk," in *Constructing Identity in Contemporary Spain. Theoretical Debates and Cultural Practice*, ed. Jo Labanyi (New York: Oxford University Press 2002), 227–228.
[13] Bianciotto, "Flor rara," 12.

housewife and sings how fun it would be to see it all explode, which actually occurs at the end.

Alex and Christina eventually split up owing to personal and musical differences and, in the early 1990s, Rosenvinge moved more in the direction of rock with a new band called Christina y Los Subterráneos, who took their name from a Jack Kerouac novella, *The Subterraneans*. In the mid-1990s, international producers Steve Jordan and Niko Bolas came onto the scene, and Rosenvinge started to work with new musicians from outside of Spain—musicians like Lee Ranaldo from Sonic Youth, whom Rosenvinge met at a festival with the writer Ray Loriga, her spouse and the future father of her two children.[14]

This was how Rosenvinge started to spend time in New York alternative music circles, and she ended up living there between 1999 and 2003. Her music was described in the music media in terms of being art pop/rock, while her collaboration with Sonic Youth members Lee Ranaldo and Steve Shelley was often mentioned. In the United States, she was often compared to Nico (Christa Päffgen) (also by the Velvet Underground's Lou Reed). Rosenvinge found her time in the United States professionally inspiring, as she was experimenting in different things with the encouragement of other musicians,[15] but in the end, she returned to Spain.

It was in Spain that she came together with musician Nacho Vegas to record the album *Verano fatal* (Fatal summer) in 2007. She released four solo albums between 2008 and 2018, and also, in 2011, a collection of her works called *Un caso sin resolver* (The case unsolved). In 2018, Rosenvinge was rewarded with the National Prize of Contemporary Music (Premio Nacional de las Músicas Actuales) by Spain's Ministry of Culture. In March 2019, she published *Debut*, and in 2020 she played the leading role in a film, *Karen*, about the Danish author Karen Blixen.[16] As this short biography demonstrates, Rosenvinge has had a long and versatile career, which makes her book an interesting object of analysis in relation to memory, truth, and narrative ethics.

---

[14] Ibid., 14, 16.
[15] Such as Tim Foljahn, Georgia Hubley, and Jeremy Wilms.
[16] Rosenvinge had previously acted in three other films: *Dragon rapide* (1986), *Todo es mentira* (1994), *La pistola de mi hermano* (1997).

Electrified Memory, Rock, and Gender

In *Debut*, songwriting and memory are creatively linked; Rosenvinge the storyteller states that memory is selective and not a perfect machine, therefore questioning the trustworthiness of her own stories. The sections of the memoir are arranged chronologically by album and lyrics, beginning in 1992 and ending in 2018. Each chapter begins with the name and title of an album and is followed by a story, the subject of which may range from describing how a song emerged to what life was like then. Some stories are simply a collection of diary notes or email exchanges, where songs are discussed; they may be interviews, in which questions have been answered either conventionally, or more truthfully. Each story is then followed by that album's complete lyrics. The chapters vary greatly, giving the memoir an apparently incoherent air.

The title *Debut* points, in Rosenvinge's case, to her first public appearance on the literary stage. In one interview, Rosenvinge states that she wanted the focus of the book to be on lyrics, and therefore, it is to the lyrics that the chapters seek to give context. She did not wish to write "a proper autobiography," meaning that we are provided with only sketches of periods when she was writing songs. Also, Rosenvinge wanted the chapters to stand by themselves by using a strong literary voice, so that the book could even be read as fiction. The literary emphasis is also clear in the choice of the publisher, Literatura Random House: it was not published merely for music fans, but was aimed at a wider, more literary audience.[17]

Rosenvinge has stated in interviews that she had literary ambitions. Moreover, in her 2011 collection *Un caso sin resolver*, there is a short monologue, in which she is in an imaginary court, trying to justify her life as a musician to all the other people (men) in the room. The monologue is written in an ironical style and employs stream-of-consciousness, ending with the declaration that she does not care if she is being judged or not, as long as she can continue playing music. To some extent, *Debut* maintains this theme: why making music is so important, and at the same time, so difficult, especially for a woman.

It is significant that the hostility that Rosenvinge remembers encountering becomes more marked when she enters the genre of "rock," which is historically considered masculine terrain, an area in which questions of authenticity

---

[17] Christina Rosenvinge, interview by Marika Ahonen, Madrid, June 20, 2019.

can become an obstacle—and especially so for a woman artist.[18] In *Debut*, before the album lyrics of *Cerrado* ("Closed," 1997), the chapter consists of "diary notes" with references to depression and sadness. The events of this chapter took place at that point of Rosenvinge's journey when she was working toward more rock-oriented music. Soon afterward, Rosenvinge left her former record label Warner and started to look for a direction elsewhere, with the help of her new connections in the United States.

However, Rosenvinge recalls answering questions about her credibility—especially in the rock world—not only due to her gender, but also because of her past in pop music. Rosenvinge believes that this issue has plagued her ever since; in *Debut*, there is a reference to the issue in a chapter where Rosenvinge responds to typical journalist questions first conventionally, but then, in italics, to suggest the way she herself "really" thinks:

> Do you think that with this album you will overcome the prejudices that weigh on your past?
> Joseph Mengele has a past, I just did "Chas!"
> *Fuck.*[19]

A further gender-specific difficulty emerged when Rosenvinge became a mother and had to return from New York to Spain. There were many reasons for this: key among them, as Rosenvinge narrates at length, were the 9/11 attacks, after which the United States became hostile to foreigners and obtaining a visa became more difficult. Family obligations as a new mother created particular challenges for a life on the road; she found the lifestyle in New York expensive, competitive, and exhausting to raise a child in. When Rosenvinge returned to Spain, she contemplated ending her career; she had already considered this possibility while in the United States, at least on a philosophical level, while struggling to be a mother and a musician at the same time. Rosenvinge writes in *Debut*:

> . I fully understand Sylvia Plath and all the women who have felt the frustration that motherhood sequesters their lives, but I do not intend to put my head in the oven. First, because it is electric—it would be a very painful

---

[18] See, e.g., Sheila Whiteley, *Women and Popular Music: Sexuality, Identity and Subjectivity* (Oxford: Routledge, 2000); Marion Leonard, *Gender in the Music Industry: Rock, Discourse and Girl Power* (Hampshire: Ashgate, 2007).
[19] Rosenvinge, *Debut*, 149.

death—and second, because I am very lucky. What I am living through is extraordinary, and although I regret not being able to seize the moment, I am very happy. I am at the epicenter of the most interesting alternative pop and what's more, they are paying attention to me.[20]

Such references to women writers and artists are scattered throughout the book. Here, with a sense of irony Rosenvinge tackles the difficult issue that all women musicians seem to face when becoming a mother: how to take care of the children when you are supposed to be on the road. It's an issue, of course, that is seldom a problem for male musicians. As the narration indicates, the realities of childcare come at a cost. Making music is not that simple, especially without the support of family or society.

However, music becomes the key to survival. If Rosenvinge questions the trustworthiness of memory at the beginning of her book, she connects the theme of "remembering well" to songwriting in particular. Just as she indicates that one remembers the "electrocutions" better than the everyday, songwriting often happens when connected to such moments. These "electrocutions" are clear at many points throughout the book, since much space is devoted to those troubled times in which Rosenvinge is struggling with her own mind, and indeed with her ability to continue as a musician, as the above examples demonstrate. She also narrates events such as breakups and the time when she started to write the song about her dead father, with whom she had a complicated relationship, as he was both violent and alcoholic. In each of these traumatic life events, it is the practice of making music that helps with and sheds light on Rosenvinge's every day, providing comfort before finally becoming song.

Autobiographical Truth

Somewhat paradoxically, *Debut* can be seen as revealing because of its literary form while not revealing any very personal information. For example, in the chapter on the album *Continental 62* (2006) we find Rosenvinge answering questions she has been asked continually, of which the following in particular play with the notion of truth and autobiography:

---

[20] Ibid., 120.

> Do you lie a lot in interviews?
> I do not.
> Yes.[21]
> I've counted five break-up songs on this record.
> Heartbreak songs are my favourites, but it's not autobiographical at all.
> *The damn prophetic power of the songs.*[22]

As these answers indicate, besides acknowledging that her memory is not completely trustworthy, Rosenvinge indicates that she tells what she wants to, which is not always the truth. But the question of autobiographical truth is not clear-cut. As Sidonie Smith and Julia Watson state, life narrators can present varying or ever-changing views of themselves and even, as Rosenvinge does, question the "truth" of their experiences.[23] According to Robert Edgar, Fraser Mann, and Helen Pleasance, when music memoirists turn the past into text, they are performing experiments, which involve, for example, "undermining the importance of facts by overtly lying to get at metaphorical 'narrative truth.'"[24]

With specific regard to autobiographical truth, Smith and Watson pose important questions: "How do we know whether and when a narrator is telling the truth or lying? And what difference would that make?"[25] They suggest that the answer to these questions depends on our expectations of the life narrators. In other words, it depends on whether readers are "expecting fidelity to the facts of their biographies, to lived experience, to self-understanding, to the historical moment, to social community, to prevailing beliefs about diverse identities, to the norms of autobiography as a literary genre itself? And truth for whom and for what?"[26] These are all essential questions, which concern the relationship between the writer and the reader, as "autobiographical truth resides in the intersubjective exchange between narrator and reader aimed at producing a shared understanding of the meaning of a life."[27] Rosenvinge does not seek to offer simple facts or make objective truth claims, but rather acknowledges the subjectivity of her

---

[21] Ibid., 149.
[22] Ibid., 147.
[23] Sidonie Smith and Julia Watson, *Reading Autobiography: A Guide for Interpreting Life Narratives*, 2nd ed. (Minneapolis: University of Minnesota Press 2010), 15.
[24] Robert Edgar, Fraser Mann, and Helen Pleasance, Introduction to *Music, Memory and Memoir*, ed. Robert Edgar, Fraser Mann, and Helen Pleasance (London: Bloomsbury Academic 2019), 3.
[25] Smith and Watson, *Reading Autobiography*, 15.
[26] Ibid., 15.
[27] Ibid., 16.

stories. According to Smith and Watson, "The authority of the autobiographical, then, neither confirms nor invalidates notions of objective truth; rather, it tracks the previously uncharted truths of particular lives."[28] In this way the authors underline the concept of intersubjective truth:

> Commitment to self-narration, not as an act for calculated gain in fortune or fame but as an epistemological act of thinking through what one as a subject knows to be or not to be, remains a basis of both writerly tact and readerly trust. It does not rule out the use of the found, the fabricated, the strategic, the consciously invented. But it asks that "my experiments with truth," Mahatma Gandhi's fine title for his autobiography, be in the service of a project larger than personal gain, opportunism, an overt political agenda, or a desire to obfuscate and impress. If indeed intersubjective truth, always tentative and provisional, emerges in autobiographical acts, its nurturance is a project requiring the care and active engagement of both readers and writers.[29]

Music memoirs are clearly about famous persons whose books are targeted at an audience in order to gain fortune and fame, but there is more to them than that. The genre of memoir is strongly nuanced, since their writers have differing aims and emphases. On the subject of truth telling regarding musicians, and indeed artists in general, Kimi Kärki and Maarit Leskelä-Kärki remind us that lived life is always relational and subjective, and that therefore to find an objective truth is impossible. It is more important to analyze the ways in which musicians talk about their art and truth, and which themes are emphasized.[30]

Like, for example, Patti Smith, Rosenvinge seems to cherish the literary style, rather than offering truth claims or going into great detail in her life narrative. She is best known for her lyrics, and a memoir is a step toward a more "literary" way of expressing herself. Besides this, given that someone will eventually tell it anyway, and for their own purpose, autobiographical writing also gives the writer some control over her own life story. As Rosenvinge has stated, she hates nostalgia; but even before the memoir, in

---

[28] Ibid., 16.
[29] Ibid., 18.
[30] Kimi Kärki and Maarit Leskelä Kärki, "'I Am Not Confessing': Joni Mitchell, Leonard Cohen ja laulettu elämä," in *Musiikki ja merkityksenanto: juhlakirja Susanna Välimäelle*, ed. Sini Mononen, Janne Palkisto, and Inka Rantakallio (Turenki: Tutkimusyhdistys Suoni ry, 2020), 285–286.

her collection *Un caso sin resolver*, she considered that if she had not done it herself, her record company would have done it anyway, following her death.[31] Memoir thus gives her the chance to narrate her vision of her life for herself, and in this way, intersubjective truth becomes the key element: in the end, it is the reader's choice whether to accept or reject that truth.

Moreover, writing a memoir can also work as an easier way to tackle complex traumatic issues. Rosenvinge starts her book by questioning memory's truthfulness by connecting it particularly to painful events, how they stand out from the day-to-day ones, and this connection is present throughout, with Rosenvinge often using irony and making tragic events comic, as the reference to Sylvia Plath demonstrates. Thus, in the final section of this chapter, I want to examine the meaning of songwriting to Rosenvinge's survival, a concept that connects to ethical questions also.

Narrative Ethics and Possible Selves

Ethical issues of many kinds can be found in women's rock memoirs. In Joan Baez's two memoirs, for example, emphasis is placed on the theme of pacifism, while her music is employed more as a tool to get the antiwar message through.[32] Moreover, as memoirs written by other women in rock demonstrate, music is frequently connected to the possibility of acting out issues such as the prejudice and dangers that women-identified musicians have to face when entering the rock world, and their different responses to it. Rosenvinge's memoir is no different: she too writes about the difficulties she has faced not only in the male-dominated music world, but in patriarchal society in general. But in my interpretation, the key theme in Rosenvinge's memoir concerns songwriting and survival, which connects to ethical questions also.

Songwriting and its connection to survival are present throughout, but the final chapter is dedicated specifically to the subject. Here Rosenvinge guides the reader in how to write songs. This is an engrossing way to end the book: a reflection on life-writing not in terms of what it *is*, but of what it *does*.[33] This

---

[31] Interview by Núria Martorell, January 2, 2012, http://www.elperiodico.com/es/noticias/musica-directa/christina-rosenvinge-ordena-discografia-caso-sin-resolver-1298620.

[32] Marika Ahonen, "Joan Baez ja tarina verenpunaiseksi piirtyneestä maailmasta" (Joan Baez and the story of a world turned into a color of blood), in *Toivon ja Raivon vuosi 1968* (The year of hope and rage 1968), ed. Maarit Leskelä-Kärki, Marika Ahonen, and Niko Heikkilä (Helsinki: Työväen historian ja perinteen tutkimuksen seura, 2019).

[33] G. Thomas Couser, *Memoir. An Introduction* (Oxford: Oxford University Press, 2011), 178.

begs the question of whom the memoir is written for, and why; of how it might, through its narration, be shaping culture and history. Rosenvinge's book, it becomes apparent, seeks to tell the reader—in this case, a potential songwriter—how to find one's own path, and what needs to be taken into consideration when doing so. I take Rosenvinge's choice to discuss her songwriting in this way to be an ethical act, since life-writing is not simply a recounting of one's life, but is ultimately concerned with values.[34]

Perhaps unexpectedly, writing about songwriting is not such a common theme in music memoirs; it is not, for example, considered as interesting as issues related to the writer's personal life. This is perhaps unsurprising when we consider that in recent years, praise for Rosenvinge has focused on her lyrics. On a larger scale, the emphasis on lyrics in the book can also be explained by the growing overall appreciation of popular music lyrics following Bob Dylan's Nobel Prize in Literature in 2016.

Throughout the final chapter, Rosenvinge is guiding the process of writing songs in a personal, autobiographical way, almost as if to say there is nothing mystical about it, as through practice you can learn it. This is important when considering, as Oliver Lovesey reminds us, that "the rock star imaginary has become one of defining myths of our time."[35] This also concerns creativity in music writing: Kärki, for example, states that both music journalists and artists have mythologized the process of creativity.[36] Thus, demystifying the process, and in this way opening the door to those wanting to learn the secrets of songwriting, Rosenvinge is broadening the possibilities of acting out for her readers too.

Songwriting is thus examined in *Debut* with a special emphasis on the perspective of the reader. This can be considered an ethical act, since Rosenvinge sharing her knowledge with readers is simultaneously opening up and demystifying the process. Such guidance to songwriting is also present in Finnish singer-songwriter Iisa Pajula's book *Itke, kirjoita, laula* (Cry, write, sing)—rather than being a memoir, Pajula's book is essentially a guide to autobiographical songwriting.

Like Rosenvinge, Pajula begins her book by emphasizing the theme of how memory is untrustworthy. The two writers share similar experiences

---

[34] Smith and Watson, *Reading Autobiography*, 19.
[35] Oliver Lovesey, *Popular Music Autobiography. The Revolution in Life-Writing by 1960s' Musicians and Their Descendants* (London: Bloomsbury, 2021), 1.
[36] Kimi Kärki, "Confessions of Metal and Folk: Remembering and Contextualizing the Creative Process," in *Music, Memory and Memoir*, ed. Robert Edgar, Fraser Mann, and Helen Pleasance (London: Bloomsbury Academic 2019), 226.

of a music industry in which women lyricists have been undervalued, and neither had professional training when entering the music world; they are self-taught and have learned by trial and error. Both encourage the reader by acknowledging that songwriting is difficult and requires work and practice—but once you find your own way, they agree, anything is possible. It is finding your own voice that matters, a notion more generally applicable in feminist thinking and in the ethics of care.[37] It is worth noting that both Rosenvinge and Pajula also started giving songwriting classes after publishing the books. The stories in their books, then, are not survival stories per se, but quite the contrary: they are guiding from the middle of it all, still struggling with songwriting. By focusing on songwriting in their books, they emphasize that writing a great song is the best reward, one that makes it worth continuing.

The ethical negotiation of the possibility of acting out is highlighted, too, in Simone de Beauvoir's writings. Beauvoir was essentially interested in the paradox of subjectivity in terms of its existential dimension, that is, its relation to freedom. We, as humans, are free to set ourselves goals and give our actions meaning, but we employ our freedom within a historical-material framework that both enhances and diminishes the possibility of any potential actions. Our freedom is also limited to the extent that other people must give recognition to it. Beauvoir describes this dual nature of human existence through the concept of ambiguity (*ambiguïté*).[38] Rosenvinge too—a longtime figure in music who has attained the status of author—is using her freedom to enhance others' potential actions. Concerning artistic work, Rosenvinge writes the following:

> The artistic work is an investigation into the human nature where frequently the artist simultaneously occupies the position of narrator and subject. Which is a matter of trust and credibility rather than narcissism. An artist is a scientist and a rat at the same time. One dissects oneself to understand how the human being works, where it hurts and why. With whom else are you going to have the confidence to stir the viscera and expose them in that way? The personal is a perfect starting point. Even when the song is not

---

[37] In Rosenvinge's writing the influence of the feminist tradition can be seen, and she has stated from the beginning of her career that her literary role models derive from feminist writers such as Simone de Beauvoir, Virginia Woolf, and Margaret Atwood. Moreover, traces of the ethics of care, which derives from feminist philosophy, can be seen in many memoirs analyzed in this book—in, e.g., Astrid Swan's.

[38] Simone de Beauvoir, *Moniselitteisyyden etiikka* (*Pour une morale de l'ambiguïté*, 1947), trans. to Finnish by Erika Ruonankoski (Helsinki: Tutkijaliitto, 2011).

autobiographical, it usually contains some drop of our essence to make it credible.[39]

The essence of songwriting, for that matter of writing a memoir, is an intertwining of the autobiographical with the imaginary, so that an intersubjective exchange between narrator and reader, aimed at producing a shared understanding of the meaning of life, becomes possible. In this process, as Rosenvinge suggests, the personal can be a good starting point. Moreover, the performative nature of Rosenvinge's narration concerns the possibilities of acting out in a creative profession and its existential-ethical dimension: what type of creative person/singer-songwriter does one want to be, and why? Memoir is the appropriate site for consideration of this, as it provides a viewpoint of how one experiences and locates oneself in a certain place and time. In the same way, it helps one to achieve understanding, which gives meaning to one's actions, and to explore what are the limits and possibilities, in a certain time and place, of acting out. The ethical significance of memoir—whether to academic research or the wider public—thus depends on its capacity to construct the past from the present toward the future, and so to negotiate possible selves for its readers.

Bibliography

Ahonen, Marika. Christina Rosenvinge, interviews by Marika Ahonen, Madrid: December 4, 2018; June 20, 2019; November 8, 2021.

Ahonen, Marika. "Joan Baez ja tarina verenpunaiseksi piirtyneestä maailmasta" (Joan Baez and the story of a world turned into a color of blood). In *Toivon ja Raivon vuosi 1968* (The year of hope and rage 1968), edited by Maarit Leskelä-Kärki, Marika Ahonen, and Niko Heikkilä, 175–189. Helsinki: Työväen historian ja perinteen tutkimuksen seura, 2019.

Ahonen, Marika. "Sirens, Narrative Ethics, and Christina Rosenvinge's '*Mi vida bajo el agua*'." *Cultural History* 12, no. 1 (April 2023): 120–138.

Allinson, Mark. "Alaska. Star of Stage and Screen and Optimistic Punk." In *Constructing Identity in Contemporary Spain. Theoretical Debates and Cultural Practice*, edited by Jo Labanyi, 227–228. New York: Oxford University Press, 2002.

Beauvoir, Simone de. *Moniselitteisyyden etiikka (Pour une morale de l'ambiguïté* [1947]). Translated to Finnish by Erika Ruonankoski. Helsinki: Tutkijaliitto, 2011.

Bianciotto, Jordi. "Flor rara." In *Un caso sin resolver*. Madrid: Warner Music Spain, 2011.

Couser, G. Thomas. *Memoir: An Introduction*. Oxford: Oxford University Press, 2011.

---

[39] Rosenvinge, *Debut*, 325.

Del Val, Fernán, and Green, Stuart. "Transitions of the *Cantautor*: Aesthetics, Politics and Authenticity in Spanish Popular Music from the Late Franco Dictatorship to the Present Day." In *The Singer-Songwriter in Europe: Paradigms, Politics and Place*, edited by Isabelle Marc and Stuart Green, 163–176. New York: Routledge, 2016.

Edgar, Robert, Fraser Mann, and Helen Pleasance. "Introduction." In *Music, Memory and Memoir*, edited by Robert Edgar, Fraser Mann, and Helen Pleasance, 1–9. London: Bloomsbury Academic, 2019.

Green, Anna. *Cultural History*. New York: Palgrave Macmillan, 2008.

Holt, Fabian. *Genre in Popular Music*. Chicago: University of Chicago Press, 2007.

Kärki, Kimi. "Confessions of Metal and Folk: Remembering and Contextualizing the Creative Process." In *Music, Memory and Memoir*, edited by Robert Edgar, Fraser Mann, and Helen Pleasance, 223–239. London: Bloomsbury Academic, 2019.

Kärki, Kimi, and Leskelä-Kärki Maarit. "'I Am Not Confessing': Joni Mitchell, Leonard Cohen ja laulettu elämä." In *Musiikki ja merkityksenanto: juhlakirja Susanna Välimäelle*, edited by Sini Mononen, Janne Palkisto, and Inka Rantakallio, 279–300. Turenki: Tutkimusyhdistys Suoni ry, 2020.

Leonard, Marion. *Gender in the Music Industry: Rock, Discourse and Girl Power*. Hampshire: Ashgate, 2007.

Lovesey, Oliver. *Popular Music Autobiography: The Revolution in Life-Writing by 1960s' Musicians and Their Descendants*. London: Bloomsbury, 2021.

Martorell, Núria. "Christina Rosenvinge ordena su discografia en *Un caso sin resolver*." *El Periodico*, January 2, 2012. http://www.elperiodico.com/es/noticias/musica-directa/christina-rosenvinge-ordena-discografia-caso-sin-resolver-1298620.

Meretoja, Hanna. *The Ethics of Storytelling. Narrative Hermeneutics, History, and the Possible*. New York: Oxford University Press, 2018.

Pajula, Iisa. *Itke, kirjoita, laula*. Keuruu: Nemo/Otava, 2021.

Rosenvinge, Christina. *Un caso sin resolver*. Madrid: Warner Music Spain, 2011.

Rosenvinge, Christina. *Debut: Cuadernos y canciones*. Barcelona: Literatura Random House, 2019.

Smith, Sidonie, and Julia Watson. *Reading Autobiography: A Guide for Interpreting Life Narratives*. 2nd ed. Minneapolis: University of Minnesota Press, 2010.

Whiteley, Sheila. *Women and Popular Music: Sexuality, Identity and Subjectivity*. New York: Routledge, 2000.

PART II
AUTHENTICITY, SEXUALITY, AND SEXISM

5
Jayne County, Laura Jane Grace, and the HerStory of Transgender Punks in America

Karen Fournier

Over the past decade, a proliferation of autobiographies by female punk musicians and scene-makers has invited long-overdue conversations about the important contributions of women to punk scenes in New York, Los Angeles, and London during their formation in the mid-to-late 1970s. In his history of British punk, Matthew Worley (2017) notes that, at its inception, punk was unique in providing "a space where feminist ideas were culturally played out. This meant engaging with themes integral to feminist discourse: the male gaze, mediated depictions of sexuality, processes of gender conditioning and deconditioning, the personal politics of social relationships. But this also meant exposing tensions and intersections between competing sociocultural identities (class, race, sexuality, religion)."[1] Worley's comments suggest that first-person female perspectives on the subculture can help to reframe punk histories in ways that acknowledge the significant roles played by women in the early subculture and that interrogate their unique experience of social alienation both within and outside punk as it emerged at the intersection of classism and sexism. Female punk autobiographies serve as important correctives for existing punk histories, where women have tended to be under- or unrepresented, and they invite scholars to reconsider and rewrite those histories either to include females as co-creators of the subculture or to retell the story of punk's creation from the female point of view.[2]

---

[1] Matthew Worley, *No Future: Punk, Politics and British Youth Culture 1976–1984* (Cambridge: Cambridge University Press, 2017), 193.
[2] See, for example, Helen Reddington (2007) and Vivien Goldman (2019).

Despite the significant gaps that they help to fill in punk histories, recent female punk memoirs do little to contest the cisgender, hetero-dominant reading of punk offered by existing histories of the subculture. Any assertion of a female form of punk that warrants historical attention assumes a dominant male form of punk but overlooks participation within the subculture by those whose gender identity might lie somewhere on a continuum between these two gender categories and/or whose sexual identity might resist dominant heterosexuality. While women may be marginalized in many punk histories, nonbinary participants in punk are nearly absent from those histories.[3] This essay will begin to redress the exclusion of transgender voices in punk histories by examining the memoirs of the pioneering punk artist Jayne County (*Man Enough to Be a Woman*, 1996; repr., 2021) and the contemporary punk artist Laura Jane Grace (*Tranny: Confessions of Punk Rock's Most Infamous Anarchist Sellout*, 2016). I contend that historical exclusions of nonbinary contributions to punk reflect the heteronormative, male perspective of early punk historians like Jon Savage, who dismissed County as one of "a whole clutch of rejects from [the New York punk club] Max's Kansas City."[4] In *England's Dreaming: Anarchy, Sex Pistols, Punk Rock, and Beyond*, Savage challenges the enthusiastic reception that County received when she headlined a show at London's Marquee Club on May 25, 1977, supported by The Police. According to him, "none of these acts had much to do with the new age [i.e., punk]."[5] Other early histories of the punk subculture are dismissive of artists like County by omission. Foundational punk histories like *Subculture: The Meaning of Style* (1979), *One Chord Wonders* (1985), and *Lipstick Traces* (1989) provide insights into meanings that might be ascribed to the performance of sexual ambiguity by (largely straight) punks but shine no light on meanings that might arise within the subculture by the embodiment of gender variance or gender nonconformance by those with a legitimate claim to these forms of difference. Instead, these early studies of punk tend to explain difference in ways that reiterate and reinforce the centrality of heterosexual male identity to the creation of punk. Dick Hebdige's study of punk "style," for example, argues that British punk youth, inspired by the precedent set by glam artists like David Bowie, embraced camp and

---

[3] Consistent with historical naming practices, I will use the acronym LGTBQ+ when speaking of the punk subculture from the 1990s onward.
[4] Jon Savage, *England's Dreaming: Anarchy, Sex Pistols, Punk Rock, and Beyond*, 2nd ed (New York: St. Martin's Griffin, 2002), 301.
[5] Ibid., 302.

queerness to add color and excitement to the "drab provincial cinemas and Victorian town halls" in which they congregated and to "challenge the notoriously pedestrian stereotypes conventionally available to working-class men and women."[6] The youth to whom Hebdige appears to refer embraced tokens of queerness to be provocative, but not to transgress against their own heteronormative and cisgender privilege: Hebdige's study assumes straightness even as it discusses punk queerness. Matthew Worley's recent history, *No Future: Punk Politics and British Youth Culture 1976–1984*, takes important first steps toward (re)asserting the gay male presence in punk and explores how the sexual identities of such punks as Pete Shelley, Andy Martin, and Tom Robinson shaped, and were shaped by, the music scenes that each inhabited. Despite the important contributions that it makes toward a recuperation of gay male identity in early punk, however, Worley's study largely defines "otherness" in terms of same-sex preference. Gender identity is largely missing from this presentation, though Worley cannot be faulted for the oversight: by the time his history appeared in 2017, County had been all but erased from histories of punk not only because she was disdained by those who (like Savage) wrote early accounts of punk from within the scene, but also because her work had failed to attract the attention of mainstream record labels that might have increased distribution of her music beyond the scene and that would have guaranteed access to her music today. Without an account of punk that includes this formative transgender artist, the exclusion of more recent nonbinary punk voices from accounts of punk seems inevitable.

In this essay, I argue that the erasure of County (and transgender voices more broadly) from punk's history reflects a conservative attitude within punk regarding gender that sidelined its female participants and erased those whose transgender identities defied both punk's hegemonic patriarchy and its heteronormativity (a conservatism that also conflated transgenderism with homosexuality and rejected the former on the basis of this false equivalency). I will show that while gay male punks found some space for self-expression in the early subculture because markers of their gay identity could be appropriated by straight male punks to cue "social alienation," transgenderism appeared to be a step too far because it transgressed the gender binary that straight, cisgender male punks policed in the interest of maintaining their privilege and power within the subculture. Consequently,

---

[6] Dick Hebdige, *Subculture: The Meaning of Style* (London: Routledge, 1979), 60.

the marginalization of transgender artists in punk has resulted in their near erasure in chronicles of punk until recently, with the publication of these two important memoirs that both document moments in the history of punk from a new set of perspectives and challenge the myth of punk's DIY claim to inclusion.

Trans Exclusion in Punk and Its Histories

Tavia Nyong'o (2008) has argued that "punk may be literally impossible to imagine without gender and sexual dissidence."[7] Despite this observation, most histories of punk have tended to privilege male sexual dissidence in ways that reinforce the gender binary, consistent with representations of identity within the subculture. Punk draws connections to gay male sexuality in the ways that punks name themselves, in song titles and lyrics, in certain modes of dress and self-ornamentation, and in topics explored in the subculture's visual art. The word "punk," itself, has deep historical resonances not only to outcasts, drop-outs, or criminals, but also pejoratively to homosexuals, whose sexual practices were believed to align them with the other three alienated groups in the view of the dominant culture. Certain song titles or song narratives also signal male same-sex preference, for example through their exploration of the gay hustler (the Ramones' "53rd and 3rd" or the Dicks' "Off Duty Sailor") and the closet (the Ramones' "We're a Happy Family" or the Germs' "What We Do Is Secret"). Mark Sinker (1999) also notes the impact of gay male sexuality on punk fashion when he observes that "in mid-70s New York, the Ramones and Richard Hell took their barely coded look from the boy hustlers on 53rd and 3rd Streets, ripped jeans and T-shirts, adorably mussed-up hair. It was the refusal to recognize any community politics in this self-locating gesture... that gave this scene its pulling power."[8] Through their mimicry of the gay hustler, these (and other male) punks presumably aimed to challenge the dominant heteropatriarchy and its narrow conceptions of allowable male sexual behaviors by embracing the practices of the homosexual "other."

---

[7] Tavia Nyong'o, "Do You Want Queer Theory (Or Do You Want the Truth)? Intersections of Punk and Queer in the 1970s," *Radical History Review* 100 (2008): 107.

[8] Mark Sinker, "Concrete, so as to Self-Destruct: The Etiquette of Punk, Its Habits, Rules, Values, and Dilemmas," in *Punk Rock: So What?*, ed. Roger Sabin (New York: Routledge, 1999), 128.

Despite its outward embrace of the gay community, punk's relationship with same-sex male sexuality has always been contradictory. It is noteworthy that none of the punk musicians whose work I have cited identified as gay and, despite the subculture's nod to queerness, some male punks were openly hostile toward anyone who conflated punk with homosexuality. In 1978, Legs McNeil famously posted his "punk manifesto" in the *Village Voice* to denounce media portrayals of punk as the embodiment of, or even as sympathetic to, homosexuality. In terms that expose a troubling undercurrent of homophobia and racism in punk, McNeil's manifesto contends that

> punk started as an attitude that celebrated American culture and the teenager as the Master Race. It wasn't asexual f****t hippie blood-sucking ignorant scum as the media would have you believe. Elements of that behavior pattern has infiltrated this country from England. The English bands with their uncool need for media attention have perverted the term *punk*, and the media, which is always looking for a sensational story to print, was glad to oblige.[9]

McNeil's "corrective" to the media's (mis)reading of punk was to assert that its intention was to uplift American teenagers who were disillusioned by mass media, consumerism, and the social conservatism that marked the country in the 1970s. The manifesto stresses that punks were emphatically *not* queer but merely appropriated tokens of gay culture to signify social alienation and to fuel moral outrage among those who observed the subculture from the outside. The truth for many punks was that queerness was merely a pose that they expressed in fashion or song lyrics. It is noteworthy that the protagonist in the Ramones' song "53rd and 3rd" hustles for drug money in whatever way he can, but ultimately expresses shame and revulsion about the sexual act in which he, as a heterosexual male, is forced to engage to feed his habit, or that the off-duty sailor described by the Dicks is the subject of a night of same-sex passion with a straight protagonist who dismisses the event as a drunken aberration in his otherwise heterosexual life. These examples illustrate what Nyong'o has described as "a history of antagonisms between punk attitude and a male homosexual desire variously cast as predatory and

---

[9] Legs McNeil, "The Punk Manifesto," *Village Voice*, May 8, 1978, 30. I have erased the pejorative that appears in the original. The term "Master Race" refers to a song by the Dictators, the connection to which I will explain below.

pitiable."[10] Both songs disavow queerness, despite the alterity and alienation that it provides, so that the male punk can reclaim and confirm his dominant position within a heteropatriarchy that punk paradoxically claims to repudiate. Moreover, in historical accounts of punk, the brand of difference embraced in the subculture is one that continues to privilege masculine identity: lesbians and gender-nonconforming individuals remain largely absent in early punk narratives (and, by extension, the histories that document punk), despite stories about trans women by such protopunks like Lou Reed. Punk's refusal to pick up where Reed left off in his descriptions of gender nonconformity illustrates the challenge posed by queer and/or trans women to punk's default heteropatriarchy and cis-maleness. It is incumbent on punk historians to interrogate this default and to contest punk's claim to inclusion through DIY. Histories of punk must consider why expressions of gender difference have been erased and how that erasure has continued to make punk an inhospitable space for certain forms of self-expression. I would argue that the absence of a significant figure like Jayne County from punk histories, whose memoir I discuss below, has contributed to uncertainties about the safety of punk for current trans artists, like Laura Jane Grace, whose memoir largely documents her struggle for self-acceptance in a cis-male subculture despite being written almost fifty years after County arrived in New York to begin her career in early punk.

Jayne County, *Man Enough to Be a Woman*

Jayne County (b. 1947) is a self-described "drag queen" and "transsexual" who first made her mark as an actor in New York City in the experimental theatre scene of the late 1960s and, later, as the first trans punk in the city's nascent scene.[11] Her memoir, *Man Enough to Be a Woman*, describes how she embraced her gender identity and sexual interest in men from an early age, how she later viewed herself as "transsexual" after reading the autobiography of Canary Conn, *Canary: The Story of a Transsexual* (1974), and how she eventually refused to be categorized altogether. "I'm happy in between the sexes," she writes, "I'm comfortable and I actually like the idea. The whole

---

[10] Nyong'o, "Do You Want Queer Theory," 107.
[11] I will use County's self-affirmed name throughout this paper. County's dead name is Wayne Vernoy Rogers, which was initially changed to Wayne County in reference to the county that contains the city of Detroit and in homage to the Michigan-born protopunk Iggy Pop.

thing of being neither male nor female, of being a mixture of both... pleases me."[12] Despite this self-acceptance, County describes how her public presentation as a woman singled her out for discrimination both by members of the dominant heteronormative culture of the time, where she was stigmatized as "perverse," and within the homonormative gay community, where her visibility was viewed as a threat to those who were afraid to be identified as gay at a time when homosexuality was criminalized.[13] County existed at the periphery of both communities, and her memoir describes how her marginalization extended into the musical scenes in which she participated, where she was subjected to physical abuse and exploitation. Two episodes selected from her memoir illustrate the point.

County entered the music field through theater and began her career in New York as an actor in Warhol's first and only play, *Pork*, which opened at La Mama Experimental Theatre Club on May 5, 1971, before moving to London's Roundhouse Theatre for a six-week run in August 1971. During its London run, the play caught the attention of David Bowie, who arranged for several cast members to sign to the MainMan Group, which had been formed by the impresario Tony Defries in 1972 and which managed Bowie's career. County was contracted by Defries on January 21, 1974, to produce her first album, but the recording was beset by delays that she blames on Bowie. She recalls that "Bowie was very jealous of his status as Freak Number One and didn't want anyone else muscling in on that territory.... In 1973, I was on the cover of *Melody Maker* in Britain... Bowie was furious that another MainMan artiste [sic] was stealing his limelight, so there was another delay on the album."[14] MainMan eventually decided to record Wayne County and her punk backup band, then known as the Backstreet Boys, in live performance at the Westbeth Theatre on the Manhattan riverfront in an area that was infamous for gay cruising. The album would be entitled *Wayne County at the Trucks!* to refer both to the trucks that would park along the loading docks across from the theater and to a code word used to cue the area to those in New York's gay community. County's performance was a sexually explicit send-up of the area's cruising subculture, featuring songs with titles like "Surrender Your Gender," "Queenage Baby," and "Stick It in Me." She has

---

[12] Jayne County, *Man Enough to Be a Woman: The Autobiography of Jayne County* (London: Serpent's Tail, 2021), 181.
[13] See Genny Beemyn, "US History," in *Trans Bodies, Trans Selves: A Resource for the Transgender Community*, ed. Laura Erickson-Schroth (New York: Oxford University Press, 2014), 501–536.
[14] County, *Man Enough*, 123.

since compared the industry reactions to *the Trucks!* to critical reactions to the *Exorcist*, which had opened a few months earlier: namely, as a combination of shock and disgust. According to Marky Ramone, who was at the show, it was apparent from the industry response to County's "outrageous crossdressing combined with the risqué subject matter of the songs . . . [that] there was no future in the mainstream for a transvestite singer."[15] The music producer Kenny Kerner, whose work with KISS might have made him an ideal collaborator for a theatrical performer like County, echoed the Ramone's observation and the reactions of many at the show. Ramone recalls that "Kenny's ears were into Wayne County. He liked the music. As for his eyes, not so much."[16] Kerner knew that while the mainstream consumer might have been willing to embrace KISS's theatrical performance of rock machismo, they would be less receptive to a performer who sounded male but whose transgender identity challenged rock's dominant masculinity. Critical responses to *the Trucks!* prompted MainMan to abandon the recording project, and any demos from the time were believe to have been lost. County has always claimed, however, that the subject material and the chorus of Bowie's 1974 hit "Rebel Rebel" bears striking thematic resemblances to her (then unreleased) song "Queenage Baby," to which he would have had access through MainMan as part of *the Trucks!* demo. It would take three decades for demos from *the Trucks!* recording session to be found and released, when they appeared on July 24, 2006, on the independent Spanish label Munster Records. Without this chance discovery, punk fans and scholars would have no way to reconstruct this important moment in County's early musical career and in the protopunk scene more broadly.

County's early experiences with David Bowie, Defries, and the MainMan management firm invite questions about identity, representation, and appropriation that become central themes in her memoir. She conjectures that her acceptance in the music industry in the early 1970s was hampered by her gender identity and that her early attempts to secure a future in music were thwarted not only because of rock's misogyny, but also because of its homophobia and transphobia. While Bowie might have been regarded with suspicion by a parental generation that was confused by his performance of androgyny, young consumers nonetheless propelled him to stardom despite (and perhaps because of) his "freak" status. County notes that this

---

[15] Marky Ramone and Richard Herschlag, *Punk Rock Blitzkrieg: My Life as a Ramone* (New York: Touchstone, 2016), 86.
[16] Ibid., 87.

"freakishness" owed a tangible debt to the trans community through various instances of borrowings as Bowie crafted his otherworldly alter ego, Ziggy Stardust. After seeing *Pork*, for example, County observed that Bowie "started painting his nails and shaving his eyebrows just like we did ... he took his subtle Lauren Bacall androgyny and pushed it into a blunter, more flamboyant area."[17] But unlike the drag queens and transsexuals who inspired his new look, Bowie was able to diffuse any threat posed by his onstage identity by creating a theatrical spectacle that revolved around this alter ego. Writing about Bowie, Peraino (2012) notes that "from the point of view of the poseur, the donning of a new name and new identity offers aesthetic satisfaction—a lifestyle that does not actually impinge on life."[18] In fact, speculations about the degree to which Bowie's art imitated his life merely drew more attention toward him. Bowie's claim to homosexuality in a 1972 interview in *Melody Maker* became a topic of debate in the popular press, since he appeared to be queer but had recently married, fathered a child, and rejected all invitations by gay rights activists to participate in their causes. Bowie would eventually confirm his sexual orientation in 1983, when he revealed in an interview with *Rolling Stone* magazine that he had always been a "closeted heterosexual," but his career was not hampered by the speculation that had taken place in the decade preceding this disclosure. For Bowie, the Ziggy Stardust character provided access to queerness through the alienation that it represented, but this identity was performative: while his appropriations of queerness and androgyny might have transgressed rock's dominant masculinity, Bowie was nonetheless identifiably male and, as he later revealed, straight.[19] By contrast, Jayne County was not an alter ego that had been constructed to play a part in an onstage gender-bending pantomime but was a person who embodied her trans identity both on- and offstage. A history that included Jayne County might invite visual comparisons between Ziggy Stardust and the cast of *Pork* or might examine musical influences on Bowie, who had access to County's recording, *the Trucks!*, as he prepared material for Ziggy to perform. County's absence from histories about Bowie and early glam has foreclosed on any critical study of these potential creative intersections and merely reinforces Bowie's status as a rock innovator.

---

[17] County, *Man Enough*, 110.
[18] Judith A. Peraino, "Plumbing the Surface of Sound and Vision: David Bowie, Andy Warhol, and the Art of Posing," *Qui parle* 21, no. 1 (2012): 159.
[19] Kurt Loder, "David Bowie: Straight Time," *Rolling Stone*, May 12, 1983, https://www.rollingstone.com/music/music-news/david-bowie-straight-time-69334/.

While Bowie and Defries might have obstructed County's access to the music industry and appropriated facets of her identity for their own theatrical use, County's experience of exclusion was often more overt and, at times, violent in the punk subculture. During one of her early performances at CBGBs, in March 1976, she was heckled and spat on by "Handsome" Dick Manitoba, the lead singer of the Dictators, who had allegedly been drinking heavily. As Manitoba charged the stage, County struck him with the microphone stand in defense, inadvertently breaking his collarbone. A brawl ensued and Manitoba was taken away in an ambulance while County returned to close her set, covered in blood, with a song appropriately entitled "Rock & Roll Resurrection." In an interview with *Creem* magazine in June 1976, Manitoba was given the opportunity to tell his side of the story. He portrayed himself as the innocent and defenseless victim when he claimed, in a statement that revealed both his cis-male privilege and his bias against the gay and trans communities, that "all I did was say 'Fuck you, you homo. Fuck you, you queer.' The next thing I remember—I wasn't facing him and I wasn't ready for it—I got smashed with the microphone stand."[20] The *New Musical Express* also sided with Manitoba when it suggested that "Dick met with less luck . . . at a CBGB's concert featuring that unpleasant, off-the-wall pervert Wayne County. . . . Manitoba got some satisfaction later when at a CBGB's benefit someone spiked County with an unhealthy dosage of demon blotter acid."[21] Detained on assault charges, County went into hiding by dressing as a man: "I cut my hair short, dyed it black, went up to the wig store and bought a glue-on beard, put on an army jacket and dark glasses."[22] The implication that County felt safer to default to the masculine identity during a time when she felt under scrutiny in the punk community reveals the power of the dominant gender to instill respect. The exchange caused a sharp rift in the budding punk scene between those who organized a benefit concert for County's mounting legal bills as she faced charges laid by Manitoba and those who believed that Manitoba was justified in his attack, like Legs McNeil, who was inspired by the event to write his "punk manifesto." Ervin (2019) states that

---

[20] Sarah Whitall, "Wayne County and Handsome Dick Manitoba: War of the Gargantuas," *Creem*, June 1976, retrieved March 30, 2022, http://www.rocksbackpages.com.proxy.lib.umich.edu/Library/Article/wayne-county-and-handsome-dick-manitoba-war-of-the-gargantuas. Manitoba, quoted in Whitall.
[21] Max Bell, "The Dictators: The Handsomest Man in Rock and Roll," *New Musical Express*, October 16, 1976, retrieved March 30, 2022, http://www.rocksbackpages.com.proxy.lib.umich.edu/Library/Article/the-dictators-the-handsomest-man-in-rock-and-roll.
[22] County, *Man Enough*, 109.

"the brawl played out a tension that was formative, not just in New York in the 1970s, but in 40 years of punk history since. Simply put, punk has perennially been defined by a fraught relationship to queerness. On the one hand, punk appears substantially queer.... On the other hand, punk resists queerness."[23] County and Manitoba were merely the embodiment of a tension that was brewing, and that continues to brew, in punk. In the end, Manitoba refused to appear at court and County was exonerated, but at a pivotal moment when queerness might have found advocates among punks who might have lobbied for a more inclusive environment for a transsexual artist like County, lack of critical engagement with this this event in the punk subculture suggests that the incident was not seen to be important enough to trigger systemic change in punk: punk's patriarchy and heteronormativity remained intact, while histories of the subculture have relegated this moment to a footnote. In County's memoir, by contrast, the event is pivotal for a very different reason, since it merely confirmed the sense of exclusion that she felt within the punk subculture.

Laura Jane Grace, *Tranny: Confessions of Punk Rock's Most Infamous Sellout*

Jack Halberstam (2005) has argued that "the gender-ambiguous individual of today represents a very different set of assumptions about gender and gender-inversion than the gender-inverted subject of the early twentieth-century . . . as a model of gender inversion recedes into anachronism, the transgender body has emerged as a kind of futurity itself, a kind of heroic fulfillment of postmodern promises of gender flexibility."[24] Despite this utopian description of the modern trans experience, Laura Jane Grace (b. 1980) describes a journey to self-discovery that was fraught and uncertain in her 2016 memoir, *Tranny: Confessions of Punk Rock's Most Infamous Sellout*.[25] Grace's narrative largely recounts her confusion about how to rationalize her

---

[23] Jarek Paul Ervine, "The Sound of Subterranean Scuzz-Holes: New York Queer Punk in the 1970s," *Popular Music and Society* 42, no. 4 (2019): 485.

[24] Jack Halberstam, *In a Queer Time and Place: Transgender Bodies, Subcultural Lives* (New York: New York University Press, 2005), 38.

[25] Grace abandoned her dead name, Tom Gabel, when she came out as a transgender woman in a 2012 interview with *Rolling Stone* and adopted the name of her great-grandmother and the name that her mother had in mind when she was pregnant. Grace's surname is that of her mother. This essay will use her self-affirmed name.

sexual attraction to women with the gender dysphoria that she experienced from puberty. Most of her memoir is devoted to a description of her struggle to embrace a gender identity that conforms with her biological sex. "I was going to be a man," she writes, "a husband to a wife, a father to a child, a front man [sic] to a band with a hit record. A man."[26] The memoir leads the reader through two failed marriages (first to her teenage sweetheart, Danielle Kay, and later to the artist Heather Hannoura, with whom she had a child in 2009) and describes the impact of Grace's attempts at gender conformity on her intimate relationships.

The memoir targets the anarcho-punk scene in which Grace participated as a fan and a musician as the main hurdle to her self-acceptance. Where County entered a scene that often played with queerness and gender ambiguity to signify alienation (even though her identity ultimately proved to be a hindrance to her success), the scene in which Grace participates purports to embrace diversity but, in practice, continues to be marked as cis-gender and male. Grace notes that while

> sex politics and queer culture were openly discussed in the radical activist punk scene, . . . gender identity was still a taboo. The acceptance and open-minded politics were part of what drew me to [the scene]. Show spaces were supposed to be open to everyone regardless of age, race, class, sex, or sexual preference, but for the most part it was just white kids oblivious to the privilege they came from. It also became clear to me that while these were the politics heralded by the scene, often they were not actually practiced.[27]

The scene perpetuated male "rock" stereotypes that were performed uncritically by members of her band, Against Me!, and which she felt obliged to embrace as she worked to suppress her identity. On early tours, Grace describes episodes of male bonding that involved such rock-star antics as wrestling, stealing beer, chasing women, and trashing hotel rooms. An incident while on tour in Italy in 2004 illustrates the feelings of shame and guilt that Grace experienced after joining her bandmates in transphobic shaming of three trans women that they encountered at a truck stop café. Eight years before she made her own transition, she felt compelled to participate as her bandmates humiliated the trio and she recalls that "I laughed at them along

---

[26] Laura Jane Grace with Dan Ozzi, *Tranny: Confessions of Punk Rock's Most Infamous Anarchist Sellout* (New York: Hachette Books, 2016), 202.
[27] Ibid., 37.

with everyone else, the whole time knowing the truth about myself, that I wished I were so brave. Not knowing who you are is a terrible feeling. I've been called a 'sellout' many times in my life for the choices I've made in my musical career. But this experience, that moment—that's what it feels like to truly sell out."[28]

Grace's other musical influence, grunge, can also be targeted as unwelcoming to an artist who was struggling with gender identity because, like anarcho-punk, it was underpopulated by women and exclusive of transgender performers. For Grace, grunge would help to explain certain behaviors that emerged as she struggled to suppress her abject body. In her study of Nirvana, Jessica Wood (2011) notes that the grunge subculture signaled social alienation through the performance of "illness," and she argues that grunge "illness" was modeled by Kurt Cobain through various physical and emotional ailments that ultimately led to his suicide in 1994. According to Wood, the "sick body [in grunge] . . . came to stand for a life of hardship, intensity, and physical risk" and was metonymic with social ills (like poverty, homelessness, and hopelessness) that deprive certain bodies of the right to exist and thrive.[29] I would add that the grunge body was gendered unequivocally as cis-male and that rare female exceptions, like Courtney Love, were also unambiguously cisgendered. In the early days of her career, Grace performed a cis-male variant of grunge "illness" through such stylistic references as loose-fitting thrift-store clothing, band T-shirts, combat boots, and a pallid and disheveled look that cued street culture. Behind the scenes, the outward performance of rock masculinity proved to be the source of Grace's "sick body," as she stoked her self-denial with drugs and alcohol and tried to release some of her inward tension in oblique allusions to gender dysphoria in such songs as "Searching for a Former Clarity" (2005), "The Ocean" (2007), or "Violence" (2011). Sickness is a recurring theme in the early parts of her memoir in ways that are reminiscent of Cobain. In a diary entry reproduced from November 2004, she writes that "if I were to say how I really feel, what I really think, people would think I was mentally ill. Cross-dressing feels like self-mutilation. I can never be anything more than a pervert dressed up in women's clothes. So sick, sick, sick. I want to black it all out. I do not care if I am alive or dead."[30] Ten years earlier, and just before

---

[28] Ibid., 64.
[29] Jessica Wood, "Pained Expressions: Metaphors of Sickness and Signs of 'Authenticity' in Kurt Cobain's 'Journals,'" *Popular Music* 30 (2011): 332.
[30] Grace, *Tranny*, 74.

his suicide, Cobain had disclosed in an interview in *Esquire* magazine that "I hate myself, I want to die."[31] Of course, Cobain's struggles were not rooted in feelings of gender dysphoria or fears of humiliation in a scene that rarely accommodated women, let alone trans women. However, as Shevory (1995) has noted, "in the ideology of grunge, the enemy turns out to be the self," irrespective of how that self might be construed.[32]

The title of Grace's memoir also alludes to the personal and professional struggles that she documents as she builds to the transition that she describes in the closing pages of the text. Her deliberate use of the pejorative term "tranny" in the title shocked her transgender fans and required a preemptive explanation, which Grace provided in a 2016 interview in *Noisey* magazine prior to the release of the book. "I don't want the word to have any power," she explained, "I don't want to ask permission to use it. I don't want to be afraid of it."[33] The term alludes to many episodes in the autobiography when Grace directed the epithet at others as a strategy to align herself with punk's normative masculinity, but it also signifies the self-loathing that she experienced as a closeted trans woman. The term "sellout," which also appears in the title, alludes not only to Grace's disappointment with herself, but also to fan reactions to the commercial success that was enjoyed by Against Me! in the mid-2000s. Anarcho-punks decried the band's decision to sign a lucrative deal with the mainstream Sire label to produce their fourth and fifth studio albums, *New Wave* (2007) and *White Crosses* (2010), with Butch Vig, who had gained international recognition as the producer of Nirvana's 1991 blockbuster album, *Nevermind*. Grace recalls that, on tour, "we'd play a new song, and someone would yell out 'sellout!' or hold up a sign that said YOU FAILED US above an anarchy symbol, and I'd stumble through the rest of the song, tripping up on lyrics."[34] Self-loathing and "selling out" had become inextricably linked during the period in Grace's career when she relinquished her right to self-determination and embraced the markers of rock masculinity that were more likely to ensure her commercial success. Paradoxically, it was through her commercial success that Grace eventually re-evaluated her life and realized that money, marriage, and fatherhood could do nothing to mitigate her gender dysphoria. In February 2011, she shared her intention

---

[31] Cobain, quoted in Stephen Wright, "The Big No," *Esquire*, July 1, 1994, 60.

[32] Thomas Shevory, "Bleached Resistance: The Politics of Grunge," *Popular Music and Society* 19, no. 2 (1995): 34.

[33] Grace, quoted in Kristen Carella and Kathryn Wymer, "'You Want Me to Surrender My Identity?': Laura Jane Grace, Transition and Selling Out," *Punk & Post-Punk* 8, no. 2 (2019): 194.

[34] Grace, *Tranny*, 189.

to transition with the members of her band and, soon after, with Hannoura. At the same time, Against Me! ended its five-year deal amicably with Sire Records and launched their own record label, Total Treble, which would enable them to produce music on their own terms. Grace came out publicly as a woman in an interview with *Rolling Stone* magazine on May 31, 2012, and set to work on a series of songs about her gender transition for the band's sixth studio album *Transgender Dysphoria Blues*, which was released on January 21, 2014, to critical acclaim. The personal and creative turn described at the end of the memoir represent a return to the spirit of anarcho-punk that marks Grace's early work. In songs like "Transgender Dysphoria Blues," "True Trans Rebel," and "Black Me Out," the band addresses the issues of inclusion, diversity, and equity that purportedly lie at the heart of punk's DIY ethos. Grace's unique embodiment of punk, as expressed in her memoir, contests that central tenet of the subculture and invites a re-evaluation of historical readings of punk as accepting, inclusive, and diverse.

Conclusion

The punk scholar and literary theorist Gerfried Ambrosch (2016) suggests that punk histories are complicit in telling the story of punk from the straight, cisgender male perspective of their authors and in reinforcing punk's conventional attitudes about gender and sexuality through their exclusion of other voices. He notes that for "idealists who see punk as an emancipatory project and believe that it can, and should, be used as a tool to change social conditions, patriarchy, heteronormativity, and the strictly binary gender model are incompatible with the punk ethos. However, this position only reflects one, very particular ideological construction within the larger punk culture that was not yet present in the mid-1970s, when punk first emerged."[35] According to Ambrosch, punk only began to address issues of social justice with the emergence of anarcho-punk in the 1980s and, even then, punk "has not been a 'united front' against sexism and homophobia—on the contrary, there has always been bigotry and misogyny in it. . . . In fact, the idea that punk is inherently 'politically correct,' a moral category established in the 1990s, is a myth."[36] The point is echoed by County, who

---

[35] Gerfried Ambrosch, "'Refusing to Be a Man': Gender, Feminism and Queer Identity in the Punk Subculture," *Punk & Post-Punk* 5, no. 3 (2016): 247.
[36] Ibid., 248.

wrote in 2021 that "rock and roll is such a macho world, they don't want people like me to be part of their history."[37] Despite the promise of inclusion and diversity in punk, the subculture and the histories that describe it have been, and remain, largely unwilling or unable to divorce themselves from social hierarchies that privilege some voices in the subculture while subordinating others, particularly those in the scene who were genuinely alienated because of their gender identities and/or their sexual preferences. To keep true to the promise, scholars must examine the narratives of those who have been excluded to interrogate the reasons for these exclusions and to bring silenced voices into dialogue with punk's history. Memoirs by marginalized members of the punk community, like County and Grace, encourage punk historians to reflect upon the biases that they bring into the stories that they create—and that their readers receive—about the punk subculture, its social hierarchies, and the opportunities it provides (or denies) for participation.

Bibliography

Ambrosch, Gerfried. "'Refusing to Be a Man': Gender, Feminism and Queer Identity in the Punk Subculture." *Punk & Post-Punk* 5, no. 3 (2016): 247–264.

Beemyn, Genny. "US History." In *Trans Bodies, Trans Selves: A Resource for the Transgender Community*, edited by Laura Erickson-Schroth, 501–536. New York: Oxford University Press, 2014.

Bell, Max. "The Dictators: The Handsomest Man in Rock and Roll." *New Musical Express*, October 16, 1976. Retrieved March 30, 2022, from http://www.rocksbackpages.com.proxy.lib.umich.edu/Library/Article/the-dictators-the-handsomest-man-in-rock-and-roll.

Carella, Kristen, and Kathryn Wymer. "'You Want Me to Surrender My Identity?': Laura Jane Grace, Transition and Selling Out." *Punk & Post-Punk* 8, no. 2 (2019): 193–207.

County, Jayne. *Man Enough to Be a Woman: The Autobiography of Jayne County*. London: Serpent's Tail, 2021.

Eells, Josh. "The Secret Life of Transgender Rocker Laura Jane Grace." *Rolling Stone*, May 31, 2012. https://www.rollingstone.com/music/music-news/the-secret-life-of-transgender-rocker-laura-jane-grace-tom-gabel-99788/.

Ervin, Jarek Paul. "The Sound of Subterranean Scuzz-Holes: New York Queer Punk in the 1970s." *Popular Music and Society* 42, no. 4 (2019): 483–500.

Grace, Laura Jane, with Dan Ozzi. *Tranny: Confessions of Punk Rock's Most Infamous Anarchist Sellout*. New York: Hachette Books, 2016.

Halberstam, Jack. *In a Queer Time and Place: Transgender Bodies, Subcultural Lives*, New York: New York University Press, 2005.

Hebdige, Dick. *Subculture: The Meaning of Style*. London: Routledge, 1979.

---

[37] County, *Tranny*, 258.

Loder, Kurt. "David Bowie: Straight Time." *Rolling Stone*, May 12, 1983. https://www.rollingstone.com/music/music-news/david-bowie-straight-time-69334/.

McNeil, Legs. "The Punk Manifesto." *Village Voice*, May 8, 1978.

Nyong'o, Tavia. "Do You Want Queer Theory (Or Do You Want the Truth)? Intersections of Punk and Queer in the 1970s." *Radical History Review* 100 (2008): 103–119.

Peraino, Judith A. "Plumbing the Surface of Sound and Vision: David Bowie, Andy Warhol, and the Art of Posing." *Qui parle* 21, no. 1 (2012): 151–184.

Ramone, Marky, and Richard Herschlag. *Punk Rock Blitzkrieg: My Life as a Ramone*. New York: Touchstone, 2016.

Savage, Jon. *England's Dreaming: Anarchy, Sex Pistols, Punk Rock, and Beyond*. 2nd ed. New York: St. Martin's Griffin, 2002.

Shevory, Thomas. "Bleached Resistance: The Politics of Grunge." *Popular Music and Society* 19, no. 2 (1995): 23–48.

Sinker, Mark. "Concrete, so as to Self-Destruct: The Etiquette of Punk, Its Habits, Rules, Values, and Dilemmas." In *Punk Rock? So What?*, edited by Roger Sabin, 120–140. New York: Routledge, 1999.

Whitall, Sarah. "Wayne County and Handsome Dick Manitoba: War of the Gargantuas." *Creem*, June 1976. Retrieved March 30, 2022. http://www.rocksbackpages.com.proxy.lib.umich.edu/Library/Article/wayne-county-and-handsome-dick-manitoba-war-of-the-gargantuas.

Wood, Jessica. "Pained Expressions: Metaphors of Sickness and Signs of 'Authenticity' in Kurt Cobain's 'Journals.'" *Popular Music* 30 (2011): 331–349.

Worley, Matthew. *No Future: Punk, Politics and British Youth Culture 1976–1984*. Cambridge: Cambridge University Press, 2017.

Wright, Stephen. "The Big No." *Esquire*, July 1, 1994, 55–63.

6

A Portrait of the Artist as a Punk

Authenticity and the Woman Musician in Debbie Harry's *Face It*

Margaret Henderson

Autobiography and rock music (here, including punk) share a powerful connection to the notion of authenticity. Autobiography promises writer and reader access to the authentic self and therefore to an authentic account of the past being narrated—"not simple verisimilitude but resemblance to the truth";[1] rock music positions itself as an authentic expression of youth culture in contrast to commercialized and hence co-opted pop music or the unrepresentative "straightness" of the mature adult cultural sphere.[2] And their coalescence as rock autobiography means that they "typically disclose previously uncirculated or private stories from an 'inside' point of view."[3] Regardless of critical work that problematizes authenticity in both forms (for autobiography, see Smith; Mack; for rock music, see Barker and Taylor; Attias)[4] autobiography and rock music continue to value and rely on authenticity's cachet. This partly explains the attractions of autobiography for women rock musicians who, as continual industry "outsiders"—already inauthentic in a male-dominated industry, can claim an authoritative speaking position

---

[1] Phillipe Lejeune and Paul John Eakin, *On Autobiography* (Minneapolis: University of Minnesota Press, 1989), 22.

[2] Helen Reddington, *The Lost Women of Rock Music: Female Musicians of the Punk Era* (Aldershot: Ashgate, 2007), 158; Lawrence Grossberg, *We Gotta Get Out of This Place: Popular Conservatism and Postmodern Culture* (New York: Routledge, 1992), 206.

[3] Thomas Swiss, "'That's Me in the Spotlight': Rock Autobiographies," *Popular Music* 24, no. 2 (2005): 288.

[4] Sidonie Smith, "'America's Exhibit A': Hillary Rodham Clinton's *Living History* and the Genres of Authenticity," *American Literary History* 24, no. 3 (2012): 523–542, doi:10.1093/alh/ajs028; Kimberley Mack, "'There's No Home for You Here': Jack White and the Unsolvable Problem of Blues Authenticity," *Popular Music and Society* 38, no. 2 (2015): 176–193, https://doi.org/10.1080/03007 766.2014.994323; Hugh Barker and Yuval Taylor, *Faking It: The Quest for Authenticity in Popular Music* (New York: W. W. Norton, 2007); Bernardo Alexander Attias, "Authenticity and Artifice in Rock and Roll: 'And I Guess That I Just Don't Care,'" *Rock Music Studies* 3, no. 2 (2016): 131–147.

Margaret Henderson, *A Portrait of the Artist as a Punk* In: *Women in Rock Memoirs*. Edited by: Cristina Garrigós and Marika Ahonen, Oxford University Press. © Oxford University Press 2023.
DOI: 10.1093/oso/9780197659328.003.0007

and potentially "create spaces for alternative voices and alternative ways of remembering" music's past.[5] As Susan Stanford Friedman explains, "Writing the [female] self shatters the cultural hall of mirrors and breaks the silence imposed by male speech," and male song, I would add.[6]

This essay explores authenticity in/and the rock music autobiography by analyzing punk/new wave singer Debbie Harry's *Face It* (2019).[7] As the contours and meanings of authenticity differ depending on music genre— I return to this soon—I wish to see if there is a homology between punk's version of authenticity and that encoded (or not) in her autobiography. As a woman musician's autobiography, gender emphasizes the salience and the complexity of the nexus between music, text, and authenticity. Regardless of women's increased participation in the rock music industry—partly attributable to punk—women remain in a circumscribed number of roles,[8] and, even more so in the historical period recounted by Harry,[9] women are largely eccentric subjects to rock's masculinist practices and self-imaging.[10] Moreover, women's relationship to authenticity in rock music is vexed: their marginality to rock and their traditional alignment with the supposedly less authentic genre of pop music[11] makes access to authenticity more complicated than for men. A textual analysis of Harry's punk memoirs allows me to trace the ways in which a white, lower-middle-class American woman renegotiates gender identity, the music industry's "hall of mirrors," and punk authenticity in the closing decades of the twentieth century.

I argue that there is a homology between punk's version of authenticity and the codes inscribed in the memoir, and that these codes provide insights into the fraught position of women punk (and rock) musicians, as well as their agency in a novel moment in recent history. Sidonie Smith's exploration of the performativity of all autobiographical subjects—literally, in the

---

[5] Robert Edgar, Fraser Mann, and Helen Pleasance, "Introduction," in *Music, Memory, and Memoir*, ed. Robert Edgar, Fraser Mann, and Helen Pleasance (New York: Bloomsbury Academic, 2019), 2.

[6] Susan Stanford Friedman, "Women's Autobiographical Selves: Theory and Practice," in *The Private Self: Theory and Practice of Women's Autobiographical Writings*, ed. Shari Benstock (Chapel Hill: University of North Carolina Press, 1988), 41.

[7] Debbie Harry with Sylvie Simmons, *Face It* (London: HarperCollins, 2019).

[8] Marion Leonard, "Putting Gender in the Mix: Employment, Participation, and Role Expectations in the Music Industries," in *The Routledge Companion to Media and Gender*, ed. Cynthia Carter, Linda Steiner, and Lisa McLaughlin (London: Taylor & Francis, 2013), 129–131.

[9] Simon Frith and Angela McRobbie, "Rock and Sexuality," in *On Record: Rock, Pop, and the Written Word*, ed. Simon Frith and Andrew Goodwin (New York: Pantheon, 1990), 373–374.

[10] Marion Leonard, *Gender in the Music Industry: Rock, Discourse and Girl Power* (Farnham: Ashgate, 2007), 22–25; Reddington, *The Lost Women of Rock Music*, 158.

[11] Reddington, *The Lost Women of Rock Music*, 158; Frith and McRobbie, "Rock and Sexuality," 375.

case of the woman musician—helps us to read Harry's memoir.[12] To understand changes in autobiographical form, Smith draws on Michel De Certeau's work regarding the power differentials and related political tactics of different groups of social subjects that he terms "weak" and "strong." Smith argues that "a specific [weak] autobiographical subject seizes the occasion to effect a timely adjustment of the norm."[13] In our case, Harry, as the outsider and therefore relatively weak subject of rock autobiography, adjusts the norms of the woman musician and of the rock memoir. "Through tactical dis/identifications" Smith explains, "the autobiographical subject adjusts, redeploys, transforms discourses of autobiographical identity."[14] Harry's locus in New York punk culture and its "authentic inauthenticity"[15] mean alternative sources of authenticity and a method of dis/identification. As did many punk women in everyday life, her autobiography performs a refusal of gendered conventions of text and of self.

Harry's deliberate figuration of the self as artist frees herself from her traditional confinement in the masculinist rock imaginary as a blonde, white, passive sex object. Rather, Harry as artist delineates the potential of punk culture for women at that time, as she profits from and transcends her self-appointed persona to become a serious cultural worker, a persona that also manages to defuse punk's and Blondie's status as commodities. *Face It* thereby decenters and reconfigures the personal to provide a detailed, informal chronicle of times and places, and detached observations on the female self as image: a social relationality replaces a more typically feminine intimate relationality.

Keeping It Real, Keeping It a Little Unreal

For Lawrence Grossberg, authenticity is constitutive of rock music and guarantor of its value for fans: "Rock's special place was enabled by its articulation to an ideology of 'authenticity'" with this authenticity "defined by rock's ability to articulate the historical condition to the experience of postwar youth: . . . its ability to articulate private but common desires, feelings and experiences into a shared public language."[16] The critical role for authenticity

---

[12] Sidonie Smith, "Performativity, Autobiographical Practice, Resistance," *AB: Auto/biography Studies* 10, no. 1 (1995): 17–33.
[13] Ibid., 21.
[14] Ibid., 21.
[15] Grossberg, *We Gotta Get Out of This Place*, 224.
[16] Ibid., 205, 206–207.

is to divide rock from "mere entertainment,"[17] thus enabling rock to negotiate the contradiction between being an artistic expression centering on an ethos of rebellion against mainstream values, and rock's (and music, more broadly) status as a reproducible mass commodity and industrial practice.

Rock authenticity relies on a set of codes on and off stage: for Grossberg, authenticity "was measured by its sound and, most commonly, its voice,"[18] producing what Simon Frith terms "rock naturalism"[19]—the sense that rock music is an unmediated expression of feeling—derived from and signifying rock's origins in rhythm and blues.[20] The centrality of rebellion and rock's implicitly male teenage subject,[21] the particular codes and practices of rock authenticity—guitars and drums, guitar solos, the physicality of live performance, the emotional release, the fantasy of existential freedom, for instance—and rock's history as a male-dominated art form and industry have meant that rock authenticity is coded as masculine.

Rock authenticity, however, by the 1970s is eroded by corporate and cultural factors, losing its privileged place as the youth musical form of "the real thing." For Grossberg, rock's sensibility changes to cynicism and irony, which he locates as part of the broader post–World War II epoch of postmodernity and its emphasis on the manipulation of the image as constructing and supplanting the real (as in Jean Baudrillard's culture of the simulacra or Guy Debord's society of the spectacle)[22]: Madonna is one of his examples. There is now "a logic of 'ironic nihilism' or 'authentic inauthenticity,'" and a recognition that "all images become equal," as are all musical styles.[23] As befitting punk's early 1970s emergence in the bloated, corporate stage of rock in which rock's role as an authentic expression of youth appears less credible, and in the same time that postmodernism approaches being a cultural dominant, punk is premised on an alternative reading and figuring of authenticity, whether in terms of affect, performance strategies, or musical content.[24] And this has implications for gender.

---

[17] Ibid., 207.
[18] Ibid., 207–208.
[19] Simon Firth, "The Real Thing—Bruce Springsteen," in *Music for Pleasure: Essays in the Sociology of Pop* (New York: Routledge, 1988), 91.
[20] Allan F. Moore and Remy Martin, *Rock: The Primary Text: Developing a Musicology of Rock*, 3rd ed. (New York: Routledge, 2019), 79–80.
[21] Dick Bradley, *Understanding Rock'n'Roll: Popular Music in Britain 1955–1964* (Buckingham: Open University Press, 1992), 11.
[22] Jean Baudrillard, *Simulacra and Simulation* (Ann Arbor: University of Michigan Press, 1994); Guy Debord, *The Society of the Spectacle* (New York: Zone Books, 1994).
[23] Grossberg, *We Gotta Get Out of This Place*, 224, 225.
[24] Barker and Taylor, *Faking It*.

Ryan Moore argues that punk has two tendencies: "the culture of deconstruction" and authenticity.[25] Deconstruction refers to "the semiotic assault of punk," in which punk is aware of, and uses, the stream of images that now make up everyday life and lived experience, and to a related sensibility of "self-reflexive irony."[26] For Crispin Sartwell, "Punk culture might be looked upon as a rejection of every aspect of the spectacle,"[27] responding with a politicized, reflexive, and often humorous use of images—both visual and verbal. Consequently, punk's use of the image produces distance between the subject and the viewer/reader, and negates any self-evident authenticity provided by the image. Instead, manipulating the image is a marker of punk authenticity. Related to this critique of the image, punk no longer believes in music's ability to offer an unmediated transcendence or a direct expression of self. And it may also be the case that punk is suspicious that expressions of an authentic self are even available for articulation.

Yet punk has its version of authenticity—its "utopian element," namely, "a search for authenticity [cultural and personal] free from the culture industries"[28]—including corporate rock, with a resultant core anxiety for punk being whether a band had "sold out" to the system. Philip Lewin and J. Patrick Williams argue that "Punk . . . forged a construction of authenticity that distinguished 'real' from 'fake' by virtue of the extent to which one created versus consumed."[29] As Rebecca Daugherty observes,[30] punk's interest in the manipulation of cultural images as creative practice opened up space for critiques of gender identities and ideologies, evident in punk women's creation of bad girl and bad taste personae (Poison Ivy, Poly Styrene, and so on). Similarly, punk's search for authenticity outside of mainstream culture meant a potentially more liberating space for women musicians, artists, and fans.[31] So it is more accurate to use the term punk in/authenticity to capture this relationship between the authentic and the inauthentic in punk culture—the authentic being at the heart of, but masked as well as

---

[25] Ryan Moore, "Postmodernism and Punk Subculture: Cultures of Authenticity and Deconstruction," *Communication Review* 7, no. 3 (2004): 307.

[26] Ibid.

[27] Crispin Sartwell, *Political Aesthetics* (Ithaca, NY: Cornell University Press, 2010), 103.

[28] Moore, "Postmodernism and Punk Subculture," 323, 307.

[29] Philip Lewin and J. Patrick Williams, "The Ideology and Practice of Authenticity in Punk Subculture," in *Authenticity in Culture, Self, Society*, ed. Philip Vannini and J. Patrick Williams (London: Routledge, 2009), 76.

[30] Rebecca Daugherty, "The Spirit of '77: Punk and the Girl Revolution," *Women and Music* no. 6 (2007): 29–33.

[31] Mavis Bayton, *Frock Rock: Women Performing Popular Music* (Oxford: Oxford University Press, 2003), 64–65.

expressed by, the inauthentic. This nexus is critical to the ways in which *Face It* "scrambles" the codes and boundaries of women's rock memoir.[32]

Face It: The Lead Singer's Portrait as an Artist

Early in her memoir Debbie Harry states that her primary desire from high school on was "to be some kind of artist or bohemian"[33] rather than a rock musician; music happened to be the medium that she worked in, and her early punk scene of New York was characterized by the art/music/writing hybridity.[34] Yet she was also aware of being physically attractive in an industry that was expert at, and reliant upon, objectifying women into sex symbols: "But I'm not blind and I'm not stupid: I take advantage of my looks and I use them."[35] This self-identification and milieu produces major implications for her autobiography.

Harry explains that at the time of Blondie's formation, "hardly anyone in the midseventies [sic] was doing that kind of retro thing we were doing. We put our own downtown spin on it that made it a kind of crossover between glitter-glam and punk."[36] Rather than the authentic core to rock—its seemingly unmediated nature—Blondie's retro, crossover music is self-consciously revisiting and adapting existing musical forms.[37] And as for her persona: "well, I had been bleaching my hair again and when I walked down the street the construction guys and truck drivers would yell, 'Hey, Blondie!' There was a famous comic strip character from the thirties named Blondie, a flapper—the dumb blonde who turns out to be smarter than the rest of them. Okay, I could play that role on stage."[38] Thus, from its beginnings, the band and its singer deployed artifice strategically to make music and as a means of controlling exploitation, thematics that structure *Face It*. Accordingly, our narrator takes a position of authority: not just an artist but a gallerist curating a cool and careful image.

---

[32] Smith, "Performativity, Autobiographical Practice, Resistance," 31.
[33] Harry, *Face It*, 29.
[34] Bernard Gendron, *Between Montmartre and the Mudd Club: Popular Music and the Avant-Garde* (Chicago: Chicago University Press, 2002), 7.
[35] Harry, *Face It*, 343.
[36] Ibid., 92.
[37] Her earlier band, the Stillettoes, was also relatively theatrical; see ibid., 84.
[38] Ibid., 91.

Considering the importance of packaging a band through record covers, photographs, and videos—even if the band is anti-image, as in punk's case—the autobiography as a material object becomes another element that requires careful curation as part of the image making/control process.[39] Gerard Genette's concept of the peritext as part of a book's public presentation aids us in decoding *Face It*'s material qualities as critical to constructing Harry's punk in/authenticity. Peritext is a "spatial and material . . . zone" produced by publishers, and refers to "(the cover, the title page, and their appendages) and with the book's material construction (selection of format, of paper, of typeface, and so forth), which is executed by the typesetter and printer but decided on by the publisher, possibly in consultation with the author."[40] *Face It*'s materiality plays a crucial role in constructing the punk singer as an artist by emphasizing the centrality of image-making, manipulation, and control to the narrating punk self, and functioning as a form of cultural distinction. This artifact signals that it is closer to art than to being a commodity.

Face It's cover goes for punk minimalism: the only text is the title and the author's name, with a black and white photo of Harry and some handwritten drawings superimposed on it—the first sign of a punk manipulation of the image. The paper is glossy—at least in the hardback edition, providing weight and luxeness, and the typeface is eye-catching in its unconventionality. The title page's listing of a creative director (Rob Roth) and Sylvie Simmons, the respected rock journalist, as interviewer—denoted as "in collaboration with Sylvie Simmons," is another marker of distinction. This is not a typical ghostwritten memoir of a celebrity, more a serious work of art—a curated and collaborative project: again, an echo of Blondie as a creative collective.

The book's aesthetic qualities are reinforced by its intense visuality. While the inclusion of photographs of family, friends, and professional acquaintances are a convention of musicians' autobiographies, "forming a parallel discourse to the narrative,"[41] Harry's text takes it to another level both in quantity and in the treatment of the photographs. Typically, autobiographies include a dedicated section or more of photographs; in contrast, each chapter of *Face It* begins with a photograph of Harry, and more photographs are interspersed within chapters. These are often set off from

---

[39] Katja Lee, "Not Just Ghost Stories: Alternate Practices for Reading Coauthored Celebrity Memoirs," *Journal of Popular Culture* 47, no. 6 (2014): 1260.

[40] Gerard Genette, *Paratexts: Thresholds of Interpretation*, trans. Jane E. Lewin (Cambridge: Cambridge University Press, 1997; French ed. 1987), 16.

[41] Matthew Sutton, "Amplifying the Text: Paratext in Popular Musicians' Autobiographies," *Popular Music and Society* 38, no. 2 (2015): 208.

the text with a border or contrasting colored background, giving the appearance of being either or both a page from a photo album or a piece of art on a gallery wall. Having photos taken by Robert Mapplethorpe, Mick Rock, and Chris Stein also adds to the serious art cachet, yet Harry makes a typically punk gesture of writing speech bubbles or scribbling on some of the photos—a type of graffitiing of the self. A baby photo of Harry starts the chapter, "Born to Be Punk": two safety pins are drawn on the baby as well as some childlike drawings of what could be punks looking at her.[42] Rather than providing straightforward intimacy for the reader, Harry is acknowledging the constructedness of any identity—even that of the baby, and including hers as a punk. As she comments, "So much of what has been written about me has been about how I look. It's sometimes made me wonder if I've ever accomplished anything beyond my image."[43] In meeting the importance of her visual image *almost* face-on, however, she also is taking control of it through a self-reflexivity and irony, a type of punk control.[44]

Complementing the photos are four sections (twenty-six pages in total) of full-color fan art: drawings of Harry done by fans and sent to her. Harry explains their inclusion thus: "Every musician, actor, artist I've ever met always says, 'It's the fans that make it happen for us.' . . . For me it's a way of saying thank you."[45] While these drawings can be read as filler or as evidence of Blondie's pop star status, they are framed by Harry to illustrate punk's reconfiguration of the relationship between band and audience[46]—its breaking of the fourth wall in the service of egalitarianism, and that amateurism in creative practices is acceptable—its DIY ethos, with Harry serving as muse.[47] That she devotes four pages of musings on them suggest the importance of these images and of the amateur artist—reiterating that she is foremost an artist: "Who knows if any of my Fan Art artists carried on into the future with their interests in portraiture or other schools of art. . . . Very likely I'd be glad if they did."[48] This fan art functions as both an egalitarian, grassroots

---

[42] Harry, *Face It*, 94.
[43] Ibid., 230.
[44] Interestingly, Tomasz Sawczuk notes that self-reflexivity is a distinctive quality of other women's rock memoirs. " 'I've Been Crawling Up So Long on Your Stairway to Heaven': The Rise of the Female Rock Memoir," *Crossroads: A Journal of English Studies* 15 (2016): 71–81.
[45] Harry, *Face It*, 134.
[46] Jon Savage, "A Punk Aesthetic," in *Punk: An Aesthetic*, ed. Johan Kugelberg and Jon Savage (New York: Rizzoli International, 2012), 146–149.
[47] Toby Mott, "A Punk's Progress," in *Oh So Pretty: Punk in Print, 1976–80*, ed. Sara Bader (London: Phaidon, 2016), 16.
[48] Harry, *Face It*, 134.

supplement to the self-authored figure and the professionally photographed image of Debbie Harry, and as a deflection of the potential rawness of "authentic" autobiography. They are another way of letting Harry (and the readers) not quite face it.

The book explicitly states that it is based on interviews with Simmons, suggesting an authenticity to the recollections, and indeed the text has more of an oral rather than literary quality, with the "voice" of Harry prominent and an impression that editing is light. American punk culture arose out of a fascination with B-grade culture, suburbia, junk food, etc.[49]—a specifically American form of quirkiness, while the New York scene had an art school, intellectual element to it[50]—the Talking Heads met at Art School and Richard Hell was both poet and musician. These twin aspects of American punk come through in Harry's voice and anecdotes. We have quirkiness and sardonic humor as markers of punk authenticity, and of readerly intimacy. Here's Harry recalling being mugged:

> That night, when I got to the last block at St. Mark's Place, the bag hanging on my shoulder, two kids came running and in a flash I was down on the sidewalk, flat on my back, being dragged by the bag strap. I hung onto that fucking bag like I was going for a touchdown. I think the only reason they didn't get the bag was because it was made so well and didn't tear. And fortunately, no knives were pulled or guns drawn, just a snatch-and-run. It's been fifty years and I still have that bag.[51]

Or when she donates her stash of cocaine to David Bowie and Iggy Pop on tour: "So I went upstairs with my vast quantity of cocaine and they just sucked it right up in one swoop. After they did the blow, David pulled out his cock—as if I were the official cock checker or something. Since I was in an all-male band, maybe they figured I really was the cock-check lady."[52] This is a female punk's take on rock and roll masculine excess, and echoes punk's irreverent stance toward criminality, drugs, and sexual deviancy.[53] As a female punk, she is neither outraged nor traumatized, and instead uses this excess as humorous fodder for stories of the self.

---

[49] Isabelle Anscombe, Robert Bayley, and Dike Blair, *Punk* (New York: Urizen, 1978), 90.
[50] Gendron, *Between Montmartre and the Mudd Club*.
[51] Harry, *Face It*, 119.
[52] Ibid., 154.
[53] This attitude is displayed in song titles like Blondie's "X Offender" and the Ramones' "Cretin Hop" and "Now I Wanna Sniff Some Glue."

Her sardonic humor is matched by a coolness of tone, in the sense of the cool (because marginalized) subject's detached emotional disposition toward the straight world.[54] There is intimacy in her humor, but there is also detachment in the narration. A cool tone is another method of dealing with personal pain, and/or for controlling the image of the self and, like her irreverence, is indicative of an aspect of an American punk sensibility—its ironic and self-reflexive take on the world. As Harry reflects: "Memory, what did you do to the fun times? Really, the first seven years of Blondie felt insane. Total madness. But I keep thinking there must have been some good times. Feels like I'm always remembering the hard times. . . . Maybe I'm just demented and the horror stories are more entertaining for me."[55] Accordingly, she recollects a series of traumatic events: being raped, mugged, almost dying in a house fire, and nearly being the victim of the infamous serial killer Ted Bundy. Furthermore, she was financially ruined by poor band management, used hard drugs, and while she kept her health—more or less—she did have to nurse her seriously ill partner, Chris, for an extended period. Rather than emotion and confession, however, Harry uses a matter-of-fact, cool way to narrate these events. This, in addition to her sardonic humor, is a critical marker of a guarded, self-conscious, streetwise narrator, as exemplified in her account of being robbed and raped with Chris present:

> He [the rapist, "Jimi"] piled up the guitars and Chris's camera and then he untied my hands and told me to take off my pants. He fucked me. And then he said, "Go clean yourself," and left. " 'Jimi' has left the building." . . . I can't say that I felt a lot of fear. I'm glad this happened pre-AIDS or I might have freaked. In the end, the stolen guitars hurt me more than the rape. I mean, we had *no* [emphasis in original] equipment.[56]

The rape is recounted as a series of events, with the emotions secondary, and Harry's response is pragmatic and ironic: " 'Jimi' has left the building."

Harry's version of punk authenticity is reiterated in the foci (and the omissions) of the autobiographical events, particularly its quality of "withholding."[57] Paralleling and reinforcing her cool tone and detachment are the events that don't find much space in the text. Harry's family, for instance,

---

[54] Dick Pountain and David Robins, *Cool Rules: Anatomy of an Attitude* (London: Reaktion Books, 2000), 19, 23.
[55] Harry, *Face It*, 96.
[56] Ibid., 96–97.
[57] Pamela Fox also notices this quality of withholding in Chrissie Hynde's memoir, *Reckless*. Note that Hynde is a contemporary of Harry. "Born to Run and Reckless: My Life as a Pretender: Rewriting

features mainly at the start. Once Harry narrates adulthood, they play little part in the narrative, although being adopted does seem important to her self-image, and to explain her lifelong fear of abandonment. This fear, and her failed attempt to connect with her birth parents, however, is only briefly mentioned. Similarly, her break-up with her longtime partner and soul mate, Chris, is a deliberately minor presence. Harry, being "too goddamned independent," as her mother observes,[58] presents as an autonomous self in the world, and embodies the female punk's rejection of the conventional expectations of femininity, family, romantic love, and emotionality. For Harry, the project of the self is the project of being an artist; as she says, for her (and Blondie) "in those days, it was about making something happen."[59] Art is *the* mode of authentic being for this woman, even as it plays with inauthenticity.

Accordingly, and given the decentering of the private self, what Harry does give space to is the trajectory and milieu of Blondie, and her reflections on being the "Blondie" of the band. In a possible defensive gesture, given Blondie's and Harry's mainstream success, Harry takes on the authoritative position as insider chronicler of the early East Coast American punk scene. She sets out the venues, the personalities, the Band's tours, the way the industry operated, the pitfalls, and the music made by Blondie, suggesting autobiography's referential impulse to place the individual in history and as history,[60] and her social and collective form of relationality. She represents Blondie's career as a slow and difficult rise to fame—"Blondie was an underdog"[61]—thereby maintaining its punk cred. And she emphasizes the cutting edge quality of the band:

> I've been trying to think what the best of Blondie was for me. I've come to the conclusion that it was the early days of the band when we were struggling artists, scuttling around the Lower East Side just trying to get something going, walking home from work before dawn through the dark, dusty, sweet-dirt smell of the city. Everybody got by on no money. Nobody talked about mainstream success. Who wanted to be mainstream? What

---

the Political Imaginary of Rock Music Memoir," in *Popular Music and the Politics of Hope*, ed. Susan Fast and Craig Jennex (London: Routledge, 2019), 133.

[58] Harry, *Face It*, 87.
[59] Ibid., 173.
[60] Paul John Eakin, *Touching the World: Reference in Autobiography*, coursebook ed. (Princeton, NJ: Princeton University Press, 1992), 144.
[61] Harry, *Face It*, 97.

we were doing was so much better than that. We felt like pioneers. We were cutting new paths instead of taking the tried and tested roads.[62]

And, "by the eighties, new wave had already been co-opted by the mainstream, just as punk had been and the hippies before that. You couldn't move for glossy, major-label new wave bands. It was all too safe for our liking."[63] She sets out the punk/new wave ecosystem as if it is her neighborhood—which it was: all the bands, the venues, and musos are there: Television, Patti Smith, CBGBs, Max's Kansas City, the New York Dolls, the Ramones, Joan Jett, and so on. Though she also, in best punk style, debunks some myths: "There wasn't really a particular sound you could define as punk until much later on—because at first there were many different styles. . . . The New York punk scene didn't have one particular look either. When Blondie started, the guys all had long hair."[64] Her detailed and colloquial anecdotes and local, grassroots perspective mark the account as authentic.

Face It's other major emphasis is Harry's reflections on her image as the only woman and lead singer in a band, and in "a highly macho game."[65] Using a similar strategy to her contemporary Grace Jones's memoir,[66] rather than being taken behind the Blondie image to the real Debbie Harry, as punk bricoleuse Harry details how the image arose and was constructed, and the work it did for this woman artist.[67] As if to deflect criticism of her self-objectification, she discusses how she likes magazine centerfolds—doing an ironic one for the punk magazine *Creem*;[68] Chris's photoshoots of her; what is really like to work as a Playboy Bunny ("hard work")[69]; how she developed her look via secondhand clothes and castoffs; and having a Barbie doll made in your image: "The Barbie people liked that pink dress [from the 1970s]. I think I would have almost preferred the zebra dress. But maybe animal print is one of the things that Barbie doesn't do."[70] And she explains the Marilyn Monroe image: "My character in Blondie was partly a visual homage

---

[62] Ibid., 213.
[63] Ibid., 200.
[64] Ibid., 107.
[65] Ibid., 105.
[66] Hannah Yelin, "'I Am the Centre of Fame': Doing Celebrity, Performing Fame and Navigating Cultural Hierarchies in Grace Jones' *I'll Never Write My Memoirs*," *Celebrity Studies* 12, no. 1 (2021).
[67] Dick Hebdige identifies bricolage as typifying punk style, a method of punk's "semiotic guerrilla warfare," in *Subculture: The Meaning of Style* (London: Routledge, 1979), 105.
[68] Harry, *Face It*, 124–125.
[69] Ibid., 60.
[70] Ibid., 332.

to Marilyn, and partly a statement about the good old double standard."[71] With these complex, humorous reflections, she is confronting a simplistic reduction of her to her image, or as an unreflexive victim of (self-)objectification. Instead, Harry is smart and political about the power of the image, and what it is like to be in a male-dominated industry: "But I wanted to do music and I didn't give a shit if that meant being in a boys' club.... [G]enerally, I've been able to turn that sexual disrespect around and make it work *for* (emphasis in original) me, rather than against me."[72] Her self-reflexivity and seeming sincerity suggest an authentic account of a female punk's mobilization of feminine inauthenticity as valuable parody. Her quest to be an artist and to make "something happen" meant that the collage of images of the singer is intrinsic to the broader project: part of the "big Dadaist up-yours" to society's hypocrisies she sees as core to punk.[73]

The Song Remains the Same, Doesn't Remain the Same

As Bernard Gendron observes, New York punk enabled rock music to merge into the visual arts,[74] expanding notions of what is an artist. Harry's memoir, with its carefully "curated" account of an American white woman's desire to be an artist—simultaneously as an image and as an image maker—exemplifies this late twentieth-century phenomenon from a gendered perspective. And *Face It* also captures the way in which punk functioned as another emanation of the early twentieth-century historical avant-garde in that the function, institutional rules, codes, and rules of rock music were up for grabs[75]—a space where authenticity for women might be realized by the devices of image manipulation, from the microlevel of the word to the macrolevel of the band and the self. This ethos is textualized in what is included in and excluded from *Face It*: we have Harry's unapologetic but reflective voice, an emphasis on the importance of the times and places of punk and new wave rather than the personal, the familial, and the intimate, and the New York punk sound captured in her cool, ironic, unpretentious, and quirky narrative of the artist

---

[71] Ibid., 105.
[72] Ibid., 306.
[73] Ibid., 107.
[74] Gendron, *Between Montmartre and the Mudd Club*, 321.
[75] Greil Marcus makes a similar argument in *Lipstick Traces*, linking punk to preceding moments and movements of cultural protest. Greil Marcus, *Lipstick Traces: A Secret History of the Twentieth Century* (London: Secker & Warburg, 1989).

as an image of a beautiful woman in a masculinist, frontier culture industry. Harry's punk agency to live unconventionally as a woman emanates in her seemingly authentic account of inauthenticity.

As befits Harry's performance as artist, *Face It* demonstrates that the grain of the music genre finds its way into the grain of the literary text and into the voice of the narrator (thus extending Barthes's influential work on the grain of the voice).[76] The grain of the genre can include, but is more than, the formal qualities of a genre's typical song, as in Stein and Butler's notion of "musical autobiographies";[77] it is in the fibers and textures of the genre as a lived and embodied experience, mythology, set of intertexts, and intermedial domain. And given the rapidly evolving cultural memorialization of punk, Harry's memoir is a critical counternarrative of and hence intervention into this process. *Face It* performs critical memory-work in "a media ecosystem that otherwise proliferates unauthorised exposés about [famous] women's lives and their meanings,"[78] telling us much about women in rock by telling us less than we might expect.

Moreover, to read this memoir in a post-#MeToo era is a disconcerting reminder of an earlier stage of the rock music industry as a type of frontier patriarchal capitalism, with sexual abuse, overwork, and exploitation of workers—both men and women—by male entrepreneurs a systemic feature, and the libertarian, or at least, anarchic orientation of musicians feeding into this: the culture industries profiting in another way from bohemianism and the desire to rebel. Regardless of punk's attempts to subvert the commodification of the image and to create alternative economic circuits,[79] exploitation appears to be a consistent marker of "the real deal" for musicians.

Bibliography

Anscombe, Isabelle, Roberta Bayley, and Dike Blair. *Punk*. New York: Urizen, 1978.
Attias, Bernardo Alexander. "Authenticity and Artifice in Rock and Roll: 'And I Guess That I Just Don't Care.'" *Rock Music Studies* 3, no. 2 (2016): 131–147.

---

[76] Roland Barthes, "The Grain of the Voice," in *Image—Music—Text*, trans. Stephen Heath (New York: Hill & Wang, 1977), 179–189.

[77] Daniel Stein and Martin Butler, "Musical Autobiographies: An Introduction." *Popular Music and Society* 38, no. 2 (2015): 118, https://doi.org/10.1080/03007766.2014.994324.

[78] Hannah Yelin, *Celebrity Memoir: From Ghostwriting to Gender Politics* (Cham: Springer International, 2020), 42.

[79] See Stacy Thompson for a pessimistic analysis of punk's attempts to create an alternative economic model. "Market Failure: Punk Economics, Early and Late," *College Literature* 28, no. 2 (2001): 48–64.

Barker, Hugh, and Yuval Taylor. *Faking It: The Quest for Authenticity in Popular Music*. New York: W. W. Norton, 2007.

Barthes, Roland. "The Grain of the Voice." In *Image—Music—Text*. Translated by Stephen Heath, 179-189. New York: Hill & Wang, 1977.

Baudrillard, Jean. *Simulacra and Simulation*. Ann Arbor: University of Michigan Press, 1994.

Bayton, Mavis. *Frock Rock: Women Performing Popular Music*. Oxford: Oxford University Press, 2003.

Bradley, Dick. *Understanding Rock'n'roll: Popular Music in Britain 1955-1964*. Buckingham: Open University Press, 1992.

Daugherty, Rebecca. "The Spirit of '77: Punk and the Girl Revolution." *Women and Music* no. 6 (2007): 27-35.

Debord, Guy. *The Society of the Spectacle*. New York: Zone Books, 1994.

Eakin, Paul John. *Touching the World: Reference in Autobiography*. Coursebook ed. Princeton, NJ: Princeton University Press, 1992.

Edgar, Robert, Fraser Mann, and Helen Pleasance. Introduction to *Music, Memory, and Memoir*, edited by Robert Edgar, Fraser Mann, and Helen Pleasance, 1-10. New York: Bloomsbury Academic, 2019.

Fox, Pamela. "*Born to Run* and *Reckless: My Life as a Pretender*: Rewriting the Political Imaginary of Rock Music Memoir." In *Popular Music and the Politics of Hope*, edited by Susan Fast and Craig Jennex, 123-142. London: Routledge, 2019.

Friedman, Susan Stanford. "Women's Autobiographical Selves: Theory and Practice." In *The Private Self: Theory and Practice of Women's Autobiographical Writings*, edited by Shari Benstock, 34-62. Chapel Hill: University of North Carolina Press, 1988.

Frith, Simon. "The Real Thing—Bruce Springsteen." In *Music for Pleasure: Essays in the Sociology of Pop*, 94-101. New York: Routledge, 1988.

Frith, Simon, and Angela McRobbie. "Rock and Sexuality." In *On Record: Rock, Pop, and the Written Word*, edited by Simon Frith and Andrew Goodwin, 371-389. New York: Pantheon, 1990.

Gendron, Bernard. *Between Montmartre and the Mudd Club: Popular Music and the Avant-Garde*. Chicago: Chicago University Press, 2002.

Genette, Gerard. *Paratexts: Thresholds of Interpretation*. Translated by Jane E. Lewin. Cambridge: Cambridge University Press, 1997.

Grossberg, Lawrence. *We Gotta Get Out of This Place: Popular Conservatism and Postmodern Culture*. New York: Routledge, 1992.

Harry, Debbie, with Sylvie Simmons. *Face It*. London: HarperCollins, 2019.

Hebdige, Dick. *Subculture: The Meaning of Style*. London: Routledge, 1979.

Lee, Katja. "Not Just Ghost Stories: Alternate Practices for Reading Coauthored Celebrity Memoirs." *Journal of Popular Culture* 47, no. 6 (2014): 1256-1270.

Lejeune, Philippe, and Paul John Eakin. *On Autobiography*. Minneapolis: University of Minnesota Press, 1989.

Leonard, Marion. *Gender in the Music Industry: Rock, Discourse and Girl Power*. Aldershot: Ashgate, 2007.

Leonard, Marion. "Putting Gender in the Mix: Employment, Participation, and Role Expectations in the Music Industries." In *The Routledge Companion to Media and Gender*, edited by Cynthia Carter, Linda Steiner, and Lisa McLaughlin, 127-136. London: Taylor & Francis, 2013.

Lewin, Philip, and J. Patrick Williams. "The Ideology and Practice of Authenticity in Punk Subculture." In *Authenticity in Culture, Self, Society*, edited by Philip Vannini and J. Patrick Williams, 65–83. London: Routledge, 2009.

Mack, Kimberly. "'There's No Home for You Here': Jack White and the Unsolvable Problem of Blues Authenticity." *Popular Music and Society* 38, no. 2 (2015): 176–193.

Marcus, Greil. *Lipstick Traces: A Secret History of the Twentieth Century*. London: Secker & Warburg, 1989.

Moore, Allan F., and Remy Martin. *Rock: The Primary Text: Developing a Musicology of Rock*. 3rd ed. Abingdon: Routledge, 2019.

Moore, Ryan. "Postmodernism and Punk Subculture: Cultures of Authenticity and Deconstruction." *Communication Review* 7, no. 3 (2004): 305–327.

Mott, Toby. "A Punk's Progress." In *Oh So Pretty: Punk in Print, 1976–80*, edited by Sara Bader, 15–17. London: Phaidon, 2016.

Pountain, Dick, and David Robins. *Cool Rules: Anatomy of an Attitude*. London: Reaktion Books, 2000.

Reddington, Helen. *The Lost Women of Rock Music: Female Musicians of the Punk Era*. Aldershot: Ashgate, 2007.

Sartwell, Crispin. *Political Aesthetics*. Ithaca, NY: Cornell University Press, 2010.

Sawczuk, Tomasz. "'I've Been Crawling Up So Long on Your Stairway to Heaven'": The Rise of the Female Rock Memoir." *Crossroads: A Journal of English Studies*, no. 15 (2016): 71–81.

Smith, Sidonie. "'America's Exhibit A': Hillary Rodham Clinton's Living History and the Genres of Authenticity." *American Literary History* 24, no. 3 (2012): 523–542.

Smith, Sidonie. "Performativity, Autobiographical Practice, Resistance." *AB: Auto/biography Studies* 10, no. 1 (1995): 17–33.

Stein, Daniel, and Martin Butler. "Musical Autobiographies: An Introduction." *Popular Music and Society* 38, no. 2 (2015): 115–121.

Sutton, Matthew. "Amplifying the Text: Paratext in Popular Musicians' Autobiographies." *Popular Music and Society* 38, no. 2 (2015): 208–223.

Swiss, Thomas. "That's Me in the Spotlight: Rock Autobiographies." *Popular Music* 24, no. 2 (2005): 287–294.

Thompson, Stacy. "Market Failure: Punk Economics, Early and Late." *College Literature* 28, no. 2 (2001): 48–64.

Yelin, Hannah. *Celebrity Memoir: From Ghostwriting to Gender Politics*. Cham: Springer International, 2020.

Yelin, Hannah. "'I Am the Centre of Fame': Doing Celebrity, Performing Fame and Navigating Cultural Hierarchies in Grace Jones' *I'll Never Write my Memoirs*." *Celebrity Studies* 12, no. 1 (2021): 119–131.

7
"Mothers aren't sexy," "What is that you're wearing?," "What's it like to be in an all-girl band?"
Memoirs as Histories of 1980s Music Industry Sexism

Wayne Heisler Jr.

By the mid-1980s, Pat Benatar, Kathy Valentine, and Cyndi Lauper attained artistic and commercial feats. Singer and songwriter Benatar (born Patricia Mae Andrzejewski, 1953) had released six platinum-selling albums. Valentine (born 1959), bassist, guitarist, and songwriter, achieved with the Go-Go's the first US number-one album by an all-female band, *Beauty and the Beat* (1981). And Lauper (born 1953), singer, songwriter, actress, and activist, was the first solo artist to chart four top-five singles in the United States from a debut record, *She's So Unusual* (1983). Such accomplishments do not occur in a gender vacuum, especially given the misogynist corporate music culture of the 1980s. Indeed, accounts of sexism loom large in their memoirs: Benatar's *Between a Rock and a Heart Place: A Memoir* (2010), *Cyndi Lauper: A Memoir* (2012), and Kathy Valentine's *All I Ever Wanted: A Rock 'n' Roll Memoir* (2020).[1]

I first consider how Benatar, Valentine, and Lauper framed their memoirs by establishing gender and feminist consciousness, which derives from parallel generational experiences. I then concentrate on their encounters with sexism in the music industry of the 1980s in relation to image and music. These musicians have unique visual styles and have worked in distinct, if overlapping, musical subgenres: Benatar's signature sound is guitar-driven

---

[1] Pat Benatar and Patsi Bale Cox, *Between a Rock and a Heart Place: A Memoir* (New York: William Morrow, 2010); Cyndi Lauper and Jancee Dunn, *Cyndi Lauper: A Memoir* (New York: Atria Books, 2012); Kathy Valentine, *All I Ever Wanted: A Rock 'n' Roll Memoir* (Austin: University of Texas Press, 2020).

mainstream rock; the Go-Go's are associated with the post-punk pop-rock of *Beauty and the Beat* and their live performances; and although Lauper has explored numerous genres, the new wave sound of *She's So Unusual* is arguably Lauper's signature. While all three are songwriters, Benatar and Lauper are primarily singers, while Valentine is an instrumentalist. The diversity of their images, musical styles, and roles underscores systemic sexism in the industry and the ubiquity of its effects. All three women encountered barriers to songwriting, arranging, and/or production; the lower status of interpretation and performance versus authorship; and gendered genre and image "branding." I highlight their struggles in a male-dominated industry at transitional moments in their careers, with albums that have gone under the radar of popular music history: the Go-Go's *Talk Show* (1984), Benatar's *Seven the Hard Way* (1985), and Lauper's *A Night to Remember* (1989). These releases provide evidence of their creators' obsolescence. But just as female artists are represented by a male-dominated industry, that industry can be mediated by women through accounts of lived experiences of sexism. Of course, Benatar's, Lauper's, and Valentine's memoirs mostly center on their sides of their stories. They are a legacy of the popular "memoir boom" that began in the late 1990s, marked by a turn away from literary experimentation in life-writing to more realist self-confession—"*me*-moirs" that, as Stephanie Burt has summarized, risk coming off as "an advertisement, or a means of self-aggrandizement."[2] I believe, however, that this risk has value, virtue even, as a counterbalance against overbearing misogynist narratives—erasure, effectively—in the male-dominated music industry, as well as critical and academic commentaries. Benatar's, Lauper's, and Valentine's memoirs offer powerful firsthand perspectives that nuance and rectify sexist commercial, critical, and historical discourses surrounding 1980s popular music by affording these musicians stronger voices regarding their music and legacies.

Memoirs as History

There are similarities and differences between the women whose voices fill these memoirs, in terms of ethnicity, geography, education, and familial environment.

---

[2] Stephanie Burt, "Literary Style and the Lessons of Memoir," *New Yorker* (July 26, 2017). See also J. Nicole Jones, "Why's Everyone So Down on the Memoir?" *Salon* (January 14, 2013).

The strongest intersectional correspondences between these musicians concern gender and generation. Born in the 1950s, they were teenagers and young women in the late 1960s and early 1970s. As Linda Nicholson summarizes, "Something happened in the 1960s in ways of thinking about gender that continues to shape public and private life."[3] Accordingly, Benatar, Valentine, and Lauper began their memoirs by foregrounding gendered challenges to creativity, sorority among female musicians, and sexual assault, respectively. These life experiences were formative for their personal histories and add important subjective perspectives to their place in popular music history.

New York City, 1979. Discovered at the Catch a Rising Star club, twenty-six-year-old Benatar was in a recording session for a debut album, *In the Heat of the Night*. Something was off: "I sounded like Julie Andrews trying to sing rock."[4] Benatar's diagnosis (wrong voice for the genre) and the barriers to a solution are consistent with rock's traditionally narrow access to women. "My dream," Benatar recalled,

> was to be the singer in a rockin' band, like Robert Plant was to Led Zeppelin or Lou Gramm to Foreigner. I wanted a partnership, like Mick Jagger and Keith Richards had. . . . The sound I heard in my head was raucous, with hard-driving guitars speeding everything forward. I was a classically trained singer with a great deal of musical knowledge, but I had no idea how to make that visceral, intense sound happen.[5]

Studio musicians, producers, and "suits"—attorneys, business manager, label executives—reportedly disregarded Benatar's concerns: "Chrysalis had signed a chick singer, and a chick singer was what they expected me to remain."[6] Benatar clearly understood "chick singer" to be a subordinate category: neither musician (instrumentalist) nor collaborator, but rather a mouthpiece for men and (female) body at which to gaze.

Valentine's memoir begins in 1980 at the age of twenty-one in Los Angeles, where she pursued the goal of "making it in a band."[7] At the Whiskey a Go

---

[3] Linda Nicholson, "Introduction," in *The Second Wave: A Reader in Feminist Theory*, ed. Linda Nicholson (New York: Routledge, 1997), 1.
[4] Benatar and Cox, *Between a Rock and a Heart Place*, 1.
[5] Ibid., 2.
[6] Ibid., 2.
[7] Valentine, *All I Ever Wanted*, 1.

Go, guitarist Charlotte Caffe, from the Go-Go's, approached Valentine: "Girls who played in bands took notice of each other," Valentine relates, believing that sorority was necessary for survival in rock. Then came the invitation to substitute as bassist in the Go-Go's for four nights at the Whiskey starting New Year's Eve 1980. In her memoir, Valentine remembers:

> The next morning, I woke up early, wasting no time, not one minute. I called Charlotte and made a plan for her to bring a recording of the Go-Go's so that I could learn to play bass on their songs. . . . Making my way through the tape, one thing became clear through the distortion of the tape player: the Go-Go's had some really good songs. . . . They blended punk, pop, surf, and rock like no one else.[8]

Valentine had played guitar, not bass, in several bands, but now the dream of "making it" with fellow female musicians suddenly seemed to come into reach.

While Benatar and Valentine frame their stories at the precipice of fame, Lauper's memoir begins earlier: "I left home at seventeen. I took a paper bag with a toothbrush, a change of underwear, an apple, and a copy of Yoko Ono's book *Grapefruit* . . ., my window for viewing life through art."[9] Lauper's childhood home in Queens housed her younger brother, mother, and stepfather; Lauper's older sister had left after their parents' divorce. As Rosalyn Baxandall characterizes it, family's power is "contradictory . . ., at once so destructive and so sustaining."[10] Lauper felt the family was bonded by love: "I used to watch my dad shave over [the bathroom] sink before he left for work. And I once saw my mom sit on the edge of the tub and sing the most beautiful rendition of Al Jolson's 'Sonny Boy' to my little brother."[11] That same space also held devastating memories. There was a hole in the bathroom door's window that "was made by my mother's platinum wedding band the day my stepfather threw her," and one afternoon, Lauper was bathing and

> heard a creepy giggle and saw my stepfather's pear-shaped shadow against the frosted glass. I even saw his crazy eye looking through the hole. . . . It

---

[8] Ibid., 2–3.
[9] Lauper and Dunn, *Cyndi Lauper*, 1.
[10] Rosalyn Baxandall, "Historical Life Stories," *Feminist Studies* 34, no. 3 (2008): 418.
[11] Lauper and Dunn, *Cyndi Lauper*, 2.

was worse than him beating the dog when she cried and making us keep her on a leash tied to the kitchen door. It was worse than him standing behind the furnace at night in his robe with that creepy giggle when I had to go into the basement to hang up the wet laundry. It was worse than him touching himself, right outside our bedroom window.[12]

Lauper fled to the sister's apartment, beginning a journey away from a world in which she perceived that "Survival seemed to be all anyone around me could handle."[13]

The passages I quote above from the introductory chapters of these memoirs illustrate a confessional, conversational, and thereby realist tone that is a mark of contemporary popular memoirs, and that all three of these stories have in common. Moreover, given their generation's newfound gender consciousness, it is unsurprising that Benatar, Valentine, and Lauper all introduced their stories in spaces charged with misogyny: recording studio, rock scene, the family home. They all also came of age in matriarchal environments in which women faced hardships, and which sowed sensitivity to gender inequity and affinity with the contemporary Women's Rights Movement.[14] Gender and feminist consciousness thus constitute the backdrop for their memoir accounts of sexism in the music industry during the height of their careers in the 1980s. Such experiential testimony has implications for how we understand and tell popular music history. As Baxandall emphasizes, "consciousness raising" is afforded by women who "came to understand that many of their 'personal' problems such as insecurity about appearance and intelligence exhaustion, and conflicts with fathers, husbands, and male employers—were not individual failings but a result of the systematic discrimination that is sexism."[15] While personal accounts are not immune from lapses of memory or traces of solipsism, they gain credibility when they resonate with readers' experiences and expose the tendentiousness of ostensibly objective tellings. Acknowledgement of the trappings of the memoir form do not let us off the hook. Simply put, our histories are complicit if we ignore individual stories.

---

[12] Ibid., 3–4.
[13] Ibid., 9.
[14] See, e.g., Benatar and Cox, *Between a Rock and a Heart Place*, 27, 159; Valentine, *All I Ever Wanted*, 109; and Lauper and Dunn, *Cyndi Lauper*, 20.
[15] Baxandall, "Historical Life Stories," 414.

Music Industry Sexism

As Peter Tschmuck defines it, "The music industry consists of a network involving the production, distribution, dissemination, and consumption of music in a variety of forms, as well as the promotion of live music performances."[16] Musical and image branding are central to the industry, whose fundamental goal is to make money. While all artists are branded, female musicians often are branded in sexist ways owing to the hegemony of men in industry leadership.[17] That is, the gendering of music is "mediated by the structures and discourses of the music industry" in ways that are consistent with "broader patterns of female experience."[18]

It is important to note that Benatar, Valentine, and Lauper acknowledged that they did not encounter sexism from all men with whom they worked. Benatar had an all-male band, and she and guitarist-songwriter Neil "Spyder" Giraldo became each other's muses when forging a guitar-driven style, although executives objected to their romantic involvement (they married and raised a family) because, as Benatar understood it, "record labels . . . want solo stars unattached and seemingly available."[19] Valentine's memoir contrasted musicians' camaraderie—female *and* male—with the industry: "the skepticism and sexism came from the non-artists, where the audience was hootin' to 'take it off' or suits in the office were telling you there was no audience for your female band."[20] Lauper collaborated with trusted male musicians but was truly a solo artist, in that studio players were mostly different for each album and largely distinct from the live lineup. Lauper reflected in her memoir on misogyny from male musicians, including being raped by a bandmate in the 1970s: "I realized that maybe it was because this guy had started the band, and then the power slipped away from him, and it had come to me."[21] As was the case for Benatar, the perception of agency and

---

[16] Peter Tschmuck, "Music Industry," *Grove Music Online*, July 1, 2014, www.oxfordmusiconline.com/grovemusic/view/10.1093/gmo/9781561592630.001.0001/omo-9781561592630-e-1002262804.

[17] Jordan McClain and Christie Thompson, review of *Gender, Branding, and the Modern Music Industry: The Social Construction of Female Popular Music Stars*, by Kristin J. Lieb (2013), *Popular Music and Society* 38, no. 4 (2014): 531–533.

[18] Nicola Dibben, review of *Gender in the Music Industry: Rock, Discourse and Girl Power*, by Marion Leonard (2007), *British Journal of Music Education* 26, no. 3 (2009): 339–341.

[19] Benatar and Cox, *Between a Rock and a Heart Place*, 71.

[20] Valentine, *All I Ever Wanted*, 79, 146.

[21] Lauper and Dunn, *Cyndi Lauper*, 63–64.

power that a female singer exudes is sometimes countered by retaliation;[22] or, as Lauper put it, "When men see women singing so powerfully..., it can scare the shit out of them."[23] Lauper also narrated sexist behavior by her first touring band. The singer wanted to perform with women, but manager (and boyfriend) Dave Wolff maintained that "They don't play as good as men."[24] It is clear from Lauper's account that Wolff was not referring to any specific female musicians, but rather to the entire category of female musicians. Regarding these "good" players, Lauper alleged that, "I'd hear about guys sleeping with a mother and daughter.... I was like, 'What the fuck is that? The people are all coming here because of me, and I'm preaching women's lib onstage, and look what you guys are doing.'"[25] In contrast to Benatar and Valentine, then, Lauper was not a member of a band that was distinct from the male-dominated industry: often, Lauper's musicians were *of* the industry.

Divergences regarding their experiences with male musicians aside, all three women experienced parallel effects of industry sexism surrounding image and music. For Benatar, a sense of sexist disempowerment reached a head upon becoming pregnant during the recording of *Tropico* (1984). Benatar quoted a litany of sexist directives from Chrysalis in her memoir, including: "No one wants to see a rocker who's someone's mother. Mothers aren't sexy."[26] Benatar's branded image as a sex symbol was at odds with male perceptions of pregnancy and motherhood, which were consistent with biases against mothers across the music industry, from singers whose image is at the forefront to women behind the scenes, for example, producers and engineers.[27] Benatar took credit for initially forging an image from "a 1953 D-movie titled *Cat-women of the Moon* that inspired me to dress up in black spandex with a lot of eye makeup." Recounting a Halloween costume contest Benatar won in New York's Greenwich Village in the late 1970s, the singer remembered having

> to go back uptown for a show at Catch [a Rising Star], and to celebrate, I decided to perform in costume.... That night, though, something changed. I don't know if it was because I felt like I was playing a role or I simply

---

[22] See Helen Reddington, *She's at the Controls: Sound Engineering, Production and Gender Ventriloquism in the 21st Century* (Sheffield: Equinox, 2021).
[23] Lauper and Dunn, *Cyndi Lauper*, 99.
[24] Ibid., 144.
[25] Ibid., 148.
[26] Benatar and Cox, *Between a Rock and a Heart Place*, 163.
[27] See Reddington, *She's at the Controls*.

removed my personal shell, but I had a newfound bravado, a sexual swagger that wasn't there before. The notes were the same, but they had an attitude to them, an aggression.[28]

Benatar embraced the "campiness" of this appropriated look and how it contributed to a desired *sonic* image as a rocker, with a confident sexuality that situated the singer in early third-wave feminism. On the other hand, Benatar's image fit stereotypical fantasies of the hetero-male-centric industry and rock's (male) fan base: a strong, attractive woman who seems sexually available. The record company's role in exploiting the latter, sexist default became obvious to Benatar when they promoted her sophomore album, *Crimes of Passion* (1980): Chrysalis placed an ad in *Billboard* magazine and, using the cover image from the record, airbrushed off Benatar's tank top, replacing it with a sign announcing the album's release date that barely covered photoshop-enhanced breasts. "I felt like I'd been raped,"[29] the singer stated. Benatar reflected on the "cat-women" image: "I never meant for it to be the focal point.... Chrysalis only wanted the sexy part. It was offensive but also boring—typical of most men's thinking in postfeminist America,"[30] by which the singer was targeting larger cultural ambivalence toward sexual objectification. Indeed, according to Benatar, Chrysalis's label head once chided the singer during a disagreement about image: "I hope that you don't think people are actually coming to your concerts to listen to you sing."[31] Benatar slapped him in the face, but despite the singer's feminist consciousness, institutional and legal barriers complicated resistance.

Benatar described how the contract from Chrysalis contained a suspension clause stipulating that the singer "had to do [the] next album in a certain time frame or [else they] could hold back royalties and delay payments."[32] In order to meet contractual terms, Benatar recorded five studio albums and one live album between 1979 and 1984. Reflecting back to 1985, when Benatar was caring for a newborn daughter while Chrysalis was demanding a new album, the singer expressed frustration with trying to maintain a career and family: "[T]here is a big lie about how you can easily have it all as a working mother.... And *that* was the part the feminists conveniently left

---

[28] Benatar and Cox, *Between a Rock and a Heart Place*, 47.
[29] Ibid., 89.
[30] Ibid., 95.
[31] Ibid., 129.
[32] Ibid., 51, 76.

out.... I was up and down at all hours breast-feeding... and living in a perpetual state of exhaustion. I was in no position to... write, rehearse, and record an album."[33] The result of Benatar's balancing act was the album *Seven the Hard Way* (1985), the title of which was reportedly derived from the dice game craps: "Since you can't roll doubles and get an odd number," Benatar explained, "'seven the hard way' is slang for an impossible bet."[34]

Throughout Benatar's career, obstacles were in place to songwriting and releasing music on the singer's own terms. For example, in the late 1970s when trying to get a foot in the door of record companies, a manager matched Benatar with a songwriter:

> I spent the next hour being chased around the piano—literally. At every turn the guy kept trying to put his hands all over me, refusing to let me out of the apartment. I finally began to cry, and with the tears, he seemed to realize how green and young I was. He took pity on me and let me leave, but the damage had been done. I rode the crosstown bus back to the East Side, shaking and crying the whole way home.[35]

Songwriting has traditionally been a territory of male gatekeepers in the industry, and here, authorial power was bound up with sexual domination. It is ironic that Benatar's breakout single, "Heartbreaker," in which the lyrics call out a man for using a woman for sex, was written by two men. The singer claimed to have "rewritten so many of the lyrics.... But the writers wouldn't go for giving me credit. I was an unknown, and Chrysalis did not stand with me."[36] Moreover, due to the terms of Benatar's contract, "it seemed like I was scheduled round the clock for publicity photo shoots and in-store events.... Touring and promoting an album are counterproductive to creating new material, and I've never been able to write when I'm in performance mode."[37] The singer's account of the contractual obligation to release a new album annually explains why Benatar's co-writing of songs amounted to just thirteen of forty-nine tracks over five studio albums.

Therefore, Benatar had to accept material for outside songwriters for *Seven the Hard Way*. When the singer and the band went into the studio in 1985 with

---

[33] Ibid., 162, 165.
[34] Ibid., 166.
[35] Ibid., 45.
[36] Ibid., 60.
[37] Ibid., 76.

a newborn baby in tow, they had no original material prepared. That meant that Benatar and the band were trying to write songs as they recorded them, resulting in "a general lack of cohesion."[38] Complicating Benatar's awareness was a confessed internalization of sexism: "after hearing this chorus for long enough, I started to believe it. They made me feel that by becoming a mother, I'd risked my entire career.... I started to convince myself that the only way to stay on top was to rush back into things."[39] Thus, following the release of *Seven the Hard Way*, Benatar acquiesced to the demands of the powers-that-be to tour. The singer recounted how "All this would have been fine if I'd been in great physical shape, but I wasn't. Of course, when I asked them if I could take a few dates off so that my voice could recover, their answer was a resounding no. 'Look, if you don't do these five shows, here's how much we'll lose. You've got to look at the bottom line.'"[40] Caring for a baby while on tour, Benatar felt unable to do the usual rigorous promotion, which played a factor in reduced record sales. Informed by the singer's perspective, it certainly seems that the aggressive, sexist tactics that Chrysalis took against Benatar in order to maintain the "bottom line" ultimately resulted in her losing creative and commercial momentum.

Like Benatar, Lauper reported confronting sexism before becoming famous, including the sexual assault discussed above. The culmination of Lauper's ongoing struggles for agency as a solo female artist came with the album *A Night to Remember* (1989), which the singer referred to in her memoir as "A Night to Forget, because it was ... destined to be doomed because the record company was changing again."[41] Back in 1982, Lauper had signed with Portrait Records, a subsidiary of CBS. When CBS was bought out by the Sony Corporation in 1988, record company executives allegedly targeted Lauper's image: "one of the new heads at Sony turned to me in a meeting and said 'What is that you're wearing?'"[42] In contrast to Benatar's sultry *Cat-Women of the Moon* look, Lauper cultivated an eclectic mix of retro and punk fashion that often obscured, distracted from, or distorted the body. Lauper described how music and "looks" were artist-generated in the early 1980s and attributed fashion choices to feminist convictions, for example, the ankle and hip chains on the cover of *She's So Unusual* "to stress that

---

[38] Ibid., 166.
[39] Ibid., 163–164.
[40] Ibid., 171.
[41] Lauper and Dunn, *Cyndi Lauper*, 194.
[42] Ibid., 188–189.

woman is the slave of the world. . . . for Sicilian women, slavery was a mind fuck, a way to keep them in the house, as domestic slaves and bearing a man's children."[43] Lauper asserted that "I was never a sex symbol. . . . I was selling freedom of expression and the freedom to be different—not sex. I'm telling ya, there were no men who chased after me. Instead, I got the sad people, because that's who I was trying to heal when I sang."[44] Lauper's elucidation of "sex symbol" here is rooted in rather narrow heteronormative terms. Still, based on self-analysis, Lauper, like Benatar, believed that music (and voice) held ultimate sway; and like Benatar, Lauper's realization that image was a focal point came as a surprise, despite being attuned to female objectification. When Lauper crossed over into movies and was filming *Vibes* in 1987, the singer overheard a male producer asking someone, "Would you fuck her? Is she fuckable?"[45] In this context, the Sony executive's question "What is that you're wearing?" seems motivated by the desire to rebrand Lauper for a sexualized male gaze.

Male gatekeepers in the industry have long controlled what and how popular music is consumed, so that "vital elements of the public profile of female artists, both visual and sonic, are not within their control."[46] As regards Lauper's *A Night to Remember*, the image rebranding was intertwined with controlling Lauper's music; the singer sensed that record company executives "were trying to remake me after the perceived lack of success of [her sophomore album] *True Colors* [1986] . . . [B]ecause they thought they were more important than the artist, they wanted to make the sounds."[47] Lauper had long been waging the battle for creative control via songwriting. After singing in cover bands, Lauper co-wrote most of the material for the sole, self-titled album by band Blue Angel (1980). However, when Lauper signed a solo contract with Portrait, the singer "said I wanted to write, but [manager and boyfriend] Dave [Wolff] said, 'Sing first, and then you can write.'"[48] Lauper trusted this managerial advice and turned energy to song choices and arranging, articulating to Wolff that "my name is pretty big on the front of the record and the producers' names are pretty small on the back. Once this thing is done, they go on to something else, but I have to sell it. If this is going

---

[43] Ibid., 121.
[44] Ibid., 148.
[45] Ibid., 180–181.
[46] Reddington, *She's at the Controls*, 131.
[47] Lauper and Dunn, *Cyndi Lauper*, 188–189.
[48] Ibid., 184.

to be my thing, . . . I want it to be great and my fuckin' vision."[49] Thus, Lauper wrangled to put an original spin on covers (such as the reggae-inflected feminist anthem "Girls Just Want to Have Fun") but also fought to include co-written material (e.g., the ballad "Time after Time"). Lauper's fight to realize a vision extended to iconic music videos as well because "I wanted a sound and a look that worked together. Which quickly became a pain in the ass to the corporate people and managers, because they just wanted me to do all the promotion and have somebody else do the rest of it,"[50] the singer argued.

Again, Benatar recounted how the record company objected to a personal relationship with Giraldo. Similarly, record executives got between Lauper and manager-boyfriend Wolff. As characterized in Lauper's memoir, Wolff

> was caught between a woman who wanted things her own way and a record company that changed hands among the biggest, most sexist, most macho guys in the world who married trophy wives—women who shut the fuck up because the man is king. During the eighties, all of these powerful men seemed wildly out of control. So many of them were on coke, and everyone was sexist. . . . They'd say, "You're the man—*you* tell her what to do."[51]

While clearly recognizing the misogynist corporate power dynamic, Lauper acquiesced to industry pressure. Just as Benatar "didn't want to be a bitch,"[52] Lauper "was so used to being a good soldier that I didn't know when to say enough is enough." Therefore, with *A Night to Remember*, Lauper "tried for a more commercial album,"[53] by which I understand the singer to indicate compromises regarding creative control. Although the singer was coproducing, co-writing, and arranging alongside a few trusted collaborators, Lauper felt disempowered by Sony's A&R (Artists and Repertoire) representative—for example, "That's nice ear candy,"[54] the rep would say—and an unnamed (allegedly) alcoholic audio engineer, who reportedly commented that the sound was "just a cunt-hair off,"[55] as well as promotion staff who were in the studio directing musical choices while Lauper was recording. Lauper's account of the sessions for *A Night to Remember*

[49] Ibid., 110.
[50] Ibid., 136.
[51] Ibid., 192.
[52] Benatar and Cox, *Between a Rock and a Heart Place*, 159.
[53] Lauper and Dunn, *Cyndi Lauper*, 194.
[54] Ibid., 194.
[55] Ibid., 195.

provides a vivid illustration of Reddington's assessment that "recording environments are positioned as masculinized territory," in which "the work of female vocalists is less important than the work of male producers."[56] Although *A Night to Remember* had a hit single in "I Drove All Night," the album sold only about one third as many copies as *True Colors* in the United States. After just seven North American concerts, Lauper embarked on an extensive international tour, which she identified as the end to her mainstream success: "The record company wanted me to work Europe and the rest of the world while they broke their new acts in the States, so that they could just live off whatever I have left in me. That's how they are."[57]

Due partly to the strain of industry sexism, the Go-Go's broke up after the release of their third album *Talk Show* (1984). Formed amid the 1970s Los Angeles punk scene, the band had long experienced sexism. For instance, after moving to LA, Valentine sought a "leg up in the business" and met Kim Fowley, who had managed the all-female band the Runaways. "See that dog up there," Fowley pointed to the stage as Valentine recalled it, "She does what I say," and then instructed that Valentine "would never get anywhere in LA without his help."[58] In such a hyper-misogynist culture, the novelty of an all-female band posed difficulties for the Go-Go's when trying to obtain a recording contract: "All of the refusals were from men, all of them justified with the same rationale: there had never been an all-female band successful enough to warrant taking a chance on us."[59] The reticence of major labels to sign the Go-Go's was undoubtedly a reaction to the powerful symbol of five women musicians. Still, as Valentine acknowledged, "the Go-Go's didn't write protest songs or make political comments in our music. Reporters never asked our opinions on anything of substance. There were no conversations about sexism or feminism. The most common question remained, 'What's it like to be in an all-girl band?'"[60]

While the Go-Go's had a reputation for sex, drugs, and rock and roll on par with male bands, Valentine recounted how, by the time of their second album *Vacation* (1982), they began to recognize "A deep disconnect between the way we saw ourselves and the way we were presented to the public."[61] In the press, descriptors such as "danceable," "energetic," "fun," "exuberant," and "bouncy"

---

[56] Reddington, *She's at the Controls*, 95, 98.
[57] Lauper and Dunn, *Cyndi Lauper*, 200.
[58] Valentine, *All I Ever Wanted*, 91.
[59] Ibid., 107.
[60] Ibid., 201.
[61] Ibid., 164.

dominated and "took on a condescending and demeaning tone. Guy bands were never described as perky and chirpy or adorable and cute.... [T]he Go-Go's were anointed as America's pop sweethearts. The girls next door. The most benign of all lady boxes."[62] The band's congenial image owed in part to their "look" as branded in the press. Valentine complained that "I don't think male bands get dressed up like dolls or get handed lollipops and balloons to pose with. Sometimes, we let them. . . . Other times our strong objections and griping branded us as . . . bitches."[63] This stereotyping is so common as to go unnoticed due to "the social forces that shape and constrain choice."[64] Despite their punk origins, the Go-Go's "lady box" conformed to clichés that disempower women, similar to how Benatar's image made her seem to be more object than agent.

The branding of the Go-Go's as "pop sweethearts" also owed to their recorded sound. After securing a record deal with IRS (International Record Syndicate), the band was initially disappointed by the end-product of *Beauty and the Beat*. Valentine described how "the live Go-Go's sounded raucous, full of attitude and energy," but the recording was "wimpy and clean": "We blamed the producers. We put our trust in Richard [Gottehrer], and then he had gone and turned us into a 60s lightweight watered-down pop group. Miles [Copeland, IRS founder] and the record company staff were unconcerned with our dismay,"[65] Valentine alleged. Gottehrer had been a songwriter at New York's Brill Building and helped forge the 1960s "girl group" sound—a "sonic signature" that he seems to have transferred to the Go-Go's and an example of what Reddington termed "gender ventriloquism," that is, when "male producers use women artists as mouthpieces for their own versions of girlhood and womanhood."[66] The Go-Go's rebellious girliness was branded sonically as girliness, but minus tongue in cheek.

Though exuding toughness both on- and offstage, the Go-Go's were still a "girl band," and in Valentine's interpretation the attendant stereotypes hampered their ability to get radio play. Benatar reported that when she was doing radio promotion, programmers would "pat [their] lap" and direct her to "come right over here and sit down, honey. We'll see if we can't get that

---

[62] Ibid., 164.
[63] Ibid., 165.
[64] Erin Hatten and Mary Nell Trautner, "Images of Powerful Women in the Age of 'Choice Feminism,'" *Journal of Gender Studies* 22, no. 1 (2013): 66.
[65] Valentine, *All I Ever Wanted*, 120.
[66] Reddington, *She's at the Controls*, 7.

record played."[67] Valentine also disclosed that upon the release of the Go-Go's first single, "Our Lips Are Sealed," "enormous resistance from major radio programmers blocked every effort."[68] Underscoring the band's awareness of systemic sexism, Valentine recalled making fun of having to promote their music to the industry's all-male gatekeepers: "On the way to an interview or radio station . . ., we would discuss with straight faces whose turn it was to put on the knee pads, pretending one of us would have to blow a guy for airplay. Quite a few of the label guys didn't flinch, as if that were a perfectly normal thing for women to do."[69]

In contrast to Benatar and Lauper, the Go-Go's enjoyed authorial freedom. With three main writers (Caffey, Valentine, Jane Wiedlin), the band had not suffered from a shortage of original material, but because they felt the "need to show everyone our band isn't a fluke"[70] after the against-all-odds success of their all-female debut, they rushed to record a follow-up, *Vacation*, before any songs were written, which Valentine opined led to lower sales. Furthermore, up until that point, the Go-Go's had been managed by a woman, Ginger Canzoneri, but when the band signed with a larger managerial firm, "we had suddenly gotten stuck with an accountant and a lawyer running things."[71] This change was consistent with the trend Lauper identified of musicians being replaced by male businessmen and lawyers in record company leadership in the 1980s.

To counter their pop image and "elevate their sound" on *Talk Show*, the Go-Go's worked with producer Martin Rushent, who Valentine recalled "was pleasantly surprised to find us to be far better musicians than he had realized."[72] Still, while maintaining some degree of control as a band of five women, the Go-Go's detrimentally internalized their male-dictated brand, according to Valentine's account. For example, when Wiedlin asked to sing lead vocals on a song, the band decided that "Everyone had their role, and Belinda [Carlisle] sang,"[73] conforming to the model of a group with a lead "chick singer." Then in May 1985, in the wake of "slower sales and smaller venues,"[74] Valentine received a call to report to their management company:

---

[67] Benatar and Cox, *Between a Rock and a Heart Place*, 93.
[68] Valentine, *All I Ever Wanted*, 121.
[69] Ibid., 129.
[70] Ibid., 156.
[71] Ibid., 175.
[72] Ibid., 184.
[73] Ibid., 186.
[74] Ibid., 197.

"We've decided to break up the band." ... Andy [Slater], the proxy-manager, perched on a desk corner, looking self-important and haughty. They probably already had Belinda's solo deal in place. ... Suddenly, Charlotte proclaimed, "I write the hits and she is the voice." It enraged me. ... My self-esteem, my identity, my family, my purpose were all encased in Go-Go's wrapping, tied up in band life. The pain felt greater than any loss I had endured.[75]

Carlisle and Caffey had some agency in the Go-Go's demise, but it was exacerbated by their management, who predicted a bigger "bottom line" from Carlisle as a solo pop act. Valentine's account is poignant because Carlisle's budding solo career represented everything the band had railed against. When *Belinda* (1986) was released, "She emerged as a new streamlined, glamorous version of herself. All the rough edges had been polished and buffed, shaped and molded into a wholesome pop confection. ... Charlotte had played a big part in making Belinda's solo album. They had brought Jane into the fold. ... Now the whole breakup felt like a personal rejection."[76] The loss Valentine experienced was deep given the precious sorority that led to her identifying as being part of "the best all-female band ever."

Memoirs and Our Stories

As characterized by G. Thomas Couser, among the most rewarding offerings of memoirs is "wisdom, [and] understanding of the formation of the self"[77]—for the writer, but also, I would argue, for readers. Somewhat predictably, then, Benatar's, Lauper's, and Valentine's memoirs climax with transformative moments of self-realization. Valentine battled depression and worsening dependence on alcohol and cocaine following the Go-Go's breakup. However, recalling entering Alcoholics Anonymous (AA) and reuniting with the band in 1988, she described how "The happiness I felt being together had a purity and intensity I have never felt in our crazy wildness."[78] Benatar's renewed empowerment came in 1997, when she released an independent album, *Innamorata*, and joined the inaugural Lilith Fair, the

---

[75] Ibid., 212–214.
[76] Ibid., 225–226.
[77] G. Thomas Couser, *Memoir: An Introduction* (New York: Oxford University Press, 2011), 175.
[78] Valentine, *All I Ever Wanted*, 265.

traveling festival featuring female singer-songwriters. Benatar shared that these performances "were the best forty-eight tour hours onstage I'd ever had."[79] Lauper's epiphany came on tour in Japan in 2011 following the 9.0-magnitude earthquake that struck the main island. "I had come to learn that the sound of my voice, especially the midrange was very soothing," the singer reflected, and continued the tour because she "realized that there was something more to my voice than just singing hit songs. So if I stayed in Japan maybe the sound of my voice would help the Japanese."[80] Lauper's realization that artistic and personal worth exceeded commercial success complements Benatar's sense of independence and Valentine's reconnection with the Go-Go's. Through their memoirs, they chronicle their attainment of well-being as women and as musicians—this is, ultimately, the central commonality between their stories. Judith Taylor asserts that storytelling plays a "crucial role ... in interpreting history, constituting civic culture, and advocating for change."[81] Given that sexism is often obscured and thereby legitimized in received histories, how might these musicians' individual catharses affect *collective* catharses and be reflected in histories of female musicians?

Although music-historical narratives tend to spotlight "hits" rather than "misses," Benatar's *Seven the Hard Way* provides telling evidence of the industry's barriers to female artists' agency, and a reminder to refocus attention from songwriting as a metric of agency to interpretation and performance. Reviewing Lauper's *A Night to Remember*, Stephen Erlewine opines that studio techniques dominated under the assumption that "labored arrangements and precisely detailed production are tantamount to musical sophistication."[82] Aesthetic (mis)calculations in the studio were arguably common in the 1980s as an era of big audio production and, given the sexist climate of its creation, *A Night to Remember* offers a case study for exploring the relationships between—and gendering of—production and "musical sophistication." The Go-Go's drew mostly critical accolades for *Talk Show*, but self-proclaimed "Dean of American rock critics" Robert Christgau offers food for further thought: he accepts the "top-forty goals" of the "relationship songs" because of their "sense of possibility that might touch women who are turned off by more explicit politics, and that these women are strong

---

[79] Benatar and Cox, *Between a Rock and a Heart Place*, 211.
[80] Lauper and Dunn, *Cyndi Lauper*, 332.
[81] Judith Taylor, "The Problem of Women's Sociality in Contemporary North American Feminist Memoir," *Gender and Society* 22, no. 6 (2008): 708.
[82] Stephen Thomas Erlewine, "A Night to Remember Review," AllMusic, [n.d.], www.allmusic.com/album/a-night-to-remember-mw0000201047.

enough to put into practice."[83] Such ostensible praise fortified the Go-Go's dreaded "lady box" by championing post-feminist sensibilities. Valentine's memoir communicates that genre admixture provided tension and empowerment for the band. Indeed, for female musicians, genre is often political as it is legislated along gender lines, and the Go-Go's offer perspectives on genre in terms of musical and gender instability.

In sum, Benatar's, Valentine's, and Lauper's memoirs supplement received histories by, as Jones values in the memoir form, opening up a "dialogue . . . between the past and the present."[84] Said dialogue might echo productively in future histories of women in popular music, in which sexism and its effects on what we see and hear have not been given the range and depth of voice it demands.

Bibliography

Baxandall, Rosalyn. "Historical Life Stories." *Feminist Studies* 34, no. 3 (2008): 412–424.
Benatar, Pat. *Seven the Hard Way*. Chrysalis OV 41507, 1985, LP.
Benatar, Pat and Patsi Bale Cox. *Between a Rock and a Heart Place: A Memoir*. New York: William Morrow, 2010.
Burt, Stephanie. "Literary Style and the Lessons of Memoir." *New Yorker*, July 26, 2017.
Christgau, Robert. "The Go-Go's, *Talk Show*." Robert Christgau: Dean of American Rock Critics. [n.d.]. www.robertchristgau.com/get_artist.php?name=Go+Gos.
Couser, G. Thomas. *Memoir: An Introduction*. New York: Oxford University Press, 2011.
Dibben, Nicola. Review of *Gender in the Music Industry: Rock, Discourse and Girl Power*, by Marion Leonard (2007). *British Journal of Music Education* 26, no. 3 (2009): 339–341.
Erlewine, Stephen Thomas. "A Night to Remember Review." AllMusic. [n.d.]. www.allmusic.com/album/a-night-to-remember-mw0000201047.
The Go-Go's. *Talk Show*. I.R.S. SP 070041, 1984, LP.
Hatten, Erin, and Mary Nell Trautner. "Images of Powerful Women in the Age of 'Choice Feminism.'" *Journal of Gender Studies* 22, no. 1 (2013): 65–78.
Jones, J. Nicole. "Why's Everyone So Down on the Memoir?" *Salon*, January 14, 2013.
Lauper, Cyndi. *A Night to Remember*. Epic E44318, 1989, LP.
Lauper, Cyndi, and Jancee Dunn. *Cyndi Lauper: A Memoir*. New York: Atria Books, 2012.
Leonard, Marion. *Gender in the Music Industry: Rock, Discourse and Girl Power*. Farnham: Ashgate, 2007.
McClain, Jordan, and Christie Thompson. Review of *Gender, Branding, and the Modern Music Industry: The Social Construction of Female Popular Music Stars*, by Kristin J. Lieb (2013). *Popular Music and Society* 38, no. 4 (2014): 531–533.

---

[83] Robert Christgau, "The Go-Go's, *Talk show*," Robert Christgau: Dean of American Rock Critics, [n.d.], www.robertchristgau.com/get_artist.php?name=Go+Gos.
[84] Jones, "Why's Everyone So Down on the Memoir?"

Nicholson, Linda. "Introduction." In *The Second Wave: A Reader in Feminist Theory*, edited by Linda Nicholson, 1–5. New York: Routledge, 1997.

Reddington, Helen. *She's at the Controls: Sound Engineering, Production and Gender Ventriloquism in the 21st Century*. Sheffield: Equinox, 2021.

Taylor, Judith. "The Problem of Women's Sociality in Contemporary North American Feminist Memoir." *Gender and Society* 22, no. 6 (2008): 705–727.

Tschmuck, Peter. "Music Industry." *Grove Music Online*. July 1, 2014. www.oxfordmusiconline.com/grovemusic/view/10.1093/gmo/9781561592630.001.0001/omo-9781561592630-e-1002262804.

Valentine, Kathy. *All I Ever Wanted: A Rock 'n' Roll Memoir*. Austin: University of Texas Press, 2020.

8
The Art of Performing Authenticity
A Study of Amanda Palmer's Memoirs

Beatriz A. Medeiros

Introduction

I laughed thinking about all the nights I'd howled on concert hall stages, screaming those same old teenage songs at the top of my lungs, as aggressively and honestly and *believably* as I possibly could, to the point that I lost my voice almost every single night for a year and had to get surgery to cut away the rough, red nodes that had grown on my vocal cords as a result of too much yelling:

PLEASE. BELIEVE ME.[1]

In her book *The Art of Asking: or How I Learned to Stop Worrying and Let Other People Help*, Amanda Palmer expresses how throughout her career she has negotiated the concepts of honesty and reality with her audience. As Palmer describes it, in trying to convey a sense of truth, to make the public believe in her and her authenticity, she screams and eventually hurts her vocal cords.

Amanda Palmer is an alternative rock musician from the United States who gained visibility following her successful Kickstarter campaign in 2012, using this crowdfunding project to seek $100,000 to support the release of her already recorded album *Theatre Is Evil*. Palmer received more than $1 million from the public, provoking criticism from the specialized media and on internet channels as people questioned whether she was worth the

---

[1] Amanda Palmer, *The Art of Asking: or How I Learned to Stop Worrying and Let Other People Help* (New York: Grand Central Publishing, 2014), 34.

money she was receiving and indeed whether Palmer should be asking for it at all.

To some people, Palmer's Kickstarter success gave her a reputation as a strategic music entrepreneur, public engager, and visionary, while others considered her merely an egotist.[2] The controversy brought her so much visibility that, in 2013, she was invited to speak at TEDxTalks. To date, her presentation, *The Art of Asking*, has had over 6 million views on YouTube and over 12 million views on the TED platform.[3] Palmer used the talk to discuss the events in her personal and professional life that led her to what she calls the art of asking, or "Let Other People Help."

Following the TEDxTalks event, in 2014 Palmer wrote and released *The Art of Asking*, a memoir with motivational self-help elements, in which she seeks to show people how they can ask for help, accept receiving it, and benefit from this lifestyle choice. The book carries the same title as the talk, an ingenious marketing stunt since it makes possible the simultaneous organic promotion of both. In her own words, Palmer proposes making "connections with those around"[4] by sharing personal stories; in the memoir, she narrates events from her professional and personal life—relationships, times of struggle, and other situations—in more detail, but the key focus remains on the Kickstarter business. The musician's name started to be primarily connected to the marketing actions of crowdfunding and crowdsourcing.[5] Believing that such strategies are the future of the music industry, Palmer also raises these issues in her memoir, and she explicitly positions herself as part of this future.

Previous discussions of her work[6] have suggested that Palmer's strategy of creating intimacy between her and her fan base through online social network platforms derives, to use Bourdieu's term,[7] from the notion of trust as

---

[2] Jon Ronson, "Amanda Palmer: Visionary or Egotist?," *The Guardian*, June 2013, https://www.theguardian.com/music/2013/jun/22/amanda-palmer-visionary-egotist-interview.

[3] "Amanda Palmer: The Art of Asking," YouTube video, 13:46, posted by "TED," March 1, 2013, https://www.youtube.com/watch?v=xMj_P_6H69g. Amanda Palmer, "The Art of Asking," *TED Conference* video, 13:31, March 1, 2013, accessed June 6, 2023, https://www.ted.com/talks/amanda_palmer_the_art_of_asking.

[4] Palmer, *The Art of Asking*, 19.

[5] Much like crowdfunding, crowdsourcing is a collective aid action. However, sourcing is more associated with practical collaboration among parties, and financial support is not necessarily the final objective.

[6] Beatriz Medeiros and Beatriz Polivanov, "Female Artists, Social Media and Alternative Economy: The Case of Amanda Palmer," in *Keep It Simple Make It Fast: An Approach to Underground Music Scenes*, ed. Paula Guerra and Thiago Pereira Alberto (Porto: Porto University, 2019), 353–366.

[7] Pierre Bourdieu, "Symbolic Capital and Social Classes," *Journal of Classical Sociology* 13, no 2 (2013): 292–302.

symbolic capital, an argument developed in this chapter by analyzing Palmer's writing style and interpreting it as a performance aimed at maintaining her public's trust. Trust, indeed, is not merely symbolic capital; it is also a negotiable value. Trust can be built up from the *performance of authenticity* when the performer delivers the message, and the audience receives and decodes it. Although the connection between performance and authenticity is not a novelty in the social sciences, it can be understood as a duality. For many centuries, authenticity was deemed as trueness and performance as a pretense,[8] and Palmer reawakens this debate whenever she engages with her public; her memoir suggests that she is aware that this duality is essential to her artistic identity.

The concept of authenticity and its connection to performance deserves further debate and analysis. The word "authenticity" evokes notions of trueness, reality, originality, and, in many cases, quality—especially regarding music.[9] However, the term is not limited to these ideas, and it has, just like the very construction of self, undergone resignification.

The performance of authenticity in Palmer's book seems to be an extension of the process she started online—through forums, blogs, tweets, and posts—and offline, via compositions and performances. This strategy is clearly fundamental to her career since she needs the support—including but not exclusively financial—of her fan base. Palmer joined the crowdfunding platform Patreon[10] in 2015 after leaving Roadrunner Records in 2010,[11] and she has never since signed with another record company.

This chapter frames the discussion around the performance of authenticity and the negotiations that can be observed in the book as a strategy for approaching the public. But these performances can be disputed: the audience perceives that Amanda Palmer is constantly questioned by non-fans who criticize her behavior—how she receives money from her fans and her ruptures of performance.[12]

---

[8] Alex Neill, "Inauthenticity, Insincerity and Poetry," in *Performance and Authenticity in the Arts*, ed. Salim Kemal and Ivan Gaskell (Cambridge: Cambridge University Press, 1999), 197–214.

[9] Simon Frith, *Performing Rites: On Value of Popular Music*. (Cambridge, MA: Harvard University Press, 1996).

[10] On Patreon, producers (who may be artists, musicians, game players, etc.) sell their creations to people interested (patrons) in exchange for their continued support. Palmer calls these creations "Things."

[11] Palmer signed with Roadrunner Records when she was still part of the Dresden Dolls, in 2003.

[12] Beatriz Polivanov and Fernanda Carrera, "Perfect Bodies and Digital Influencers: Gendered Ruptures of Performance on Social Media in Brazil," *Cultural Politics* 18, no. 1 (March 2022): 28–43.

The Strategy behind Performing Authenticity

As previously pointed out, Palmer has long been building her relationship with her fan base.[13] Such connections date back to when she started playing with drummer Brian Viglione in the Dresden Dolls, a local punk-cabaret band from Boston, consisting only of Palmer (piano/vocal) and Viglione (drums). After every show, they would ask to include people's emails in the band's mailing list, through which they published updates about their live performances, new music, and videos. Later, Palmer created an online forum, The Shadow Box, and a blog: even before her Kickstarter success, she had thus built a community. In her book, she mentions this often, referring to her fan base as "Our Crowd" and reinforcing the idea that they give her a sense of security and mutual trust:

> my "special relationship" with my fans wasn't some shtick that came up with a marketing meeting.... Throughout my career, the fanbase has been like one significant other to me, a thousand-headed friend with whom I have a real, committed partnership.... I twitter to say goodnight and good morning, the way I would with a lover. They bring me food and tea at shows when I'm sick. I visit them in hospitals and make videos for their friends' funerals. We trust one another.[14]

Palmer openly treats her fans as close friends in her book and her daily posts and blogs, a strategy for legitimizing herself as an approachable person. In other words, she is performing her authenticity, creating a sense of proximity with the public, and supporting her self-narrative. This way, she keeps reinforcing her constructed identity, created by imbricating her online and offline relations with fans, an identity based on authenticity and secured by "expressive coherence."[15]

Performance and authenticity, at first, seem to be opposed values. As we see in the works of Goffman[16] and Schechner,[17] there is a strong connection

---

[13] Beatriz Medeiros and Natalia Dias, "Crowdfunding Is Not for Everybody: Performance in the Art of Asking," in *Popular Music Studies Today: Systematische Musikwissenschaft*, ed. Jenny Merrill (Wiesbaden: Springer, 2017).

[14] Palmer, *The Art of Asking*, 80.

[15] Erving Goffman, *The Presentation of Self in Everyday Life* (Edinburgh: Social Sciences Research Center, Monograph No. 2, 1956), 87.

[16] Goffman, *The Presentation of Self in Everyday Life*.

[17] Richard Schechner, *Performance Studies: An Introduction* (New York: Routledge, 2006).

between performance and theater. This constructed reality can challenge its credibility as true non-intentional actions or actions rooted in trueness.[18] The performance also depends on the audience; it needs to be recognized, engendering a relationship between the performer and the public. The audience gives meaning to what the performer is presenting, and it needs this response to be accurate.

On the other hand, authenticity can be connected with the immersion of the self. In a historical and cultural sense, in eighteenth- and nineteenth-century Europe, when authenticity started to be debated as an achievable value, denying this interiority meant denying one's essence. The creation of personality and subjectivity was understood as separate from the experience in society—it was a time when German Romanticism (*Romantik*) sought to oppose the values of the French Enlightenment and its rationalism by encouraging people to turn inward to personal emotions and feelings.[19]

From this context, one can infer that while performance can be presented as something thought through and necessarily externalized, authenticity is more connected to inner perception. However, Hall points out that, in late modernity, it is impossible to think of a way of constructing subjectivity and identity without the interference of others.[20] The very idea of a unified self, unchangeable and without contradictions, is unattainable because we are constantly influenced by others, even as we in our turn also affect them. We feel that it is possible to construct different, even contradictory, identities, depending on our identifications and the multiple "system of meaning and cultural representation"[21] surrounding us. In this sense, performance and authenticity work together to construct the self.

In her autobiography, Palmer seems to be constantly performing her authenticity so that we can perceive the construction of her identity. She writes continually about her connection with her audience and the desire to be seen while seeing others. This sense of attachment, and the understanding that it could bring her positive results, such as a loyal fan base, emerged from her experience as a street artist:

---

[18] It is not my place to debate the notions of trueness or reality in this text. Both concepts are dependent on factors such as social constructions and personal and individual beliefs.

[19] Bruno Campanella, "Celebridade, engajamento humanitário e a formação do capital solidário," *Famecos* 21, no. 2 (August 2014): 738.

[20] Stuart Hall, "Questions of Cultural Identity," in *Modernity and Its Futures—Understanding Modern Societies*, Book IV, ed. Tony McGrew, Stuart Hall, and David Helds (Oxford: Polity, 1992), 276.

[21] Ibid., 277.

> I wanted to be seen. That was absolutely true. All performers—all humans—want to be seen; it's a basic need. Even the shy ones who don't want to be *looked at*. But I also wanted, very much, to see.... I needed the two way-street, the exchange, the relationship, and the invitation to true intimacy that I got every so often from the eyes of my random street patrons.[22]

To see and be seen is a process that can be described as a performance of authenticity—a process that, in *The Art of Asking*, is represented by this expression of Palmer's need to share her personal life. This perception of performed authenticity—where she supposedly shows her true self without the fear of revealing something compromising—is a way of simultaneously coming closer to the public while gaining legitimacy as an artist of value.

Authenticity, in these terms, is constantly disputed by the artists of popular music, including those operating in the rock music genre.[23] This dispute takes place via political stances or political compositions arising from specific artists and subcultures,[24] gender discussions,[25] and even the making of live performances. The quality of audio reproduction and the proximity of live music to the recorded version are vital elements in fans' legitimization of authenticity in rock music.[26] In addition, authenticity in popular music is defined by a set of previous personal beliefs, individual notions of music quality, and the consumer's taste.[27]

Association with one or more specific rock subgenres helps to legitimize some artists because of the rules inherent to that genre. This strategy creates a performative coherence, fundamental for performance credibility.[28] Simon Frith claims that any artist who obeys genre rules can be deemed authentic. He divides Fabbri's rules neatly into "sound conventions (what you hear), performing conventions (what you see), packaging conventions (how a type of music is sold), and embodied values (the music's ideology)."[29]

---

[22] Palmer, *The Art of Asking*, 44–45.
[23] Philip Auslander, *LIVENESS: Performance in a Mediatized Culture* (New York: Routledge, 2008).
[24] Gary Clarke, "Defending Ski-Jumpers: A Critique of Theories of Youth Subcultures," in *On Record: Rock, Pop, and Written Word*, ed. Simon Frith and Andrew Goodwin (New York: Taylor & Francis, 2005).
[25] Kaylie Ann Murphy, "'I'm Sorry, I'm Not Really Sorry': Courtney Love and Notions of Authenticity," *Hecate* 27, no. 1 (November 2001): 139–162.
[26] Auslander, *LIVENESS*, 84.
[27] Frith, *Performing Rites*, 16.
[28] Goffman, *The Presentation of Self*, 87.
[29] Frith, *Performing Rites*, 94.

The disputes occur in discussions of the dynamics surrounding this set of rules and how many of them an artist can actually engage in through their work and with the public. In her narrative, Palmer incidentally associates herself with consecrated rock subgenres, such as punk rock and heavy metal: "Brian had been reared on a steady diet of metal, jazz, and hardcore punk, and he hit the drums like a smoke-choked victim pounding on the exit door of a burning building; for him, commitment to the religion of drumming was his gateway to redemption. And I played piano the same way, seeking salvation through volume."[30]

She then recounts how often she broke the piano strings by playing too strongly, seeking the volume she perceived in rock songs. This is a constant in both her music and her writing. An association is created when she recognizes her proximity with notions of Do It Yourself (DIY):

> DIY is a tricky term.
> I've been called the "Queen of DIY," but if you're really taking the definition of "Do It Yourself" literally, I completely fail. I have no interest in Doing It Myself. I'm much more interested in getting everybody to help me.[31]

By emphasizing the loud sound that she made with the Dresden Dolls and embodying cultural trends such as DIY, which is characteristic of underground (rock) music, Palmer performs her authenticity to be associated more strongly with the alternative scene. To secure her place as an authentic artist, she embodies several of the genre rules—in this case by playing strong and loud and by being recognized as part of the DIY culture. Palmer initially affirms that DIY might not be the best category for her and her idea of engaging a community, but in the end, she relents:

> Then there's "Maximal DIY," which is more about expansion and asking. The emphasis is on collectivism; you throw the problem out to your circles to see what solution will arise.... Minimal DIY doesn't rely on trust; it relies on ingenuity.
> Maximal DIY relies on trust *and* ingenuity. You have to ask with enough grace and creativity to elicit a response, and you also have to *trust* the people you're asking.[32]

[30] Palmer, *The Art of Asking*, 77.
[31] Ibid., 97–98.
[32] Ibid., 99.

As we can read, she associates her Art of Asking with a reading of DIY culture. By doing that, she again reinforces her place and coherence, strengthening her performed authenticity. She thus raises the notion of a collective construction with her fan base, the audience she is asking for attention and money.

In *The Art of Asking*, Palmer creates a sort of connection with her readers that aims for "expectations established in the verisimilitude or suspension of disbelief"[33] that categorizes her autobiographical truth. Paraphrasing Smith and Watson, she settles on a negotiation of truth with her readers to convince them of her reality, which directly affects her own identity—which has been constructed collectively. She uses her stance as an authentic rock musician to negotiate music and personal life values.

She also creates an identification by entering a particular narrative—one that tackles the struggles of being an artist and self-doubt, along with the delight in doing whatever she wants, expressing herself the way she sees fit.

I will move on to analyze the negotiations Palmer performs with her public, through her autobiography and other media.

Negotiating the Truth Using Self-Narrative

Regarding her choice to become a musician, Palmer writes: "I knew I wanted to be a musician. I know I didn't want a Real Job,"[34] and *"I WILL NEVER HAVE TO HAVE A REAL JOB AGAIN. And technically? I never really did."*[35]

The musician capitalizes "Real Job," referring to work that society supposedly considers somehow more "realistic" than those in the entertainment industry. This perception seems to come from two significant ways of thinking and experiencing life: first, she is an independent musician, an occupation that often is not considered suitable employment in the capitalist system, where one of the rules is to have a stable source of income, preferably one that pays well. Second, she is a woman that opted for a music career, producing and publicizing her material and connecting with her fan base.

What is considered a "real job" or not depends on the socially constructed concept of occupation. Clair points out that what is considered a job depends

---

[33] Sidonie Smith and Julia Watson, *Reading Autobiography: A Guide for Interpreting Life Narratives* (Minneapolis: University of Minnesota Press, 2001), 12.
[34] Palmer, *The Art of Asking*, 26.
[35] Ibid., 29.

on socioeconomic background;[36] it has always been an open debate in Western civilization and will vary according to the social construction of labor. Therefore, it is possible to assume that some artists have a "real job" regardless of gender. Hollywood actors and well-known popular musicians employed by major record companies, for example, are recognized for their work and receive their rightful payment. This, however, is not a reality for independent artists, many of whom are in constant danger of not receiving payment for their work as their contractors often see the production of entertainment as effortless.[37]

The struggle to achieve recognition as a "true" artist appears at several points in Palmer's narrative. She deems social construction and her insecurities to be imposter syndrome, which she terms "The Fraud Police"— a struggle for recognition by others and herself as a professional artist. Palmer's performance of authenticity enables her to get closer to her public and makes her feel that the music she produces is valuable. She claims that no matter how successful she becomes, or the number of positive comments she receives from specialized media or her peers, "What at last began to quiet the voices and dismiss the deep-rooted psyche-bashing work of The Fraud Police was simply this: after hundreds of signings, after talking to thousands of fans, I started to believe that what I did was just as useful as what they did."[38]

To be connected is to prove her trueness as an artist to her fans and herself. "The Fraud Police" resembles the idea of the "inner voice," as discussed by Taylor, one that we must keep in close communication with in order not to lose a sense of "true self."[39] However, Palmer proposes ignoring this inner voice and focusing on her identity construction through her exchanges with the public. Her autobiography plays a vital role in this negotiation, but the interactions through the online platforms also matter. Her online performance, as part of an online narrative, is crucial to the construction of authenticity that aids in shaping her identity.

Understanding the platforms as stages where Palmer coherently performs her authenticity, it is possible to assume that the process of construction of identity is a collective action. Goffman and Schechner already defended such a notion previously; however, this is enhanced by Palmer's online presence

---

[36] Robert P. Clair, "The Political Nature of the Colloquialism 'A Real Job': Implications for Organizational Socialization," *Communication Monographs* 63, no. 3 (September 1996), 251.
[37] Ibid., 257.
[38] Palmer, *The Art of Asking*, 155.
[39] Charles Taylor, *The Ethics of Authenticity* (London: Harvard University Press, 2003), 362.

and it also appears in the book—complementing the performance she has been constructing throughout her career. It is made obvious when she writes that she wants to see and be seen, when she mentions her "special relationship" with her fans, and when she includes herself in groups of people and demonstrates her feminism in the most practical ways.

As discussed by authors such as Farrugia,[40] Wolfe,[41] and Reddington,[42] women working in the music industry, whether in recording studios or on stages, tend to be taken less seriously than their male counterparts. This all reflects on their self-esteem, the feeling of belonging in the music market, and when seeking compensation. This idea also appears in Palmer's narrative:

> When I took the step from playing in The Dresden Dolls with Brian, I felt a huge difference between asking people to listen to ME and MY songs and help ME ME ME, versus helping our BAND. . . .
>
> In 2010, Emily Amanatullah, a graduate student in management, did a research simulation in which men and women had to negotiate starting salaries in different scenarios.
>
> When the women negotiated for themselves, they asked for an average of $7,000 less than the men did.[43]

Although Palmer seems to try to take gender out of the debate about self-doubt or public criticism throughout her book, referring to it as something every artist goes through, passages like the above suggest that she is aware of women's self-doubt in the music market. From Palmer's viewpoint, this reference to Amanatullah's research makes it possible to suggest that this self-doubt may come from a lack of recognition for female artists, a stigma that women have to fight against inside the music industry. As Farrugia[44] and Wolfe[45] have noted, many of the actions taken by women inside the music industry are driven by personal resistance. Women make efforts to increase their value by, for example, enrolling in music production and technology courses and working against gender-biased behaviors in the industry, such

---

[40] Rebekah Farrugia, *Beyond the Dance Floor: Female DJs, Technology and Electronic Dance Music Culture* (Bristol: Intellect Books, 2012).

[41] Helen Reddington, *She's at the Controls: Sound Engineering, Production and Gender Ventriloquism in the 21st Century* (Bristol: Equinox, 2021).

[42] Paula Wolfe, *Women in the Studio: Creativity, Control and Gender in Popular Music Production* (London: Routledge, 2020).

[43] Palmer, *The Art of Asking*, 171.

[44] Farrugia, *Beyond the Dance Floor*, 74.

[45] Wolfe, *Women in the Studio*, 183.

as the lower payments, without any clear justification—even if they have to resort to legal means to do so. As Wolfe explains: "the popular music industry is a very particular type of cultural industry where gender constructions are central to the branding process of making music."[46]

Palmer continues to refer to Amanatullah's work to try to make sense of why women ask for less compensation than men for their work: "Amanatullah found that women were concerned about 'managing their reputation,' worried that pushing for more money would 'damage their image.' And other research shows that it's a justified fear, that both male and female managers are less likely to want to work with women who negotiate during a job interview."[47] Personal reputation plays a central role in contracts, work arrangements, and invitations. When one is not taken seriously for one's work, these agreements lose force, reducing the significance of the professional. Palmer notices this specific problem as a reason for women feeling blocked when asking, also constructing this narrative to justify the negative response she received from the public following her successful crowdfunding project.

One point raised by critics was based on a blog post written by Palmer on August 21, 2012, when she asked for volunteer musicians to play with her on tour with the Grand Theft Orchestra. In exchange, she would pay them "beer" and "hug/high five."[48] The post angered musicians and associations who wrote open letters, which made the case go viral.

Palmer gave an interview to clean up her image, wrote a letter in response, and started to discuss openly how much she was spending on each phase of the *Theatre Is Evil* project. She also addresses the case in the book. In the early pages of the memoir, she writes:

> Apparently, it was distasteful to ask. I was targeted as the worst offender for a lot of reasons: because I'd already been promoted by a major label, because I had a famous husband, because I was a flaming narcissist.
>
> Things went from dark to darker in the months after my Kickstarter as I set off to tour the world with my band and put out my usual call to local volunteer musicians who might want to join us onstage for a few songs. We were a tight community, and I'd been doing things like that for years.[49]

---

[46] Ibid., 11.
[47] Palmer, *The Art of Asking*, 171.
[48] Amanda Palmer, "Wanted: Horn-y and String-y Volunteers for the Grand Theft Auto Orchestra Tour!!!!!" *Amanda Palmer Blog* (August 2012), https://blog.amandapalmer.net/20120821/#.
[49] Palmer, *The Art of Asking*, 11.

While stating that calling for volunteers is something that she has always done, Palmer tries to make sense of people's perceptions about her. This event presents itself as a rupture, so Palmer tries to justify her actions. Such validation of a narrative is not a new approach, and it may even be considered mandatory in autobiographical texts. As Smith and Watson point out: "Persuasion to belief is fundamental to the pact between narrator and Reader."[50] In this case, the book is vital as a tool for persuading the public that Amanda's actions were appropriate.

Not correcting a performance rupture is also a problem, especially when it influences online performance and expressive coherence. Talking about the changes brought up by the creation of virtual worlds and the digitalization of the entertainment industry, Latour[51] defends that it is not as interesting to talk about the proximities of what is real and what is a set of codes that produces a character, as much as it is highly important to talk about "traceability." In this scenario, the philosopher elaborates that in the twenty-first century, every action with an online repercussion is prone to not be forgotten or can be easily traced—a factor that changes concerns with expressive coherence.

This notably shapes Palmer's performance and worry about defusing situations that can hinder her authenticity and the trust of her fan base. Throughout her book, the blogs, and the settling of scores posted online, Palmer constructs the idea that the act of asking other people for what you need—a helping hand, a piece of advice, tampons, money—is what unites her community. Explaining the above-mentioned event, she clarifies that this is the relationship she always had with her fans, "happily exchanging: favors, flowers, dollars, music, hugs, beer, love, whatever."[52] However, the rest of the world—the people outside the community—"couldn't see the exchange for what it was: a process that was normal for us, but alien to them."[53]

It is not merely that she asks when she needs something; the conviction of the performance of authenticity creates trust inside her community, generating confidence that she will deliver a production people will enjoy while trusting in her proximity with her fan base. Palmer and her fans have

---

[50] Smith and Watson, *Reading Autobiography*, 28.
[51] Bruno Latour, "Beware, Your Imagination Leaves Digital Traces," *Times Higher Education Supplement*, April 6, 2007.
[52] Palmer, *The Art of Asking*, 202.
[53] Ibid., 203.

thus built up a two-way relationship that resembles friendship, an affinity she must reinforce by maintaining the performance—including the online one.

On Trust and the Construction of Community

As Goffman states: "In everyday life, of course, there is a clear understanding that first impressions are important," which is the way that a "social actor" can garner the trust of people around them.[54] One way to generate positive, trustable sensations from "first impressions" is by self-asserting performances protected from "failures," by which the person performing can guarantee that their performance will instill trust in the audience. In this case, the performance demands the security of "expressive coherence," a crucial requirement for both day-to-day performances and artistic ones: Goffman presents an analogy comparing everyday life to a theater. Ruptures and contradictions in the expressive coherence must be avoided so as not to cause misunderstandings between performer and audience in the performative act.[55] For Palmer, it is fundamental to be part of an artistic environment where the performance is central and conveys authenticity and expressive coherence, aiding her identity construction in that process.

As with the above-mentioned example regarding volunteer musicians, Palmer tried to deal with the event in many ways, including discussing the matter in her memoir. To ensure that the public understood her and to avoid the risk of having her authenticity questioned by her fan base, she did not let the matter go, mentioning it and clarifying once again.

Trust is a constructed affection that depends on either expressive coherence to aid maintenance and social understanding or on an agreement between the parties involved. Ahmed writes that the breaking of trust results from the social intelligence of a "subject or an object" that lacks something.[56] It is a set of processes based on the social construction of affections that question the subject's quality. Constructing trust among friends is essential for endorsing the exchange of life experiences and other forms of capital, whether material or not. Trust takes shape when an unspoken agreement

---

[54] Goffman, *The Presentation of Self*, 5.
[55] Polivanov and Carrera, "Perfect Bodies and Digital Influencers," 33.
[56] Sara Ahmed, *The Cultural Politics of Emotion* (Edinburgh: Edinburgh University Press, 2014), 27.

between people makes them believe in one another, usually through sharing personal life stories.

Palmer builds trust by inserting herself into the so-called real community, born from her interaction with her fans. The type of authenticity negotiated by the musician depends on her people, and this community enables the legitimization of Palmer as someone honest—a real artist, a real persona. This is a constant in Palmer's narrative, as when she describes how she dealt with Roadrunner Records' producers and agents who did not understand her relationship with her fans:

> I don't think you guys get it. Our website is like . . . a Real Place. It needs to exist all the time. You don't shut it down and then come back later.
>
> The whole point of being an artist, I thought, was to be connected to people. To make a family. A family you were with all the time, like it or not. . . .
>
> I knew the way to keep the fans happy was by staying present—through the forums, through sharing people's art and music back out through the Internet channels, through keeping everybody connected. . . . And when the time came to ask them to buy a record, to buy a ticket, whatever . . . if I'd been there for them, they'd be there for me.[57]

Palmer builds a community with her fans through these exchanges and tried to convey this idea to the record label. Still, they did not recognize the nature of the connection, deeming the website and social media profiles to be merely means of communication between artist and public. Her memoir, by contrast, makes it clear why engagement with the public is a central topic for the musician. Palmer is an artist who aims to capture and captivate her fan base by building trust with them. She performs to be understood as someone authentic, someone whom the public can rely on to the point where they will pay in advance for something they do not know or how or whether it will be further developed.

Her constructed identity is, therefore, dependent on a coherent performance and a necessity for the construction of narrative without fail so as to prevent ruptures, as explained by Polivanov and Carrera.[58] Her authenticity can be put into question if she does not keep the trust of the public

---

[57] Palmer, *The Art of Asking*, 106.
[58] Polivanov and Carrera, "Perfect Bodies and Digital Influencers," 36.

by avoiding controversies or substantiating very well her changes of opinion and behavior.

Palmer joined Patreon in 2015, almost one year after the book's release. She does not discuss the platform in any detail, only mentioning it briefly in conversations with other artists about ways to charge for artistic productions.[59] However, she did post a lot on her Twitter and made a few blog posts talking about her decision to join the platform. Patreon demands greater fidelity and engagement with the public because, unlike Kickstarter, the producer receives payment for their work. People actively give from $1 to $241,50 for everything Palmer publishes on Patreon today (the more you give, the more you receive). With this backup from her fan base, she has released 50 audio releases (among songs, EPs, and albums), 4479 images, 16 links, 22 live streams, 37 polls, 10 writings (among small books and short stories), and 73 videos.

The book can also be seen as more organic preparation for her Patreon. Palmer reinforces the importance of crowdfunding and of how her fan base is an integral part of the process. The conviction is based on her truth and her dependence on a solid community that will back her up, no matter what: "If you love people enough, they'll give you everything."[60] The performance of authenticity shows itself to be a strategy that engenders symbolic capital and, if the results are positive, converts it to financial capital. Therefore, the book is not only a recounting of the musician's life, not even a self-help book for minor artists to learn how to ask. It works together with her online presence as a tool for Palmer's performance of authenticity, through which she can persuade the public she deserves to receive for whatever she creatively produces while reinforcing her place as a woman inside the music industry.

Conclusion

This chapter has discussed the performance of authenticity as a strategy used by the musician Amanda Palmer to maintain the connection with her fan base. Using this strategy, she provokes and negotiates trust as a value to engage her community through the self-narrative employed in her memoir. Palmer thus builds a strong bond with her public that will help her when she

---

[59] Palmer, *The Art of Asking*, 150, 206.
[60] Ibid., 261.

needs it to lessen the damage caused by eventual ruptures in expressive coherence that influences her narratives of self.[61]

While there has been debate about whether the performance of authenticity is possible, Palmer negotiates this question with expertise, her memoir becoming a part of the process. Besides, the musician has been using the value in her online presence to create a coherent narrative of self and has repeatedly been legitimized by her fan base—the group that matters to her. In this sense, I understand that her virtual construction of self is not different from her "physical" persona when it comes to the construction of an authentic identity.

In *The Art of Asking*, Palmer reinforces authenticity, revealing how she performs to acquire validation as a good artist belonging to a trustworthy community. Following the logic that to be seen is to be real, the performance of authenticity seems to be the best way to make this happen. Palmer's grasp of this idea is present throughout the entire book. She presents herself as someone whom her fan base can rely on to engender identification, creating a connection that keeps the community strong. The book itself thus becomes a significant part of the performance process.

Using a book as a tool for the performance of authenticity is a good strategy when we consider the longevity that bibliographical material can provide to an author. Many independent artists do not engage in such a way with their public, and many others have been less successful than Palmer in their crowdfunding strategy. When she writes and makes official her views in *The Art of Asking*, the musician creates proof that sharing intimacy with her community of fans might be one way of maintaining the connection. She deconstructs the idea of an unattainable celebrity, showing herself to be on the same level as her fans, even though, of course, those fans exist only because Palmer does.

Bibliography

Ahmed, Sara. *The Cultural Politics of Emotion*. Edinburgh: Edinburgh University Press, 2014.

Auslander, Philip. *LIVENESS: Performance in a Mediatized Culture*. New York: Routledge, 2008.

---

[61] Polivanov and Carrera, "Perfect Bodies and Digital Influencers," 36.

Bourdieu, Pierre. "Symbolic Capital and Social Classes." *Journal of Classical Sociology* 13, no. 2 (May 2013): 292–302.
Campanella, Bruno. "Celebridade, engajamento humanitário e a formação do capital solidário." Famecos 21, no. 2 (August 2014): 721–741.
Clair, Robert P. "The Political Nature of the Colloquialism 'a Real Job': Implications for Organizational Socialization." *Communication Monographs* 63, no. 3 (June 1996): 249–267.
Clarke, Gary. "Defending Ski-Jumpers: A Critique of Theories of Youth Subcultures." In *On Record: Rock, Pop, and Written Word*, edited by Simon Frith and Andrew Goodwin, 68–80. New York: Taylor & Francis, 2005.
Farrugia, Rebekah. *Beyond the Dance Floor: Female DJs, Technology and Electronic Dance Music Culture*. Bristol: Intellect Books, 2012.
Frith, Simon. *Performing Rites: On Value of Popular Music*. Cambridge, MA: Harvard University Press, 1996.
Goffman, Erving. The Presentation of Self in Everyday Life. Edinburgh: Social Sciences Research Center, Monograph No. 2, 1956.
Hall, Stuart. "Questions of Cultural Identity." In *Modernity and Its Futures—Understanding Modern Societies*, Book IV, edited by Tony McGrew, Stuart Hall, and David Helds, 247–323. Oxford: Polity, 1992.
Latour, Bruno. "Beware, Your Imagination Leaves Digital Traces." *Times Literary Supplement*, April 6, 2007.
Medeiros, Beatriz, and Natalia Dias. "Crowdfunding Is Not for Everybody: Performance in the Art of Asking." In *Popular Music Studies Today. Systematische Musikwissenschaft*, edited by Jenny Merrill, 85–95. Wiesbaden: Springer VS, 2017.
Medeiros, Beatriz, and Beatriz Polivanov. "Female Artists, Social Media and Alternative Economy: The Case of Amanda Palmer." In *Keep It Simple Make It Fast: An Approach to Underground Music Scenes*, edited by Paula Guerra and Thiago Pereira Alberto, 353–366. Porto: Porto University, 2019.
Murphy, Kaylie Ann. "'I'm Sorry, I'm Not Really Sorry': Courtney Love and Notions of Authenticity." *Hecate* 27, no. 1 (November 2001): 139–162.
Neill, Alex. "Inauthenticity, Insincerity and Poetry." In *Performance and Authenticity in the Arts*, edited by Salim Kemal and Ivan Gaskell, 197–214. Cambridge: Cambridge University Press, 1999.
Palmer, Amanda. *The Art of Asking: or How I Learned to Stop Worrying and Let Other People Help*. New York: Grand Central Publishing, 2014.
Polivanov, Beatriz and Fernanda Carrera. "Perfect Bodies and Digital Influencers: Gendered Ruptures of Performance on Social Media in Brazil." *Cultural Politics* 18, no. 1 (March 2022): 28–43.
Reddington, Helen. She's at the Controls: Sound Engineering, Production and Gender Ventriloquism in the 21st Century. Bristol: Equinox, 2021.
Schechner, Richard. *Performance Studies: An Introduction*. New York: Routledge, 2006.
Smith, Sidonie, and Julia Watson, *Reading Autobiography: A Guide for Interpreting Life Narratives*. Minneapolis: University of Minnesota Press, 2001.
Taylor, Charles. *The Ethics of Authenticity*. London: Harvard University Press, 2003.
Wolfe, Paula. *Women in the Studio: Creativity, Control and Gender in Popular Music Production*. London: Routledge, 2020.

9

The Punk, the Rebel, and the Cowboy

Queering Masculine Spaces in Patti Smith's Memoirs

Amy McCarthy

The opening lines to Patti Smith's poem "notebook" read: "I keep trying to figure out what it means / to be American."[1] From "nineteenth-century / French" to "syphilitic cowpokes,"[2] both make up the American poet. To be an American poet is to take inspiration from a variety of cultures and identities; therefore the poet is a bricoleur. There is nothing that is quintessentially American; as Andy Warhol argues, "there's no such thing as being more or less American, just American."[3] In this poem, "Smith brings up the notion that being American is not something rooted in the ancestral or psychological makeup of a person," nor is it "some gritty reality of the [W]est."[4] The American poet is made up of worldly influences. Smith, as an American poet, is a melting pot of influences that crafts a version of the self.

In "notebook," Smith is represented not only as a poet, but as an individual. For decades, the cowboy has been the symbol of the American individual, representing modern American culture, and it is the essence of hegemonic masculinity. Once an "unpopular and seemingly unsavory"[5] character, the cowboy is romanticized by Hollywood and popular culture via John Wayne and Clint Eastwood. Through the cinematic experience, the masculine cowboy is mythologized. William B. Savage argues: "By taking up the gun, the cowboy ensured his future as America's most persistent, and therefore most significant, myth."[6] The difficult and laborious lifestyle of the

---

[1] Patti Smith, *Early Work: 1970–1979* (New York: W. W. Norton, 1995), 12.
[2] Ibid.
[3] Andy Warhol, *America* (London: Penguin, 2011), 223.
[4] Greg Smith, "'And All the Sinners, Saints': Patti Smith, Pioneer Musician and Poet," *Midwest Quarterly* 41, no. 2 (2000): 188.
[5] William W. Savage, *Cowboy Life: Reconstructing an American Myth* (Boulder: University Press of Colorado, 1993), 10.
[6] Ibid.

cowboy is glamorized to represent the hustle culture promoted to the everyday American. The myth of the cowboy is "the antidote to worrisome urbanization and soul-killing industrialization"[7] of American culture. What the cowboy represents is something paradoxical—the modern American but also the rejection of urbanization.

The cowboy's image is unsolidified and has shifted across time. Since the 1970s, the cowboy has been queered as the Western film genre branched out into further subgenres, such as Weird Westerns and Sci-fi Westerns. Eve Sedgwick argues that the term "queer" refers to "the open mesh of possibilities, gaps, overlaps, dissonances and resonances, lapses and excesses of meaning when the constituent elements of anyone's gender."[8] The definitions of the term "queer" exist where spaces overlap. The cowboy figure in Smith's memoir is always male and appears at the intersection between fiction, reality, and artistry. What the cowboy represents has shifted on numerous occasions in the last century. The gaps and contradictions in the figure's history makes room for the queering of the cowboy's image.

Across many of her creative endeavors, Patti Smith references and uses the image of the cowboy to construct a version of herself. The figure's presence has altered since first being referenced in the 1971 play *Cowboy Mouth*, written by Sam Shepard and Patti Smith. Ultimately, the cowboy's existence throughout the memoirs represents Smith as an artist. In *Just Kids* (2010), Smith recounts writing and performing the play with Shepard as well as using Wild West imagery to describe two key men in Smith's life at that moment: Robert Mapplethorpe and Sam Shepard. In *M Train* (2015), the cowboy has a more predominant role in the memoir and appears as a character in Smith's subconscious and drifts in and out of the narrative. The cowboy figure does not appear in *Year of the Monkey* (2019), but the memoir takes place along the West Coast and the solitary cowboy imagery is present in Smith's writing. Where the cowboy exists is significant as "the landscapes of the American West are susceptible to suffusion by nostalgia."[9] In the memoirs, the cowboy only exists in memory—a space where nostalgia and narrative building resides. Much like the punk musician and music, both the Wild West and the punk musician have versions of themselves rooted in

---

[7] Tim Lehman, "The Making of the Cowboy Myth," *Saturday Evening Post*, January 21, 2020, accessed March 11, 2022, https://www.saturdayeveningpost.com/2020/01/the-making-of-the-cowboy-myth/.

[8] Eve Kosofsky Sedgwick, *Tendencies* (Durham, NC: Duke University Press, 1993), 8.

[9] Beth E. Levy, *Frontier Figures: American Music and the Mythology of the American West* (Berkeley: University of California Press, 2012), 8.

nostalgia. Western imagery in Smith's memoirs is rooted in memory and the slippery nature of one's own memory.

In this chapter I will focus on Smith's three memoirs, with a specific focus on *M Train*. Across the memoirs Smith takes a conservative, masculine figure and usurps his mythical identity. By mapping the journey of the cowboy in Smith's memoirs, I will argue that the cowboy is a vessel used to project Smith's voice. When Smith references cowboys and the Wild West, she is referring to the artistic process and the rebellion that comes with being an artist. By making the cowboy represent the artistic process—a bohemian pursuit—Smith subverts a typical example of masculine iconography. Smith reclaims the cowboy and Wild West mythology within the memoirs and makes it a part of her own mythology. All three memoirs deal with striving toward an artistic frontier, whether that be making a name for oneself in New York or overcoming writer's block. The cowboy acts as a vessel for Smith to transcend conscious realms and only appears in fleeting moments or liminal spaces, particularly in Smith's dreamscape. Smith takes fragments of the cowboy's identity and creates a new version that subverts patriarchal heteronormativity. Through art, Smith claims authority in male-dominated spaces therefore queers a masculine space. By using the existing masculine culture surrounding the cowboy, Smith tears it up and reattaches it to create a portal to the psyche.

The Memoirist as Bricoleur

Ripping it up and starting again is central to the punk aesthetic, which Smith embodies. Robert Edgar, Fraser Mann, and Helen Pleasance argue that music memoirists can "be understood as bricoleurs and their memoirs contribute as further acts of bricolage."[10] The bricoleur presents their draft work and influences on the page. Patti Smith's music and poetry are sprinkled with allusions to literary revolutionaries, which is an act of bricolage. Whether it be the wisdoms of Louisa May Alcott or Bob Dylan, the source material and influences are present on the page. In doing so, the selves presented in music memoirs "are necessarily both real in the sense that they are the identity narratives of real historical subjects, and also new formations of identity,

---

[10] Robert Edgar, Fraser Mann, and Helen Pleasance, "Music, Memory and Memoir: Critical and Creative Engagement with an Emerging Genre," *Journal of Writing in Creative Practice* 12, no. 1–2 (2019): 185.

dependent on and, paradoxically, limited by their textual construction."[11] Stitching together fiction and nonfiction creates a version of Smith to present in the memoirs and this representation can shift.

Memoirs do not always center on the writer, as Hermione Lee states: "Autobiographers often stray into fiction, and infiltrate the lives of others into their own stories."[12] Autobiography "is a kind of fiction, its self and its truth as much created as (re)discovered realities."[13] Smith's later memoirs in particular are an amalgamation of dreams, reality, literature, and art. The mixture of different mediums offers various versions of Smith's image and personality. Smith crosses conscious and unconscious realms to merge creative life with mundane reality. Dancing through literature, dreams, and personal milestones, Smith's writing presents the layers of consciousness that create a person and place. The bricolage nature of Smith's art constructs the queering of masculine images and spaces in the memoirs, particularly in *M Train*. The overlaps are where new meaning is found and various versions of the memoirist are created.

Women's autobiographical writing is a traditionally transgressive act. Autobiographical writing is historically deemed as "fundamentally a male generic contract,"[14] whereas diaries and letters were associated with the domestic sphere and coded as feminine. Life-writing is stitched together by the private writings of diaries and letters. Letter writing, Jonathan Ellis argues, is "a form of self-portrait."[15] Ellis's argument can also be extended to memoir. The writer is creating a self-portrait. However, a self-portrait is not a stabilized entity and has the ability to change over time. An artist inevitably adapts and hones their craft over time, and no self-portrait is identical and portrays what the artist wants to convey.

Autobiography and the publication of life-writing is "a performative act,"[16] as they are public texts of a subject's private life. Autobiographical writing is subjective, as it theorizes "memory, experience, identity, space, embodiment,

---

[11] Ibid., 184.
[12] Hermione Lee, "'From Memory': Literary Encounters and Life-Writing," in *On Life-Writing*, ed. Zachary Leader (Oxford: Oxford University Press, 2015), 124.
[13] Laura J. Beard, *Acts of Narrative Resistance: Women's Autobiographical Writing in the Americas* (Charlottesville: University of Virginia Press, 2009), 12.
[14] Sidonie Smith, *A Poetics of Women's Autobiography: Marginality and the Fictions of Self-Representation* (Bloomington: Indiana University Press, 1987), 14.
[15] Jonathan Ellis, "Introduction: 'For What Is a Letter?'," in *Letter Writing among Poets: From William Wordsworth to Elizabeth Bishop*, ed. Jonathan Ellis (Edinburgh: Edinburgh University Press, 2015), 2.
[16] Sidonie Smith and Julia Watson, *Reading Autobiography: A Guide for Interpreting Life Narratives*, 2nd ed. (Minneapolis: University of Minnesota Press, 2010), 61.

and agency"[17] of a person's life and is inevitably biased. The writing must encapsulate memory and embody the identity of the subject. Whereas autobiography focuses on a large portion of one's life, memoir focuses on specific themes and does not have to be a chronological account of living. The fluidity of the memoir format works with the musician memoirist as music constructs and recollects memory in a nonlinear fashion. Lauren Istvandity argues that music can "embody something more personal" than other sounds, "due to its complexity and ability to affect emotions in strong and sometimes unexpected ways."[18] Memoir delves into the fictional world and draws thematic connections between memories. In doing so, memoir and music intertwine by mirroring the complexities of human life and emotions.

A music memoir centers on music and the musician's relationship with their life soundtrack. The publication of women's music memoirs rewrites rock's history and revises the mythology surrounding the music. By bringing the domestic space and gender inequality into the narrative, these memoirs reposition women's space in rock music. Although Abigail Gardner argues that "[a]ll of them are about the positioning of the self,"[19] Patti Smith bends this rule. Beyond the image of the punk pioneer, Smith is a difficult person to define. After three memoirs, Smith still remains an enigma and holds multiple identities but, most important, presents the artist as ordinary. Gardner argues that "[t]he 'myth' of the confessional singer-songwriter is allied to authenticity" and female music memoirs are "the telling of the real as it is experienced and the communicated, by the self."[20] Memoir presents the authentic self as the musician intends to be presented to others. The music memoir is somewhat confessional. However, the confessional narrative is crafted. Smith's memoirs are "not a 'how I got into music' memoir[s]."[21] They do not present the man behind the curtain of the musician. Rather, Smith's memoirs reveal the cogs that create Patti Smith the artist. Although Smith stands independently against other music memoirists, all memoirs are confessional as they present the self through the artist's eyes. Confession is inherently mundane. It is the mythology around the confession which is exciting. Smith and other musicians in the genre reveal this in their memoirs. Rather than presenting a life through music, Smith's memoirs present a life through

---

[17] Ellis, "Introduction," 61.
[18] Lauren Istvandity, *The Lifetime Soundtrack* (Sheffield: Equinox, 2019), 23.
[19] Abigail Gardner, *Ageing and Contemporary Female Musicians* (New York: Routledge, 2020), 29.
[20] Ibid., 19.
[21] Ibid., 21.

art. By using memoir writing as a method to reclaim personal history, Smith presents her life in a contradictory and mythological way.

Smith's queering of the written space begins in her poetry. When performing at St. Mark's Place, Smith "wanted to infuse the written word with the immediacy and frontal attack of rock and roll"[22] and merged poetry with the electric guitar. Fusing together spoken word with rock, Smith formed her own version of punk poetry. By queering an already queered genre, Smith confuses "the boundaries between poetry and popular music"[23] to create something new. This is also extended to memoir writing as Smith dismantles the norms of the genre. Music memoir writers "seek to explore what makes them artists and how their relationship with sound overlaps and comingles with language and memory."[24] Although the memoirs barely mention music, Smith stretches language and the boundaries of memoir to recollect memories which curate an artist's identity. Despite an increasing catalogue of memoirs, the image of the artist is not solidified within the pages. Rather, Smith becomes increasingly difficult to place and becomes as abstract as her art. The abstract nature of Smith's writing leaves gaps in the memoirs and allows stories to be fluid and change, which allows Smith to relinquish control over the narrative by allowing parts of it to remain a mystery. Ultimately, the cowboy is used as a tool to sculpt the self and aid Smith in her own mythmaking.

The Transgressive Cowboy in *Just Kids*

Despite the legendary status of the gunfighter, the cowboy is also stripped to a mundane existence like the musician. The cowboy myth contains multiple contradictory identities, as the cowboy is "a gunfighter, sometimes a gambler, and he may be a rancher, sheriff, or scout, even an outlaw."[25] Over time, the cowboy's mythology is revised through the lens of nostalgia, much like the mythology surrounding punk and Smith herself. Will Wright argues: "The cowboy myth is specifically American, but America represents a theory, the

---

[22] Patti Smith, *Just Kids* (New York: Bloomsbury, 2011), 180.
[23] Carrie Jaures Noland, "Rimbaud and Patti Smith: Style as Social Deviance," *Critical Inquiry* 21, no. 3 (1995): 587.
[24] Edgar et al., "Music, Memory and Memoir," 189.
[25] Will Wright, *The Wild West: The Mythical Cowboy and Social Theory* (London: Sage, 2001), 6.

theory of market society. The cowboy, then, is a market character, a symbol of individualism, not just an American character."[26]

The cowboy myth contains two stereotypes: the rancher and the outlaw. The rancher leads a humble lifestyle the urban American can only fantasize about; alternatively, the outlaw is the antithesis of the modern American— a reckless criminal attempting to undo the United States' progress. Henry Nash Smith argues: "The philosophy and the myth [of the West] affirmed an admirable set of values, but they ceased very early to be useful in interpreting American society as a whole because they offered no intellectual apparatus for taking account of the industrial revolution."[27] Depending on the media outlet, the cowboy can be anywhere on the spectrum of rancher and outlaw, and Smith also falls on this spectrum as she lives several existences simultaneously, such as both countercultural figure and a mainstream, award-winning writer. Much as the cowboy in Smith's memoirs belongs in the liminal space between conscious and unconscious realms, Smith belongs in the space between rancher and rebel. The ever-changing identity of the cowboy reveals the multidimensional nature of identity and how this is presented in memoir. The contradictory nature and mystery surrounding Smith's image presents the authentic self.

The cowboy is a "nostalgic figure of the Old West, a place that is generally considered agrarian, at the turn of the century and during the early twentieth century, the cowboy actually furthered American nationalism and the capitalist ideology."[28] Across the three memoirs, the cowboy and the Wild West play a significant role in Smith's narrative. Although the vision of the cowboy appears as the nostalgic image popularized in cinema, Smith reinvents the image to project themes of the memoir. The cowpoke in Smith's memoirs is not a conservative figure. Instead, the cowboy image is a symbol of going against the grain and finding an artistic voice. Patti Smith is the American poet in "notebook" and embraces the American philosophy of individualism. The cowboy is an extension of the artist and represents the American individualism present in Smith's work. Symbolically, the cowboy justifies and problematizes the writer's process.

---

[26] Ibid., 2.
[27] Henry Nash Smith, *Virgin Land: The American West as Symbol and Myth* (Cambridge, MA: Harvard University Press, 1999), 10.
[28] Jennifer Moskowitz, "The Cultural Myth of the Cowboy, or, How the West was Won," *Journal of American Popular Culture, 1900 to Present* 5, no. 1 (2006): 6.

There are multiple versions of the cowboy in the memoirs, and Smith undermines the figure's masculine image. Using a traditional and masculine figure like the cowboy creates a conservative and American image, which is engrained into American popular culture. However, the figure's earnest image is dismantled and molded to suit Smith's portrayal of the self. The cowboy first makes an appearance in *Just Kids* when Robert Mapplethorpe attends a movie theater to watch *Midnight Cowboy* (1969), which centers on Joe Buck (Jon Voight), a Texan cowboy who moves to New York City to become a sex worker. Joe is unsuccessful in his endeavors until he meets conman Ratso (Dustin Hoffman). The pair team together to make money and Joe becomes increasingly corrupt. Mapplethorpe describes the film as a "masterpiece" and that "[h]e felt a deep identification with the hero, infusing the idea of the hustler into his work, and then into his life."[29] Buck and Mapplethorpe draw parallels to one another with their promiscuous careers. The depiction of the cowboy in *Midnight Cowboy* is corrupted by New York City, which mirrors the countercultural narrative of *Just Kids*.

Traditionally the cowboy is "a symbol of life in the West" and the Western genre "romanticized the low-paying, hard-working, lonely existence of cattle herders by emphasizing the freedom that they supposedly experienced out in the West's wide-open spaces."[30] The cowboy is a representation of hustle culture, but Joe Buck represents the corruption of hustle culture. Both Smith and Mapplethorpe related to the cowboy lifestyle—they were overworked, underpaid, and alone in their early endeavors. They are a product of New York City in a similar way to Joe Buck in *Midnight Cowboy*.

It is important to note that *Midnight Cowboy* is the first explicit reference to cowboys that Smith makes in the memoirs, as Joe Buck does not represent the hegemonic masculine image of the cowboy. Rather than introducing the imagery with John Ford films or images of Clint Eastwood, Smith introduces the cowboy as a transgressive figure. It is the queer cowboy who represents Smith's shifting self, not the traditional masculine version of the character. Introducing the transgressive cowboy first reflects Smith's ethos as an artist: the rebel. If the cowboy is already queered, Smith can then queer the image further in future writing, which is demonstrated in *M Train*. Voight's

---

[29] Smith, *Just Kids*, 83.
[30] Kenneth W. Porter, "Black Cowboys in the American West, 1866–1900," in *African Americans on the Western Frontier*, ed. Monroe Lee Billington and Roger D. Hardaway (Boulder: University Press of Colorado, 1998), 111.

portrayal of a cowboy is the first metamorphosis of the changing character in the memoirs.

The cowboy is transported from *Just Kids* to *M Train* by the playwright, and lifelong friend of Smith's, Sam Shepard. Shepard's influence on Smith is highlighted in the section of *Just Kids* where Smith recounts writing *Cowboy Mouth*. The premise of *Cowboy Mouth* finds Slim "intoxicated with the idea" of Cavale but he "has to tell her that he can't realize her dream."[31] At the end of the play, "Slim Shadow goes back into his own world, his family, his responsibilities, leaving Cavale alone, setting her free."[32] The comparison to Shepard is not subtle, as before Shepard leaves New York City to return to his family and Smith is left alone and free. When leaving, Shepard says to Smith: "the dreams you had for me weren't my dreams. . . . Maybe those dreams are meant for you."[33] Shepard removes himself from Smith's narrative to return home to a nuclear family and advises Smith to follow her dreams. From this moment onward, the cowboy begins to occupy the dreamscape in Smith's memoirs.

The Lone Cowboy in *M Train*

Sam Shepard is one of Smith's greatest muses, and their friendship is immortalized in the pages of Smith's memoirs. Both artists embody the status and loneliness of the cowboy figure. How Smith identifies with the image has already been defined, but Shepard embodies the cowboy by living on a ranch in the West, incorporating Western imagery into his writing, and belonging on the spectrum between rancher and outlaw. The cowboy who appears in Smith's memoirs draws clear connections to Shepard, as he has a "writer's hand" that has "a crescent moon tattooed in the space between his thumb and forefinger."[34] This is a direct reference to Shepard, as the tattoo both the cowboy and Shepard have is "a souvenir from [Smith and Shepard's] younger days," with Smith's being "a lightning bolt on the left knee."[35] The cowboy donning Shepard's tattoo connects the subconscious with Smith's past; therefore reality and the dream world are connected in *M Train*. Despite

---

[31] Smith, *Just Kids*, 185.
[32] Ibid., 185.
[33] Ibid., 186.
[34] Patti Smith, *M Train* (New York: Bloomsbury, 2016), 207.
[35] Patti Smith, "My Buddy," *New Yorker*, August 1, 2017, accessed March 12, 2022, https://www.newyorker.com/culture/culture-desk/my-buddy-sam-shepard.

embodying some physical and characteristic similarities, the cowboy is not a carbon copy of Shepard. Rather, the figure represents a part of Smith's psyche. The cowboy is an extension of Smith in which "neither the person nor the text can reveal any single or final truth, but both can provide activities of interpretation."[36] Smith identifies with this Shepard-esque cowboy figure and molds him to be an extension of herself. Visualizing a part of her personality as a cowboy usurps the patriarchal nature of the figure and places Smith not only on par with her male contemporaries, but above them. Both Patti Smith and the cowboy alike are rebels against society. By using the cowboy as a figure to identify with, Smith not only subverts gender expectations through counterculture, she also transgresses the masculine image of the cowboy by using her own voice to control a traditionally masculine narrative.

The memoirist holds the ultimate control over their narrative, yet Smith shows resistance and a grappling for creative control over the story with the cowboy. Leigh Gilmore argues that "autobiography's domain of first-person particularities and peculiarities offers an opportunity to describe their lives . . . and to emerge through writing as an agent of self-representation."[37] The memoir is a space to represent the self; it is a space where the writer has autonomy over their narrative and is in control of their story. In *M Train*, Smith is stripped from that autonomy immediately as the cowboy controls the dream. In the opening scene of the memoir, Smith witnesses the cowboy write in a notebook:

> He pulled a notebook out of his pocket and started writing.
> You got to at least look at me, I said. After all, it is my dream.
> I drew closer. Close enough to see what he was writing. He had his notebook open to a blank page and three words suddenly materialized.
> Nope, it's mine.[38]

Initially, the cowboy appears to have autonomy over the narrative as the character structures the rest of the memoir. As the writer of the memoir itself, Smith has the ultimate control over the narrative, but as in *Just Kids*, Smith is able to be selective with what is revealed on the page. Smith therefore

---

[36] Susanna Egan, *Mirror Talk: Genres of Crisis in Contemporary Autobiography* (Chapel Hill: University of North Carolina Press, 1999), 226.
[37] Leigh Gilmore, *The Limits of Autobiography: Trauma and Testimony* (Ithaca, NY: Cornell University Press, 2001), 9.
[38] Smith, *M Train*, 4.

subverts the memoir genre by removing control from the "I" in the narrative and allowing someone or something else to represent the story. The cowboy guides Smith with the following parting words: "The writer is a conductor."[39] The pen is orchestrated by the conductor; it is controlled by the path the conductor creates. Smith, therefore, is the orchestrator and has ultimate autonomy in the narrative.

Although the "I" in Smith's narrative is never one-dimensionally hers, Smith is the author of the text. As the memoirist, Smith conducts the story and has the power to control the narrative even when the speaker in the text is not herself. The memoir allows the writer to have autonomy over their life story and, as an extension, Smith also has autonomy over the cowboy. In memoir, the memoirist has control over their narrative and how they are perceived by the reader. A struggle for autonomy is present, but Smith holds the pen and ultimately controls the words on the page. Although the cowboy claims to be in control of the dream, Smith is, in fact, the writer and has control over how the cowpoke is perceived in writing. Fiction, as Gilmore argues, is important in autobiography because it is needed "to challenge the assumption that honesty lies in personal revelation where one assumes that testimonial transparency is not only necessary and desirable but possible."[40] Smith's memoirs, in particular *M Train* and *Year of the Monkey*, delve into the fictional realm to present Smith's inner conflicts not only as an artist but as a person. Imagined characters and conversations allow for the memoirist to explore the multidimensional nature of memory and identity. Blurring the lines between fiction and reality makes room for these personal revelations. Fiction leads to revelations of the self. In the case of *M Train*, the revelation is the artistic process after grief.

As Smith struggles with writing and aims to overcome writer's block, the cowboy yields control of the dream. Smith's text is anchored by solitary coffee shop visits, dreams, and the memory of her late husband Fred Sonic Smith. Each aspect exists in an isolated state. The cowboy is a solitary figure—forgotten to the Western landscape—and therefore finds an appropriate home in the derelict corners of Smith's dreamscape. When Smith meets the cowboy figure in the memoir, it is in a dream. Smith encounters the "cowpoke" in a "lone café."[41] The café resembles that of a saloon in a Western movie, with an "antiquated gas pump" decorating the sparse interior of the

---

[39] Ibid.
[40] Gilmore, *The Limits of Autobiography*, 24.
[41] Smith, *M Train*, 3.

space.[42] The stagnant water in the trough and emptiness of the café draws parallels to Smith's creative struggle to write: "It's not so easy writing about nothing."[43] This dream is somewhat recurring throughout the memoir as the cowboy drifts in and out of the narrative. Dreams are key to Smith's memoirs and the dream world is crucial for working out inner creative conflict. Luke Strongman writes: "Dreams, which are figments of the imagination produced during sleep, may influence our waking states."[44] Dreams are used to transition to a different theme, location, and thought process in Smith's memoirs. A dream is usually "strange and disconcerting" and projects a "lack of logic, questionable morality, uncouth form, and apparent absurdity or nonsense."[45] Like the cowboy, the dreams are a vessel to explain Smith's subconscious thoughts, which cannot be represented in a waking state. The dreams in *M Train* are logical and when pieced together create a story arc of Smith musing over the struggle to write. By writing about her dreams, Smith ultimately has control over the portrayal of the dreams. Smith is the conductor.

M Train is about writing and the challenges of the art. The "cowpoke" at the beginning of the text allows for discussion about the inner conflict of being a writer. Throughout the memoir, Smith visits her favorite writers via fiction or traveling to one of their significant landmarks. The text creates a museum of writers. In the early chapters of *M Train*, Smith includes a photograph of Roberto Bolaño's writing chair alongside a paragraph on the "Writer's debris."[46] Smith's apartment acts as a writer's museum. In the room, Smith notes that "there are the scores of notebooks, their contents calling—confession, revelation, endless variations of the same paragraph—and piles of napkins scrawled with incomprehensible rants."[47] The fragmented notes that are scattered across the room show the writer's work-in-progress. The writer is not perfect; the writer must edit and redraft to refine their craft. Smith's recurring cowboy dream somewhat resembles the drafting stage of writing. Each time Smith enters the dream, the scenery and characters are the same but the scenario is altered and expanded slightly. The dream is the "endless variations of the same paragraph" that can be found on Smith's floor. *M Train*

---

[42] Ibid.
[43] Ibid.
[44] Luke Strongman, "Conscious States of Dreaming," *The Institute of Mind and Behavior, Inc. The Journal of Mind and Behavior* 34, no. 4 (2014): 191.
[45] Carl Jung, *Dreams* (From Volumes 4, 8, 12, and 16 of *The Collected Works of C. G. Jung*) (Princeton, NJ: Princeton University Press, 1974), 68.
[46] Smith, *M Train*, 27.
[47] Ibid.

is aware of the writer as conductor and how the writer drives the perception of the memoirist. Smith's apartment also representing a writer's museum acknowledges the meta-aspects of the text.

In this scene, Smith also shatters the illusion of the romantic writer. Smith's memoirs are not written in Bolaño's chair. Instead, they are written in bed. The writer is romanticized as an artist using pen and paper or hunched over a typewriter. Smith reveals: "Occasionally I write directly into my small laptop, sheepishly glancing over to the shelf where my typewriter with its antiquated ribbon sits next to an obsolete Brother word processor."[48] Again, *M Train* becomes self-aware as it talks about the writing process—revealing the mundane life of the writer being watched by the specter of the typewriter representing the romantic ideal of the writer. Self-scrutinizing "enables an autobiographer to be representative more than any particular set of experiences."[49] Scrutinizing the writing process allows Smith to demonstrate control of the narrative by revealing the writer's tools. No longer is the writer hitting the keys of a typewriter; now they are seated with their laptop in bed. The typewriter and "obsolete Brother word processor" are mummified artifacts of writing past. Much as how the derelict saloon is a museum of the cowboy's past, the apartment is the memorialization of Smith's.

M Train is a memoir about grief and solitude. The cowboy of Smith's dreams and the fragmented structure of *M Train* depict the painful process of writing. Beyond this manifestation, the cowpoke appears in a memory of Smith's late husband. Memory and Western imagery are therefore intertwined. Smith's memoirs center on loss: the loss of a loved one, motivation, and self. The memoirs lose a clear structure and, rather than reaching a destination, they are searching for what is lost. Toward the end of the memoir, and after several appearances of Smith's cowboy, Smith recalls a story of her husband as a child. Fred Sonic Smith had a "red plastic" cowboy as child, which disappeared and could not be found. Smith writes:

> When he set up his fort and arranged his men on the floor of his room, he felt Reddy near, calling to him. It was not his own voice but Reddy who called. Fred believed that, and Reddy became part of our common treasure, occupying a special place in the Valley of the Lost Things.[50]

---

[48] Ibid.
[49] Gilmore, *The Limits of Autobiography*, 19.
[50] Smith, *M Train*, 241.

The story of Fred's cowboy mirrors the connection between Smith and the cowboy in the dreamscape. Reddy and the cowboy both belong in the Valley of the Lost Things. Whereas Reddy is lost to the floorboards of Fred's childhood house, the cowboy is lost to Smith's dreamscape. Primarily existing in Smith's dreamscape, the cowboy is not solely tied to it and is able to adapt and inhabit different landscapes. Drifting from being an allusion of Sam Shepard to Smith's unconscious to Fred Smith's childhood room, the cowboy figure is complex and represents many things—much like Smith as an artist.

All versions of the cowboy in Smith's memoirs represent the transgressive artist, and his frontier is forever expanding. In Smith's final dream of the café in the desert, the cowpoke's final words are: "There's nothing lonelier than the land.... Because it's so damn free."[51] At the end of the final dream, Smith has overcome writer's block and no longer needs the cowboy for guidance. If the frontier is conquered, or does not exist, the cowboy no longer has a purpose. Although the cowboy's horizon is not concrete, "the cowboy needs a frontier" in order to exist.[52] Patti Smith's frontier is her writing. From poetry to lyrics to memoirs, Smith crosses literary boundaries and pushes the limits of genre. Joseph G. Rosa describes the cowboy as "The frontiersman lived off the land, abided by his own rules, and owed allegiance to no one."[53] Smith matches Rosa's description of the cowboy. In the context of memoir, Smith's memoirs are not a token of gratitude for the people who shaped her; rather they are an ongoing project of exploring identity. Documenting one's life is not the priority. Instead, Smith uses the genre as a creative workshop similarly to past writing endeavors in other genres. The words on the page are the frontier, and Smith as the conductor has the power to craft an identity through language and mold it into infinite possibilities.

The Cowboy as the Artist

In Smith's epilogue for the paperback edition of *Year of the Monkey*, she once again reflects on the writer's process and loneliness. Whereas Smith dreams too much in *M Train*, the opposite occurs in her third memoir. While staying at the Dream Motel at the beginning of *Year of the Monkey*, Smith "did not

---

[51] Ibid., *M Train*, 207.
[52] Wright, *The Wild West*, 7.
[53] Joseph G. Rosa, *The Gunfighter: Man or Myth?* (Norman: University of Oklahoma Press, 1969), 29.

dream."[54] Although this would suggest Smith is not accessing her unconscious creativity, the fragmentary structure of this memoir would suggest that conscious and unconscious realms merge. In the epilogue, Smith writes:

> We often pondered on why writers, in the pursuit of producing the unclassifiable, are generally coerced into attaching a label identifying a work as fiction or non-fiction. Both of us relished the prospect of writing a book so uniquely faceted that one would be hard-pressed to distinguish one from the other.[55]

Smith certainly achieves this in her latter memoirs through the use of Western imagery. The distinction between reality and dreams is more transparent in *M Train*, but is obscured in *Year of the Monkey* as the line between fiction and nonfiction does not always have to be opaque. In the epilogue of *Year of the Monkey*, Smith states: "I am compelled to write, with or without true destination, lacing fact, fiction, and dream with fervent hopes."[56] Destination is not the priority of Smith's latter memoirs; rather it is exploring the mind of the artist.

The physical representation of the cowboy remains the same, but the figure's identity shifts and is fluid in Smith's memoirs. Although the cowboy's being is unsolidified, it is Smith's words that are at the center of the figure's being. Smith focuses on the subversive portrayals of the cowboy and uses a destabilized version of this masculine model to queer the figure's identity. By taking a well-known identifier of masculinity and using it to represent her voice and art, Smith displays confidence in her artistry.

When discussing the reworking of the Western Frontier myth, Hillary A. Jones concludes that "the frontier myth might need not new spaces, but new heroes who can offer new forms of liminal identity."[57] Through the memoir format, Smith transforms the cowboy figure into a new hero—herself. The conservative figure helps Smith to access her artistic process and, once she accesses that, to mold the figure to look more like herself. The cowboy, then, is not defined by gendered boundaries and instead crafts their way through the world to find purpose. The men who appear as the cowboy

---

[54] Patti Smith, *Year of the Monkey* (New York: Bloomsbury, 2020), 11.
[55] Ibid., 202.
[56] Ibid., 201.
[57] Hillary A. Jones, "'Them as Feel the Need to Be Free': Reworking the Frontier Myth," *Southern Communication Journal* 76, no. 3 (2011): 243.

in the three memoirs represent Smith. Just like the cowboy, Smith is striving toward a new frontier, first, in music as a pioneering woman in punk and, second, in the reshaping of the music memoir genre. Using the cowboy as a symbol for Smith's pioneering artistry emphasizes the value of injecting fiction into life-writing. By including fictional elements in memoir and implementing similar literary tropes to novels, memoir extends itself beyond a historical account of a musician's life and gives insight into the complex nature of memory. Smith queers the masculine cowboy image to represent her life story as a pioneering woman in the punk movement and beyond.

Across the three memoirs, Smith pushes the boundaries of the memoir genre to its limits. The bricolage nature of Smith's music expands into memoir writing. Sketches remain on the page and Smith presents her influences via photographs and love letters to great artists. By claiming a masculine imagery and usurping their masculinity, Smith uses unconventional figures to construct identity and represent the psyche. The Western imagery of the cowboy is stretched as Smith plays with the memoir form to symbolize the artistic process. Essentially, the cowboy is a key to unlock different levels of consciousness and present them in autobiographical writing.

Ultimately, Smith claims the cowboy figure as a representation of herself and the artistic process. As the writer, Smith is the creator and has autonomy over the figure and is thus able to usurp and claim the cowboy's masculine image. Taking inspiration from masculine figures from real life and in literature, Smith dismantles traditionally gendered performances and removes masculinity from the character. The cowboy is no longer constricted to a masculine image. The cowboy represents only the artist.

Bibliography

Beard, Laura J. *Acts of Narrative Resistance: Women's Autobiographical Writing in the Americas*. Charlottesville: University of Virginia Press, 2009.

Edgar, Robert, Fraser Mann, and Helen Pleasance. "Music, Memory and Memoir: Critical and Creative Engagement with an Emerging Genre." *Journal of Writing in Creative Practice* 12, no. 1–2 (2019): 181–199.

Egan, Susanna. *Mirror Talk: Genres of Crisis in Contemporary Autobiography*. Chapel Hill: University of North Carolina Press, 1999.

Ellis, Jonathan. "Introduction: 'For What Is a Letter?'" In *Letter Writing among Poets: From William Wordsworth to Elizabeth Bishop*, edited by Jonathan Ellis, 1–16. Edinburgh: Edinburgh University Press, 2015.

Gardner, Abigail. *Ageing and Contemporary Female Musicians*. New York: Routledge, 2020.

Gilmore, Leigh. *The Limits of Autobiography: Trauma and Testimony*. Ithaca, NY: Cornell University Press, 2001.

Istvandity, Lauren. *The Lifetime Soundtrack*. Sheffield: Equinox, 2019.

Jones, Hillary A. "'Them as Feel the Need to Be Free': Reworking the Frontier Myth." *Southern Communication Journal* 76, no. 3 (2011): 230–247.

Jung, Carl. *Dreams* (From Volumes 4, 8, 12 and 16 of *The Collected Works of C. G. Jung*). Princeton, NJ: Princeton University Press, 1974.

Lee, Hermione. "'From Memory': Literary Encounters and Life-Writing." In *On Life-Writing*, edited by Zachary Leader, 124–141. Oxford: Oxford University Press, 2015.

Lehman, Tim. "The Making of the Cowboy Myth." *Saturday Evening Post*, January 21, 2020. Accessed March 11, 2022, https://www.saturdayeveningpost.com/2020/01/the-making-of-the-cowboy-myth/.

Lévi-Strauss, Claude. *The Savage Mind*. Chicago: University of Chicago Press, 1966.

Levy, Beth E. *Frontier Figures: American Music and the Mythology of the American West*. Berkeley: University of California Press, 2012.

Moskowitz, Jennifer. "The Cultural Myth of the Cowboy, or, How the West was Won." *Journal of American Popular Culture, 1900 to Present* 5, no. 1 (2006): 1–11.

Porter, Kenneth W. "Black Cowboys in the American West, 1866–1900." In *African Americans on the Western Frontier*, edited by Monroe Lee Billington and Roger D. Hardaway, 110–127. Boulder: University Press of Colorado, 1998.

Raha, Maria. *Cinderella's Big Score: Women of the Punk and Indie Underground*. New York: Seal Press, 2004.

Rosa, Joseph G. *The Gunfighter: Man or Myth?* Norman: University of Oklahoma Press, 1969.

Salt, Waldo. *Midnight Cowboy*. Directed by John Schlesinger. Los Angeles: United Artists, 1969. DVD.

Savage, William W. *Cowboy Life: Reconstructing an American Myth*. Boulder: University Press of Colorado, 1993.

Sedgwick, Eve Kosofsky. *Tendencies*. Durham, NC: Duke University Press, 1993.

Smith, Greg. "'And All the Sinners, Saints': Patti Smith, Pioneer Musician and Poet." *Midwest Quarterly* 41, no. 2 (2000): 173–190.

Smith, Henry Nash. *Virgin Land: The American West as Symbol and Myth*. Cambridge, MA: Harvard University Press, 1999.

Smith, Patti. *Early Work: 1970–1979*. New York: W. W. Norton, 1995.

Smith, Patti. *Just Kids*. New York: Bloomsbury, 2011.

Smith, Patti. *M Train*. New York: Bloomsbury, 2016.

Smith, Patti. "My Buddy." *New Yorker*, August 1, 2017. Accessed March 12, 2022, https://www.newyorker.com/culture/culture-desk/my-buddy-sam-shepard.

Smith, Patti. *Year of the Monkey*. New York: Bloomsbury, 2020.

Smith, Sidonie. *A Poetics of Women's Autobiography: Marginality and the Fictions of Self-Representation*. Bloomington: Indiana University Press, 1987.

Smith, Sidonie, and Julia Watson. *Reading Autobiography: A Guide for Interpreting Life Narratives*. Minneapolis: University of Minnesota Press, 2010.

Strongman, Luke, "Conscious States of Dreaming." *The Institute of Mind and Behavior, Inc. The Journal of Mind and Behavior* 34, no. 4 (2014): 189–200.

Warhol, Andy. *America*. London: Penguin, 2011.

Wright, Will. *The Wild West: The Mythical Cowboy and Social Theory*. London: Sage, 2001.

PART III
AGING, PERFORMANCE, AND THE IMAGE

10

Queens of Noise

Rewriting the "Rock Chick" Identity through *Neon Angel* and *Living Like a Runaway*

Jacqueline Dickin

Girls Who Rock: Introducing the Rock Chick

Queens of Noise may not be so different from "rock chicks": a popular terminology that refers to women who work in and are fans of rock music. As I discuss in this chapter, though, the rock chick is a complex persona rooted in histories of a misogynist rock music industry and brings with it certain expectations of aesthetics and behaviors that may never have served women in rock music, especially today. In order to examine the rock chick further I compare the memoirs of two members of the all-female teenage rock band the Runaways, lead singer Cherie Currie and lead guitarist Lita Ford. Currie's memoir *Neon Angel: A Memoir of a Runaway* was published in 2010 and adapted into the film *The Runaways*, followed by Ford's memoir *Living Like a Runaway*, which was published in 2015. While the two share formative experiences of their time in the Runaways growing up on the road and trying to find themselves in a whirlwind of fame that was extinguished just as quickly as it was ignited, the women and their memoirs could not appear more different. Currie and Ford are represented at two different extremes of the Runaways spectrum; Currie appears brightly colored and openly sexual in her writhing stage moves and corsetry and catsuits, while Ford appears clad in leather or dark washed denim with a flash of platinum blonde hair, standing in the back shredding on her guitar. Aesthetically, one appears as the quintessential image of the rock chick in leather with her guitar, while the other borders of the psychedelic mainstream of the 1970s. As teenagers and bandmates, Currie and Ford had a tumultuous relationship, and at times hated each other. Currie resisted the pull of masculine rock traditions, wanting to flaunt her femininity and embrace their difference as an all-female band, while Ford rejected Currie's ideas as commercial and mainstream, instead wanting to take the band's sound in a heavier direction. Currie gained a lot of attention from the press, which left Ford angry and frustrated that the Runaways and by extension, she, would lose her legitimacy as rock musicians. Read comparatively, the memoirs of Currie and Ford foreground their differences and tend to present the failings of the other as a legitimizing force for their very different professional personas. However, as I discuss further in this chapter, when read through the lens of the rock chick these memoirs reveal histories of oppression and trauma through which Ford and Currie attempt to rewrite and gain control back over their identities.

The rock chick memoir draws many parallels with what Hannah Yelin refers to as "glamour girl memoirs."[1] Yelin explains these as memoirs of the lives and careers of women working in the sex industry, but particularly those that both compound and contrast the masculine codes of pleasure and power that ground much of the sex industry. Yelin's discussion of glamour girl memoirs is useful for thinking about the rock chick as a performative persona/subjectivity that uses postfeminist ideas of sex and beauty work as empowerment that enables survival in a male-dominated industry. Postfeminism here is understood as a backlash against the gains of second-wave feminism, in which feminism is only identified in order to emphasize its perceived lack of necessity in today's culture. Further, Yelin identifies a mutually reinforcing relationship between postfeminism and neoliberalism seen through their focus on individualism, consumption, and choice, which I argue is also present in Ford and Currie's memoirs.[2] Evelyn McDonnell in her book-length study of the Runaways, *Queens of Noise: The Real Story of the Runaways*, disrupts the long-held assumption that the Runaways were victims of an evil music industry/producer: "That widespread narrative denies the women agency in their own life-story and simplistically demonizes Fowley, a complex figure ('I'm a bad guy who does nice things') without whom there would have been no Runaways."[3] Women's rock memoirs shed light on experiences and narratives of creativity, whose dominant themes center on the matrices of domesticity, sexuality, trauma, and musical creativity.[4] As Abigail Gardner

---

[1] Hannah Yelin, *Celebrity Memoir: From Ghostwriting to Gender Politics* (Oxford: Palgrave Macmillan, 2020), 62–63.
[2] Ibid., 34–36.
[3] Evelyn McDonnell, *Queens of Noise: The Real Story of the Runaways* (Boston: Da Capo Press, 2013), 10.
[4] Abigail Gardner, *Ageing and Contemporary Female Musicians* (New York: Routledge, 2019), 13.

argues, these memoirs feed into a neoliberal conception of the individual that maps onto myths of "rock and roll" and underplays structural systematic racism and misogyny. Additionally, they build into an equally neoliberal discourse of the individual creative and continue a discursive trajectory of the confessional artist, singer, songwriter.[5]

McDonnell explains the central theme of the Runaways story: five teenage girls coming together during the years after second-wave feminism, in the permissive environment of 1970s California, they found personal freedom and agency by doing what boys had done for years—expressing themselves through loud, sexy rock and roll.[6] But they also ran hard into the walls of exploitation, chauvinism, inequality, and misogyny that the women's liberation movement had spotlighted and denounced but scarcely toppled. The Runaways sought to "own their sexuality," as fellow Runaway Joan Jett likes to say, but as soon as they put their sexuality out there, it became a battlefield, as others in the male-dominated music industry and media—not to mention their own fans—sought to take possession of it, or at least rent/consume it.[7] Music memoir sits at a junction of celebrity writing and memoir, and these subgenres have different reader expectations that can contradict each other. Readers of celebrity writing usually expect fantasies of fame and the good life while memoir readers tend to have expectations of truth and self-exposure. Typically for music memoirs, it is the public persona that is the subject of the memoir and not the private self, but music memoirs are also generally expected by their readers to expose something new or scandalous about the private self. As Leigh Gilmore explains, celebrity memoir "may yet continue to offer readers and writers not simply the pleasure or a gaze behind the curtain of fame, but a rich engagement with autobiographical form."[8] Memoir is predominantly marketed by the promise that they expose something new, confessional, or scandalous about its author, which can be particularly enticing for readers when the author is a celebrity, popular figure, or rock star.

---

[5] Ibid., 14.
[6] McDonnell, *Queens of Noise*, 31.
[7] Ibid.
[8] Leigh Gilmore, "Just Kids/Life," review of *Just Kids* by Patti Smith, *Fourth Genre* 13, no. 2 (2011): 124.

Cherie's Corset: Representations of Agency and the Commodified Self

Questions of patriarchal power can scarcely be ignored in any discussion of women's rock memoirs, especially those that look back at the 1960s, 1970s, or 1980s from the progressive perspective of today's readers. Themes of consent, empowerment, agency, and sexual violence are prominent in both Currie's and Ford's memoirs, suggesting that the patriarchy is not just an innocent bystander but indeed a main character in each of their memoirs. Perhaps also, it is not so much the question of agency but the inevitable tension that accompanies the *representation* of agency, particularly in the case of marginalized groups, such as teenage girls who are only just discovering that they have agency at all. It seems, in both memoirs, that patriarchal power as a construct is embodied by the manager of the Runaways Kim Fowley as he comes to represent the restrictions of the rock music industry and acts as self-interested gatekeeper of male violence. The representation of Fowley in Ford's and Currie's memoirs differs slightly, and while the eccentric and self-interested core of Fowley remains consistent in both memoirs, his dealings with each of the girls are represented rather differently.

Fowley does not treat Ford, Currie, or any of the other band members as people; they are tools designed to make him money, and he treats them with disdain. When speaking to the band, Fowley does not refer to them by name but instead he calls them "dogs."[9] Ford tends to minimize Fowley's actions as a necessary evil; in her memoir she writes, "We would all soon learn that Kim was a master at getting people to do what he wanted, which would work both to our benefit and our detriment."[10] For Ford, Fowley enables access to the rock industry, and dealing with his behaviors is an acceptable trade-off if it means that she gets to continue performing. The memoir reflects Ford's attitudes by either minimizing or omitting Fowley's actions; he is represented as a tool toward Ford's fame and not a source of drama, emotion, or insecurity. Comparatively, in Currie's memoir Fowley takes on the role of the villain who relentlessly uses and abuses her and the other band members. Currie writes about an incident that followed the Runaways' first headline show at the Starwood in West Hollywood, where, at the age of sixteen, she was sold to a pop musician by Fowley for sex. Currie writes, "Last night I'd discovered

---

[9] Cherie Currie, *Neon Angel: Memoir of a Runaway* (New York: It Books, 2011), 85.
[10] Lita Ford, *Living Like a Runaway* (New York: Dey Street, 2015), E-Book, 7.

what it felt like to be a rock star. This morning I knew what it felt like to be a whore."[11] While she doesn't go into further detail, Currie suggests in her memoir that this was not an isolated incident and would happen again multiple times. Crucially, despite this incident Currie does not see this kind of prostitution as an integral part of her rock stardom; she does not consent to prostitution and Fowley threatens her career to get her to comply. How Currie is represented during this section is in stark contrast to her public persona that commands an audience only a few pages before. The tension between private Currie who is presented as a compliant victim and her public persona that flaunts her teenage sexuality on stage is palpable here, and this juxtaposition also forces the reader to confront how they read and consume Currie in this private-made-public format of memoir.

Incidents where Currie is exploited are made more complex and disturbing by their position as a punishment for her attempting to exercise her limited agency, both as a rock star and a teenage girl learning about her sexuality. Significantly, Currie and Ford appear safer experimenting with and exposing their sexuality in the public forum of rock stardom where they are somewhat protected by the industry instead of in private where they seem more vulnerable. During an anecdote about purchasing Currie's famous corset that she wears during performances of Cherry Bomb, McDonnell writes that none of the members of the Runaways was averse to provocative garb: "West drummed in tight pants with elaborate cutouts; Ford wore short shorts, with underwear and sometimes labia poking out of her spread crotch; Jett liked leather. They were real musicians but they were also young sexual beings. Often, it was hard for the press and fans to believe that they could be both."[12] Further, the rock chick persona appears to be an inherently sexual subject position, where the rock chick is secure in her own sexuality and flaunts it for, usually, male attention. Crucially, what is considered sexy and rock and roll, and what is not, is a judgment that rests with audiences who can celebrate or reject women based on this flexible, and usually unachievable, benchmark. The result for women in rock is a level of presumed sexual access, usually invisible, and expected beauty work and the constant pressure to measure up to an unattainable goal dressed up as empowerment. This is most evident in discussions and reviews of what became known as Cherie's Corset—a piece of lingerie that came to represent Currie's public rock persona.

[11] Currie, *Neon Angel*, 119.
[12] McDonnell, *Queens of Noise*, 4.

More than just a costume piece, Currie's corset symbolizes a tension at the heart of the rock chick persona, that it is the audience and not the rock chick herself who decides if she has met the standard. Significantly, Cherie's Corset received mixed reviews from fans and press. At best it was a symbol of Currie's unbridled teenage sexuality, but at worst it was a distasteful gimmick designed to sell records to young men. "Even some of the young male fans who were presumably the target demographic for Currie's outfit were turned off by its blatant shtick. Fan of the Runaways and music journalist Mike Hain remarks, 'It just wasn't sexy at all. . . . It seemed cheap. I mean wearing black leather, that was cool. That was rock and roll.'"[13] While the corset represented exactly the kind of jailbait thirst that Fowley was targeting the marketing of the Runaways toward, it just didn't translate to the teenage rock fans. Except that Cherie's Corset was not intended by the lead singer to be a sex symbol, Currie's stage moves were less provocative, and they appear psychedelic and reminiscent of her hero David Bowie or Tim Curry as Frank N. Furter from *The Rocky Horror Picture Show*. Currie writes of her first performance in the corset: "I felt like a conduit of pure power from a place I didn't know. I was no longer of this world. I had risen above it, beyond it."[14] Further, as one of the more openly bisexual and sexually progressive members of the Runaways, perhaps Currie was making more of a statement about gender than sexual exploitation. Riot Grrrl Kathleen Hanna suggests that Currie consciously desexualizes the corset: "When I watch videos of them, I'm like oh, she brings out the idea that being a woman is a role. It's like something that you can put on and take off, and if we lived in a genderless society, anybody could be a man or anybody could be a woman or whatever they want."[15] The problem, though, as McDonnell astutely points out, is that "while [Currie] projected one image, she was not in charge of how that image was perceived."[16] Hain not reading Cherie's Corset as rock and roll exposes the one-dimensionality of the rock chick persona and suggests that while the persona appears powerful, it may also be oppressive. This, too, is the penchant tension of both memoir and celebrity, and particularly memoir, that circulates in popular markets; readings are multiple and simultaneous and cannot be solely controlled by authors, publishers, readers, or even markets.

---

[13] Hain, quoted in ibid., 6.
[14] Currie, *Neon Angel*, 112.
[15] Hanna, quoted in McDonnell, *Queens of Noise*, 7–8.
[16] McDonnell, *Queens of Noise*, 7.

Becoming the rock chick and keeping up the performance begins to reveal itself as a process of objectification where the woman musician turns herself into an object of the rock industry and wider male desires. Julia Watson notes the objectification required in autobiography's imperatives of narrative and witnessing and yet, as Margaret McLaren argues, the process of critically examining "how one came to be as one is must, at the same time, be viewed as 'a process of subjectification.'"[17] This objectified subjectivity could be considered inherent to memoir, and especially celebrity memoir. However, the tension in the status of objectified subject is nowhere more evident than in the memoirs of women in the rock industry as their professional investment in their status as object of the male gaze demands a performance of eroticized subjectivity. In an adaptation of the misogynist assumption that female fans of rock music are more interested in the musicians as objects of desire than the music, the Runaways are repeatedly marketed more on their eroticized image than their musical talent. For example, Currie writes that she spent more conscious time working on her image—that is her body, stage presence, costume and makeup—than she did on becoming a better singer.[18] She *became* the Cherry Bomb. This beauty work is far more obvious in Currie's memoir than Ford's; while Ford writes about asking fitness advice from female members of the band the Tubes because she's trying to lose her "baby fat," she spends much more time practicing her guitar and partying with other rock stars.[19] Crucially, by downplaying her beauty work Ford makes her rock chick persona appear effortless—she doesn't have to work at being a rock chick, she is one. Here, Ford simultaneously reinforces and challenges neoliberal and postfeminist assumptions that individualism, consumption through beauty work, and choice represent success, power, and normality. Regardless of how much celebrity authors claim to use memoir to show new or different aspects of their identity, or a real self, the account of the life given in celebrity memoir must, to some degree, correlate with the persona that inspired readers to purchase the book. The memoir reader is always "consciously or half-consciously comparing the textual world with extratextual reality."[20]

---

[17] Julia Watson. "Towards an Anti-Metaphysics of Autobiography," in *The Culture of Autobiography: Constructions of Self-representation*, ed. Robert Folkenflik (Stanford, CA: Stanford University Press, 1993), 77; Margaret A. McLaren, *Feminism, Foucault, and Embodied Subjectivity* (Albany: State University of New York Press, 2002), 152.
[18] Currie, *Neon Angel*, 106–107.
[19] Ford, *Living Like a Runaway*, 3.
[20] Yelin, *Celebrity Memoir*, 63–64.

Ford's and Currie's memoirs continue the Runaways tradition of capturing and defying the male gaze. While sex is certainly a main theme of both memoirs, and Ford is quite explicit about her sexual escapades with the likes of Ritchie Blackmore of Deep Purple and Tony Iommi of Black Sabbath, the representation of sex is never pornographic. This suggests that Currie and Ford exercise their agency by placing a limit on their exposure and access to their bodies—something that they were unable to achieve as Runaways. Ford refuses to write in detail about her abusive marriage; instead, in an author's note she writes: "Out of respect for my children, I have chosen not to write in detail about their father, my husband of almost eighteen years. It was a very difficult decision. There is much the world needs to hear. But now is not the time."[21] Ford recounts the period as simply "one of the worst times in my life" and details her eventual escape from her husband Jim Gillette, lead singer of Nitro, but laments that Gillette retains full custody of their two children James and Rocco.[22] Ford exercises her agency by presenting a hard limit on the access to her private life; details of her marriage and abuse are also absent from any news or tabloid publications.

Currie's memoir goes a step further, with the only graphic sexual scene being one of violence and abuse when she is abducted, raped, and tortured for six hours by a crazed fan. Currie writes: "I can't even begin to explain what I went through. It's hard to tell another person some of the things that that man did to me. What I will say is that the terror, the horror and the humiliation that he inflicted upon me were even worse than what I imagine hell to be like."[23] This scene is especially jarring since other sexual encounters in the memoir are glossed over or mentioned in passing. The only time that Currie's memoir allows access to Currie's body is when it is forcefully taken, in essence flipping the male gaze back on itself and exposing it as intrusive, nonconsensual, and violent. The difference here is that Currie's memoir represents her as a person with thoughts and feelings, in contrast to her public persona as a Runaway who is perceived by mostly male fans as a sexual object. In this way, the memoir sets up a particular reading of the rape scene where readers are forced to confront how they personally read Currie as the memoir subject and not strictly as a rock and roll product. Of course, Currie is not in control of how she is perceived, even when her memoir encourages certain readings of her as the subject. Fans may still read Currie as an object,

---

[21] Ford, *Living Like a Runaway*, 17.
[22] Ibid., 21.
[23] Currie, *Neon Angel*, 259.

and even become titillated by the sexual violence represented in her memoir, and thus is the tension of most memoir written for popular markets by celebrities; readers will read what they want out of it. Like Currie, Ford also loses any control over how her memoir may be received; by omitting the details of her marriage and her abuse she also omits any ability to speak back to her abuser or set the record straight for her readers.

Not One of Your Toys: Rewriting Rock Tradition

The type of reasoning that assumes that a female musician's role models must also be female follows the binary opposition that designates males as active producers and women as passive consumers. This is the same binary opposition that is often applied to female musicians in the backhanded compliment: she's good, for a girl. The foreword to Ford's memoir destroys this binary by a male guitarist of Twisted Sister Dee Snider describing how he felt when he first witnessed Ford performing: "*Here was a girl who could really play!* And I'm not talking playing good 'for a girl,' I'm talking playing good for *anybody*."[24] This foreword by Snider sets Ford up to be read in her memoir as the exemplar rock chick and the woman who did what other women cannot. Ford writes that her introduction to the Runaways was over a phone call from the band's manager Fowley, where he describes the band as "An all-girl teenage band of rebellious jailbait rock-and-roll bitches."[25] Significantly, Fowley frames the Runaways as both a rock band and a sexual or pornographic spectacle by his use of derogatory terms like "jailbait" and "bitches" to describe the group of teenage girls. Ford writes that in Fowley's original sales pitch for her to audition for the Runaways he promised: "I can make you into one of the biggest rockstars in the world. You will fuck the best rock stars. You will tour the biggest arenas. You will be on the cover of every magazine. You will become a legend."[26] From the outset of Ford's career, sex is understood as just another part of being a rock star. Even as a female musician, Fowley is selling Ford a subordinate position to other male rock stars—as a female object with assumed sexual access. This tension is more palpable in Ford's memoir, as she is struggling to stake out a place for herself in the

---

[24] Dee Snider, "Foreword," in Ford, *Living Like a Runaway*, 2.
[25] Ford, *Living Like a Runaway*, 7.
[26] Ibid., 3.

industry as a guitarist, and as such this tension focuses on her musical talent and performance. Comparatively, Currie is often concerned about her appearance and stage performance and worries that the other members of her band may see her as just a talentless groupie.

Rosemary Lucy Hill in her book *Gender, Metal and the Media* notes that when women are fortunate enough to become successful as musicians in the world of rock and heavy metal, they are not represented in the same way that male musicians are. Women musicians are heterosexualized for a male audience, and, although men musicians are also positioned as objects of desire, they primarily appear for a male viewer: as a warrior to be admired and emulated.[27] When women fans defend musicians from what are framed as personal attacks, and when they express sexual desire for male musicians, they reinforce the message that women are primarily interested in the musicians over the music. What this amounts to, Hill argues, is a myth of women as always sexually willing.[28] Furthermore, this position reinforces the reduction of women's roles in rock and heavy metal communities as an object for men's pleasure, either through sexual access or through access to women's labor (getting drugs or alcohol, organizing parties, cleaning, cooking, and generally mothering male musicians on the road). In this way, the role of women musicians in the world of rock and heavy metal comes dangerously close to derogatory definitions of groupies who are only interested in sex with musicians, have no talent, and don't *really* understand the music enough to genuinely appreciate it. There is a troubling assumption here rooted in misogynistic ideas of men as the logical sex and women as the emotional sex that suggest women's sexual and emotional desire for the male musician overrides any ability for her to logically admire the music for what it is—music. Though, more disturbingly, the assumption that *all* women in rock and heavy metal are groupies and sexually willing is dangerous for genuine fans, as their sexual access may be expected or assumed by male musicians.

In this chapter, Ford and Currie are read not as groupies but as rock chicks because a rock chick instead brings to focus the music and musical talent of the female subject. Although the cultural, social, and industrial forces that surround the groupie also permeate the rock chick identity, as both are constructed *by* men *for* men, the rock chick is also a sexualized fantasy. Like the groupie, the rock chick identity does not only oppress or exploit women,

[27] Rosemary Lucy Hill, *Gender, Metal and the Media: Women Fans and the Gendered Experience of Music* (London: Palgrave Macmillan, 2016), 72.
[28] Ibid., 72–73.

but there are also avenues for survival, empowerment, and even success. Let's not forget that terms like "groupie" or "rock chick" designated the only *available* subjectivities at which women could enter the rock or heavy metal industries. These were not—and even still, are not—free and equal spaces for women, even if the imaginary community of rock and heavy metal privileges equality and freedom. Key here is the concept that one can choose to be a rock chick and construct one's own way of being a rock chick in ways that do not challenge or disrupt the imaginary community of rock or heavy metal. Crucially, to find female empowerment and encourage respect for female musicians, producers, journalists, and fans in rock and heavy metal is not to destroy the mythologies and ideologies on which the community is built.

Ford, particularly, as the woman who went on to be the "Queen of Heavy Metal" and created a rock chick identity with which she found power and success, never did it just because she was a woman. Even as a teenager, she did not see herself as an oddity, and she reflects that she never thought about the ratio of men to women in rock or heavy metal; she just loved the music and the guitar. Initially, I read Ford's memoir of a rock star lifestyle including consensual sex, drug use, partying, and career progression into heavy metal under the lens of postfeminist empowerment. Unlike Currie, who was forced into particular exploitative situations, Ford foregrounds her own personal choices toward her lifestyle and attributes these choices to her ability to gain respect and work as a professional musician in rock and heavy metal. However, Hill's feminist analysis of women's fan responses and practices in the heavy metal space has encouraged this researcher to read Ford's memoir differently, as the focus on her personal choice turns her empowering memoir into a postfeminist and neoliberal tale of individual success and reifies her position as exceptional, which is just another form of othering her as a woman. Additionally, upon more careful analysis it becomes clear that Ford's musical shredding style and her aesthetic reinforce the myth of the warrior, which in turn reinforces a misogynistic structure of rock and heavy metal. Significantly, Ford appears to have used the rock chick identity as an access point to the masculine warrior myth, which allows her to carve out a successful role for herself without dismantling the patriarchal structure of rock and heavy metal. Like Hill, this is not read as a kind of false consciousness by Ford becoming an unconscious ally of the patriarchy and contributing to her own subordination; that argument is too simple.

The patriarchal structures of rock and heavy metal are entrenched in nostalgic remembering of the golden days of rock in the 1960s, 1970s, and 1980s, and to uproot or dismantle these structures would mean backlash from the industry, loss of fans, and potential exile from the music subculture. Ford disrupts the myth that women are incapable of the musical knowledge or talent required to perform complex guitar solos or to shred on a guitar, but she maintained her fame by creating space for women in the warrior aesthetic. In a tradition that has been followed by Angela Gossow of Arch Enemy, she also styles herself as a warrior, complete with blackface paint, and has dismantled the assumption that women are incapable of providing a dirty vocal by screaming with the same depth and vocal range as a male lead singer. Rock and heavy metal are patriarchal and sexist structures, and women have a complicated role to play in their own empowerment in these musical subcultures, but female participation as fans, producers, and musicians has increased significantly in recent years.

There's more than one way to be rock chick just as there's more than one way to be a woman; in this way Cherie's Corset represents more than just a personal vendetta against the system and her own personal and sexual emancipation as a teenage girl. Cherie's Corset is a symbol that represents the narrow points of entry to fame and the rock industry. Ford finds a way through by appearing to conform to masculine traditions and codes of heavy metal and rock ideology; being "about the music," warrior aesthetic, raw musical talent, and appearing as constantly in control of her actions with sex and drugs. Ford may be more complex than her professional persona allows, and certainly more complex than the popularized rock chick that she appears to be emulating. Ford may instead be enacting performance of this kind of rock chick *because* it gains her access to the industry, solidifies her legitimacy, and presents the potential of lasting change. The memoir, then, struggles to keep up the performance as it introduces complex and feminine themes that are not synonymous with the traditional rock chick like vulnerability, trauma, and motherhood. Thus, the tension between the public persona and the private, remembering and forgetting, telling and not telling that structures many of the works in this volume is exposed. Ford's memoir does not seek to dismantle the structures that enabled her survival and indeed her success as these are a part of her public persona and professional identity, but it does seek to diversify understandings of the rock chick. Popular understandings of the rock chick offer fantasies of success, freedom, and lasting change while the rock music industry that initially created it denies rock chicks any fundamental ability to alter the system. What Ford and Currie, and the other rock chicks of this volume, achieve with their memoirs is a reimagining of the rock chick as a complex and multidimensional identity that enables survival and success. These memoirs provide a space for women to rewrite themselves into rock music history in ways that both counter and complement the "sex, drugs, and rock and roll" tradition of rockstar glamour.

Survival: Changing the Landscape of Rock Music

The Runaways is the story of young female artists fighting ferociously, and almost fatally, to be the subjects, not objects, of their own story.[29] A concern emerges that the novelty of female voices in a usually male-dominated space and market will wear off as quickly as fame did for the Runaways. Though similar concerns have been expressed about the memoir boom itself, with critics predicting that it would disappear as quickly as it emerged. However, the recent emergence of women's rock memoirs that spurred this volume presents not only the long tail of the memoir boom which still runs strongly, but also the continued and strengthening presence of women in rock music. In this volume we ask how female rock musicians, or female-identified rock musicians, narrate and remember their experiences in memoir, and what type of knowledge these books offer. This chapter specifically offers an alternative reading and understanding of the rock chick, not as a one-dimensional persona designed to sexualize and diminish female empowerment, but as a complex identity that makes space for diverse representation of rock music by women. I recast the rock chick as instead a Queen of Noise, who continues to push boundaries and encourage disorder while dissolving the boundaries of self and other to introduce vulnerability and emotional connection often denied by masculine rock traditions. Gardner argues that the female rock memoir is "an age-appropriate survival story which reframes the histories of punk and independent rock music."[30] Narratives of overcoming, typical of popular celebrity memoir in neoliberal times, are not the sole preserve of female rock memoirs, as similar stories of overcoming addiction, emotional turmoil, and even physical struggles permeate male musicians and band memoirs.

The Runaways records were a direct inspiration for the Riot Grrrl movement, which would lead the third-wave feminist revolution girl style in the

---

[29] McDonnell, *Queens of Noise*, 32.
[30] Gardner, *Ageing and Contemporary Female Musicians*, 8.

early 1990s. "When you hear something like that on a record, I feel like a lot of people are trained to think a full-grown man is doing that," Hanna says of Ford. "To be able to conceptualize that it's not a full-grown man, it's actually a teenage girl doing it—it changes what is possible for yourself as a girl, as a woman."[31] The memoirs and careers of Currie and Ford have provided foundations upon which continued female participation in the rock and heavy metal music industry are built. Ford, for example, was the first woman to make a career as a musician in rock and heavy metal because of her prowess with a guitar, colloquially understood by fans, the industry, and journalists as shredding. This contributed to an equalization of the playing field and began widening the avenues of access to the rock and heavy metal music industries for women. The legacy of Ford as the "Queen of Heavy Metal" is invoked in the career and performance of Angela Gossow, the former lead singer of heavy metal band Arch Enemy. Gossow's stage persona is reminiscent of Ford, with her leather pants and shock of blonde hair, which contrasts against the black outfits of the rest of the male members of Arch Enemy. Gossow is also the first female credited with the ability to perform a dirty vocal, known as screaming, as well as any other male lead of a heavy metal band. Significantly, when Gossow announced her retirement (although she is still Arch Enemy's manager), her replacement Alissa White-Guz, the former lead singer of the all-women heavy metal group the Agonist, invokes themes reminiscent of the hyperfemininity and hypersexualization of Currie. Her stage outfits are brightly colored, she wears shiny and (often impractical) jewelry, and her hair color changes every few shows (red, blonde, pink, blue, purple). There is no mistaking the quality of the new singer's vocals; she rivals Gossow in proficiency, but there is no mistaking the femininity of their new lead singer. This seamless transition from Gossow to White-Guz signals that those popular understandings of the rock chick may have also shifted to a place where, finally, Currie and Ford are both equally worthy of the persona. Though more significant, this signals a shift in audience perspectives and expectations where a more diverse representation of women in rock is needed.

---

[31] Hanna, quoted in McDonnell, *Queens of Noise*, 11.

Bibliography

Cline, Cheryl. "Essays from Bitch: The Women's Rock Newsletter with Bite." In *Adoring Audience: Fan Culture and Popular Media*, edited by Lisa A. Lewis, 69–83. London: Routledge, 1992.

Currie, Cherie. *Neon Angel: Memoir of a Runaway*. New York: It Books, 2011.

Ford, Lita. *Living Like a Runaway*. New York: Dey Street, 2015. E-Book.

Gardner, Abigail. *Ageing and Contemporary Female Musicians*. New York: Routledge, 2019.

Gilmore, Leigh. "Just Kids/Life." Review of *Just Kids* by Patti Smith, Fourth *Genre* 13, no. 2 (2011): 123–126.

Hill, Rosemary Lucy. *Gender, Metal and the Media: Women Fans and the Gendered Experience of Music*. London: Palgrave Macmillan, 2016.

Jeffreys, Sheila. *The Idea of Prostitution*. North Melbourne: Spinifex, 1997.

McDonnell, Evelyn. *Queens of Noise: The Real Story of the Runaways*. Boston: Da Capo Press, 2013. E-Book.

McLaren, Margaret A. *Feminism, Foucault, and Embodied Subjectivity*. Albany: State University of New York Press, 2002.

Watson, Julia. "Towards an Anti-Metaphysics of Autobiography." In *The Culture of Autobiography: Constructions of Self-representation*, edited by Robert Folkenflik, 59–79. Stanford, CA: Stanford University Press, 1993.

Yelin, Hannah. *Celebrity Memoir: From Ghostwriting to Gender Politics*. Oxford: Palgrave Macmillan, 2020.

11

Humanizing Icon

Collaboration and Control in Grace Jones's *I'll Never Write My Memoirs*

Satoko Naito

Jamaican-born Grace Beverly Jones (b. 1948) is a legend. A seminal fixture of the 1970s Manhattan disco scene, in the ensuing decade she moved on to record genre-bending pop, rock, and reggae fusion. Captivating and campy appearances in cult and Hollywood films further expanded her global recognizability.[1] During a varied career spanning decades, she has been featured in such high-profile events as Queen Elizabeth II's 2012 Jubilee concert, during which she hula-hooped while singing the entirety of her hit song "Slave to the Rhythm"—in her mid-sixties, as media outlets were quick to point out.[2] Jones continues to be adored by fans for her deep, resonant voice and dynamic performances, but it is her still images, overwhelmingly inflected and curated by white male artists, which have become most iconic. Jones has been most intimately associated with French-American designer Jean-Paul Goude, so much so that her agency has been continuously questioned, as in Carolyn Anderson's words: "To what extent . . . does she herself promote these images and to what extent has she been mythologized by others, such as Jean-Paul Goude?"[3] Goude's own claim to exclusive authorship of her image is provocatively outlined in *Jungle Fever* (1981), his early autobiographical retrospective that asserts that he was the genius mastermind without

---

[1] I am grateful to the editors of this volume for their invaluable insights that allowed me to complete this chapter. Jones appeared in *Conan the Destroyer* (1984), *A View to a Kill* (1985), *Vamp* (1986), and *Boomerang* (1992).

[2] Regarding Jones's resistance of the aging diva narrative, see Nathalie Weidhase, "Ageing Grace/Fully: Grace Jones and the Queering of the Diva Myth," in *Women, Celebrity and Cultures of Ageing: Freeze Frame*, ed. Deborah Jermyn and Su Holmes (London: Palgrave Macmillan, 2015), 97–111.

[3] Carolyn Anderson, "En Route to Transnational Postmodernism: Grace Jones, Josephine Baker and the African Diaspora," *Social Science Information* 32, no. 3 (1993): 493.

whose creative intervention she would have faltered as a disco has-been.[4] This chapter examines Jones's own 2015 autobiography *I'll Never Write My Memoirs* to discern the ways in which it resists and rewrites the narrative that identifies her as a model-cum-muse opposite more influential artists. As I show, Jones undermines Goude's claims of creative authority, not through a simple reclamation of agentic control but by outlining the collaborative ontology of her image and celebrity. This does not lead to, nor is it an attempt at, a self-erasure by Jones, who repeats her unwillingness to cede control over her public and private lives. The commitment to ensure ownership of her identity is at the service of a simple yet significant demand to be recognized as human, a recognition she extends to others, including Goude, in a crucial discursive strategy that promotes a shared humanity.

While seared into the public consciousness as static, two-dimensional representations, the iconicity of Grace Jones is predicated on a distinctly multimodal praxis: her most recognizable images are album covers and are reproduced in music videos, guaranteeing that her physical appearance and voice are always necessarily linked. Staged performances consistently feature visual centerpieces in a combination of theater, fashion, and commercial art. Her memoir relies on the multimodality of Jones's legacy insofar as its readers may be assumed to be familiar with her work, but as an autobiographical narrative, it is generically straightforward. As might be expected from a celebrity tell-all, it tantalizes with frequent namedrops and behind-the-scenes retellings of notorious incidents.[5] Even her claim that she is indifferent to whether readers believe her story is clichéd and leads us to wonder if the text brings us any closer to understanding Grace Jones, or if she is simply performing in the genre of celebrity memoir.[6] Furthermore, while we might refrain from declaring the autobiographical self to be complete fiction as such,

---

[4] Jean-Paul Goude, *Jungle Fever*, ed. Harold Hayes (New York: Xavier Moreau, 1981), 103. Others simply describe Jones as "basically the creation of the designer Jean-Paul Goude." Georges-Claude Guilbert, *Madonna as Postmodern Myth: How One Star's Self-Construction Rewrites Sex, Gender, Hollywood, and the American Dream* (Jefferson, NC: McFarland, 2002), 10.

[5] For example, Jones details how she and Andy Warhol arrived late to the wedding of Maria Shriver and Arnold Schwarzenegger. Grace Jones and Paul Morley, *Grace Jones: I'll Never Write My Memoirs* (New York: Gallery Books, 2015), 183. Regarding Jones as deliberately performing celebrity, see Hannah Yelin, "'I Am the Centre of Fame': Doing Celebrity, Performing Fame and Navigating Cultural Hierarchies in Grace Jones' *I'll Never Write My Memoirs*," *Celebrity Studies* 12, no. 1 (2019): 119–131.

[6] Indeed, her use of drag and identity performance have been said to "pose challenges of readability." Francesca T. Royster, "'Feeling like a Woman, Looking like a Man, Sounding like a No-No': Grace Jones and the Performance of Strange in the Post-Soul Moment," in *Women & Performance: A Journal of Feminist Theory* 19, no. 1 (March 2009): 77.

it is impossible to excavate Jones's voice with even a perfunctory claim to authenticity from an "as-told-to" memoir. In particular, as Janine Bradbury insightfully notes, that Jones's amanuensis is Paul Morley, a white music writer, "raises alarm bells for any critic, thinker, and activist wary of the ways that white men have historically exploited the labour of women of colour."[7] But because Jones's position has long been problematized and politicized, with race, gender, and sexuality always implicated in the question of her iconic imagery, her memoir provides a unique opportunity to consider agency, complicity, and consequence in the presentation of the objectified body and celebrity self.

Repositioning Goude, and the Nature of Collaboration

Jean-Paul Goude is mentioned in the opening pages of *I'll Never Write My Memoirs* as "[Jones's] son Paulo's father," a fight with whom inspired the lyric used as the book's title.[8] Introduced to readers as a "boyfriend at the time," he and Jones were in truth so deeply intertwined with and invested in one another that the casual phrasing reads like a deliberate slight. As part of the book's insert, a photo of Goude pictured alongside Jones and Paulo also identifies him as her son's father. Named in relation to her child, Goude becomes a biological necessity for progeny—not unimportant, of course, but devoid of any professional authority. Simultaneously, the genesis of the title allows that without him, the book—at least under its current title—would not exist, but the fact of its publication (which is to say she changed her mind, even if she did not technically "write" anything herself) adds a layer of signification that resists any claims he may make on her work. That the autobiography is not under Goude's artistic direction is further highlighted by the front and back cover photos, both of which stray far from his style and are almost defiantly generic. Indeed, credits confirm that he had no part in their production.[9] While his presence may be felt throughout the memoir, Goude's creative influence is pointedly undermined in its opening text and paratexts. In fact, as the father of her only child and an artistic collaborator during what was certainly one apogee of Jones's career, Goude's role in both her personal

---

[7] Janine Bradbury, "Grace Jones: Cyborg Memoirist," in *Music, Memory, Memoir*, ed. Robert Edgar, Fraser Mann, and Helen Pleasance (New York: Bloomsbury Academic, 2019), 71.
[8] Jones, *Grace Jones*, viii.
[9] Jacket photographs are credited to Greg Gorman.

and professional lives is far from insignificant. And yet, the pace with which the narrative of the memoir moves from one lover to the next—the actor Dolph Lundgren follows Goude—renders him as but one of many sexual-romantic partners. More important, Goude is similarly positioned as only one of a multitude of influential professional collaborators. To be sure, Jones does hold the dancer-turned-artist in high esteem: "I admired his work so much that I would have done anything he asked me," she says, as if in confirmation of Goude's claim made decades earlier in *Jungle Fever* that "Grace let me make her over completely, [to] use any effect I could find to turn her into what I wanted her to be."[10] She is also mindful of his critical role in generating her most widely distributed images.[11] But significantly, Goude is not the most innovative artist with whom she has worked. She deems one of her earliest professional jobs with photographer Anthony Barboza as "a moment of birth."[12] Hans Feurer, a Swiss photographer, dressed her "in men's clothing, a few years before anyone else did," which is to say before Goude had her wear suits seemingly tailored for men.[13] A hairdresser identified as Andre was "the first one to style [her] short hair," again before Goude fashioned it into the iconic marine cut, though notably it was Jones who initially shaved off most of her own hair. Andre was also "the first one to paint [her] naked body, years before Keith Haring would."[14] Incidentally, it was with Andre that Jones had her first orgasm, yet another "moment of birth." The many references to early and lesser-known collaborators suggest the difficulty, if not the impossibility, of pinpointing originality. In the memoir, this is all the more pronounced because Jones does not always identify an originary moment of innovation—as in the case with Barboza who, even before Andre, photographed her face with "dramatic, almost tribal white marks" in a style that sounds suspiciously close to the broad white lines used later by the enduringly popular Haring, who himself referenced Masai warrior body painting.[15]

The futility of establishing originality is expressed pointedly in her accolades for renowned designer Issey Miyake, who helped "set her apart

[10] Jones, *Grace Jones*, 203; Goude, *Jungle Fever*, 107.
[11] "It was through how Jean-Paul rendered me . . . that I first really entered many people's consciousness as an original being." Jones, *Grace Jones*, 207.
[12] Ibid., 70.
[13] Ibid., 114.
[14] Ibid., 83.
[15] Jones, *Grace Jones*, 70. According to photographer Tseng Kwong Chi, Haring prepared to paint Jones's body by studying photographs of Masai men. Robert Farris Thompson, "Notes on the Art and Life of Keith Haring," in *Keith Haring: The Political Line*, ed. Dieter Buchhart (San Francisco: Delmonico Books, 2015), 49.

from the standard way that pop singers moved."[16] He inspired her to study the theatrical conventions of *kabuki*, though Goude would claim that it was he who much later urged Jones to look to traditional Japanese dance.[17] In Jones's judgment, no one could copy Miyake without being immediately called out as imitation. Yet it is she who, decades later, retrospectively describes Goude's work as "a continuation of where Issey Miyake and [collaborator] Eiko Ishioka had been, exploring bodies, faces, settings, material, theater in the search for the sublime point."[18] In other words, even Miyake's legacy, like those of Barboza, Feurer, and Andre, is not immediately or universally identifiable. One cannot deconstruct an image or a performance to reliably ascertain a creator, in the same way that Jones's marine-cut hairstyle cannot be credited to a single author. We are reminded that a great deal more always lies behind and before any single performance or image, regardless of Goude's declaration in *Jungle Fever* that he singlehandedly created the mythology of Grace Jones.

In his book, Goude further depicts himself as an exceptional genius who turned the likeness of Jones and other women into works of art. Beginning with "[his] first black girl" Sylvia Waters, an Alvin Ailey dancer whose teeth he has capped and whose nose he attempts to have surgically altered, Goude embarks on his quest to "improve" the women's bodies by "doing . . . things to" them.[19] Transitive, violent language used in describing his relationship with the women's bodies marks him as the oppressive agent, the soul that controls the body in the classic Cartesian formulation. Indeed, once an aspiring dancer who was discouraged due to his short stature and general appearance, it is as if he can claim no physical body of his own to manipulate.[20] Jones too is treated as a malleable and violable object, likened to an African sculpture that "looks barely human."[21] While Goude saw her as the literal embodiment of his obsession—a "representation of all the attractiveness and beauties of . . . black women"—he acknowledges her value only in the

---

[16] Jones, *Grace Jones*, 132.

[17] "[I]t would be such a nice fresh thing for a black entertainer with such a domineering image . . . to tippy-toe around the stage like a samurai sissy, instead of boogying down or whooping and hollering like all the others." Goude, *Jungle Fever*, 105.

[18] Jones, *Grace Jones*, 204. The inclusion of Ishioka, a Japanese woman, is significant; though there are women Jones admires, the tutelage and mentorship she receives is almost exclusively male and overwhelmingly white. She identifies her "teachers" as "Sam, Tom, Andre, Antonio, Richard, Issey, Helmut, Hans." Ibid., 189.

[19] Goude, *Jungle Fever*, 31, 40–41.

[20] Dancer Robert Joffrey advised Goude that he would never make it in ballet. Ibid., 7.

[21] Ibid., 106.

possibility of "using ... as the ideal vehicle for [his] work."[22] And as with the other "vehicles" (that is to say, black women) featured in his book, at a certain point Goude claims no use for Jones, though interestingly, *Jungle Fever* ends after Jones's chapter, as if to concede that she represented the zenith of Goude's life's work and he could not effectively move on sans Jones.

Jones's memoir does not mention *Jungle Fever* by title, but it addresses Goude's claims of having created, in her, a "masterpiece":

> [Goude] would say, later, in a book he wrote, when he was angry and frustrated with me, that he had created me. I knew that wasn't the case, that I was creating myself before I met him, and that I was still creating myself during our time together and continued creating myself after we parted. . . . It's okay—I never had a problem with it, even though a lot of people around me got upset because their part in the creation of me got erased.[23]

Goude has insisted that Jones was in fact so angry with his book that they could no longer work together.[24] Regardless, here we are to understand that it was others who were upset with Goude for belittling their creative labors. When Jones reminds readers that she had already released multiple successful albums before meeting Goude, she lists work done by collaborators, rather than herself.[25] The memoir, at pains to name the legion of artists and visionaries that Jones worked with in her decades in fashion, music, and film, recognizes the frustration of such collaborators who receive no credit or, as Jones puts it, are "erased." The attitude toward artistic creation is evident in her music: though Jones writes or co-writes some songs, she proudly recognizes that many of her most widely known, including those that now seem iconically Jonesian like "Warm Leatherette," are covers of existing songs.[26] This is a marked contrast from Goude's portrayal of himself as a uniquely situated, sovereign creator possessed of a singular vision. As Ramon Lobato has succinctly put it, Jones's work "exhibits all the hallmarks of postmodernism: appropriation, simulation, irony, bricolage, pastiche."[27]

---

[22] Ibid., 107, 103.
[23] Jones, *Grace Jones*, 227–228.
[24] Colin McDowell, "Goude Heavens," *Sunday Times*, November 6, 2005, https://www.thetimes.co.uk/article/goude-heavens-t6l8sb5807t.
[25] Jones, *Grace Jones*, 203.
[26] Ibid., 222.
[27] Ramon Lobato, "Amazing Grace, Decadence, Deviance, Disco," *Camera Obscura: A Journal of Feminism, Culture, and Media Studies* 22, no. 65 (May 2007): 135–136.

Her memoir too denies originality—not only in Goude, but also in Haring, Issey, and Jones herself.

Controlling Identity, Resisting Categories

While denying any need to claim originality, Jones insists on having maintained control over her work. She calls herself "the designer," rejecting any suggestion that she was on unequal footing with any collaborator, claiming instead "responsibility for every detail."[28] Control over her work, so much of which is presented in deliberate conflation with her identity, is a crucial extension of control over her identity.

Significant in her self-identity is the contentious position of race, and throughout the memoir, Jones resists calling herself "black."[29] Soon after moving from Jamaica to Syracuse, New York, as a young adolescent, Jones rejects terminology that many in her new surroundings took for granted: "I didn't want to be thought of as 'black,'" she recalls, "and certainly not as 'negro,' because I instinctively felt that was a box I would be put in that would control me."[30] Later, she comes to understand why many, particularly in the United States, proudly embrace the identifier, but she never accepts it for herself.[31] It is not until she is told by a powerful modeling agent in Paris that as "a black model" she was not marketable that she feels confronted with limitations forced upon her due to the color of her skin.[32] No doubt partly thanks to her fierce drive to prove the agent wrong, Jones in fact achieves considerable success as a model in France. While not naïve to the insidious tenacity of racial prejudices, Jones continues to deny raced categories for herself.

This persistent refusal is perhaps most conspicuous in her personal recollection of the 1981 tour of *One Man Show*. "I never really thought of myself as black, so it wasn't as though I consciously decided that I would behave in a way that black people didn't usually behave."[33] And yet the show, which infamously opened with Jones in a gorilla suit, rather overtly evoked

---

[28] Jones, *Grace Jones*, 204, 302.
[29] I follow Jones's choice to leave the first letter of the word "black" in lower-case.
[30] Ibid., 54.
[31] "If I'd been born [in the US] and really lived it, as a black person, it would have been different. It would have absolutely defined me, but I came into it from a distance. To be honest, I don't know how black America can ever get over how its history developed with this monstruous split." Ibid., 63.
[32] Ibid., 106.
[33] Ibid., 261.

performance as used by the African diaspora to critique the dehumanization of black entertainers, as well as black individuals in general.[34] As Miriam Kershaw saw it, "[b]y quickly discarding her emphatically artificial costume, Jones insinuates that racial stereotypes are, themselves, a mask which will be manipulated throughout the performance."[35] Jones, for her part, denies consciously subverting, playing into, or making any issue of racial stereotypes, though she concedes that Goude, who produced the show alongside Jones, may have used it to channel his own ideas without openly admitting to it. As she elaborates:

> We never discussed its being about blackness, or femininity, or masculinity, about the breaking of certain taboos and traditions.... I was playing a character ... *human*, as an energy, a force, a creative act that did what creative acts are meant to do: to break outside of categorizing us sexually and racially, which causes problems.[36] [emphasis added]

Jones's intention to "break outside of" categorizations sounds precisely like "the breaking of certain taboos and traditions" that she says she refrained from discussing with Goude. Regardless, what is notable is that her resistance to taxonomies of sex and race is predicated on, and ultimately emphasizes, her foremost identity as human. While this may amount to a simplistic global humanism that ignores material, economic, legislative, and cultural histories, Jones remains unyielding throughout her memoir in reminding readers that she is indeed human.

This insistence is seen in the pithy opening statement of the first chapter: "I was born."[37] As Janine Bradbury rightly notes, such an opening phrase is a convention of narratives of the formerly enslaved, asserting the existence of a narrator who stands behind the authenticity of the text.[38] The declaration simultaneously attests to an even more fundamental fact that the narrator is a sentient, verbal individual. Jones further repeatedly distinguishes her living self as "the actual me" and "the human me" as opposed to the figure in photographs and on stage: "I was stretched, fractured, crushed, expanded,

---

[34] Royster, "Feeling like a Woman," 79.
[35] Miriam Kershaw, "Postcolonialism and Androgyny: The Performance Art of Grace Jones," *Art Journal* 56, no. 4 (Winter 1997): 21.
[36] Jones, *Grace Jones*, 261.
[37] Ibid., 1.
[38] James Olney, "'I Was Born': Slave Narratives, Their Status as Autobiography and as Literature," *Callaloo* 20 (1984): 52, quoted in Bradbury, "Grace Jones," 69.

liquefied, but always as a performance, as an effect, a consciousness, never as a real human being."[39] This insistence on repeating the fact of her humanhood is also underscored in the documentary *Grace Jones: Bloodlight and Bami* (2017), directed by Sophie Fiennes and released two years after the publication of Jones's memoir. In a memorable scene, Jones is on the phone to confirm a studio recording session but is left frustrated, ending the conversation with the repetition: "I am human, I am human."[40] In the context of the conversation it is not obvious what she intends to communicate: perhaps she means "I am (only) human" and can only deal with so much, or "I (too) am human" and should be respected as such. Either way, the statement does not fit the natural flow of the conversation, and her somewhat facile delivery suggests that she has used the line before, and perhaps often. That is to say, "I am human" seems to be a familiar refrain for Jones, and it is no accident that she repeats the phrase, in various forms, in her memoir.

Dehumanization

Jones's constant and consistent need to proclaim her humanity has apparent roots in a formative childhood spent in Spanishtown, Jamaica, under the strict authority of her grandmother's young husband. Mas P, as he was known, had replaced her parents as a guardian after they moved to the United States ahead of their children.[41] Despite occasional attempts by the grandmother to appease him, Mas P treated Grace and her siblings as if they were his property, physically tormenting them in the guise of edification. Jones notes that when she shaved her head years later, it made her look "more like a thing than a person," but that it was only appropriate: "that was how I had felt I was treated growing up—as a thing, without feeling, an object, not even human."[42] Jones comes to associate the need to be perfectly beautiful for Goude to her oppressive childhood where she needed—though she nearly always failed—to be perfectly behaved for Mas P.

---

[39] Jones, *Grace Jones*, 245, 232, 371.

[40] If it is difficult to confer intention to Grace Jones through her memoir, then it is near impossible to do so with a documentary which the subject did not see until it was finished. But the film provides unique insight into the many realities of Grace Jones (under stage lights [Bloodlight] and eating Jamaican bread [Bami] with her family) and can be productively read as another form of life-writing.

[41] Like many men in positions of power within the church, the young pastor was addressed as "mas," a painfully obvious remnant of the practice of slavery. Jones, *Grace Jones*, 17.

[42] Ibid., 82.

While we are to understand that he never physically mistreated Jones in the way that Mas P did, Goude's exploitation of Jones is blatant, at least as evinced in *Jungle Fever*.[43] Indeed, if we follow the elements of human objectification first identified by Martha Nussbaum, we note that Goude demonstrates them all toward Jones and other models by displaying ownership, denying autonomy and subjectivity, and marking the women as instrumental, inert, violable, and fungible.[44] In this way, *Jungle Fever* reads as the articulation of one artist's flagrant objectification of the Other.

The case of Goude is, of course, simply one in a long and ongoing history of such objectification. The story of Saartje (or Sarah) Baartman (ca. 1790–1815), degradingly but widely known as "the Hottentot Venus," is but one of the most infamous examples of the inhumane treatment of black women, in both life and death.[45] While Grace Jones achieved her first critical success as a model only after moving from the United States to Paris, evoking the legacies of American-born entertainers like Ada Smith (1894–1984) and Josephine Baker (1906–1975), this was not simply due to Parisian appreciation for a diversity of beauty and talent. Rather, the women were simultaneously victims to and found opportunity in a fetishistic fascination with the myth of the so-called Black Venus deriving from French colonial conquests in Africa.[46] Such a compulsion to associate African physical characteristics with sexual excess and primitive savagery, particularly in Europe and the Americas, has worked to hypersexualize and dehumanize black women.[47] The tendency in particular to dehumanize through animalization remains pervasive in mass media at large.[48]

Jones has herself taken on the role of animal, perhaps facetiously and apparently willingly. Whatever her intention, the performance in the gorilla suit mentioned above is one such example. Another infamous occasion is

---

[43] As Lola Young describes it, "Goude self-consciously uses the black female body 'as a blank space' on which to play out his racialized sexual fantasies of domination and control over otherness." Lola Young, "Racializing Femininity," in *Women's Bodies: Discipline and Transgression*, ed. Jane Arthurs and Jean Grimshaw (London: Cassell, 1999), 82.

[44] Martha Nussbaum, *Sex and Social Justice* (New York: Oxford University Press, 1999), 218.

[45] Anne Anlin Cheng, "Skins, Tattoos, and Susceptibility," *Representations* 108 (Fall 2009): 98–105. As Kimberlé Crenshaw famously declared when she coined the term "intersectionality," black women's lives are experienced not only as women nor as black citizens, but in the intersection of race and sex relations.

[46] Kershaw, "Postcolonialism and Androgyny," 19. Of course, this is not meant to deny agency or exceptional talent in Smith, Baker, or Jones.

[47] Marquita Gammage calls this the ongoing "anti–Black woman agenda." Marquita Gammage, *Representations of Black Women in the Media: The Damnation of Black Womanhood* (New York: Routledge, 2016), 19.

[48] Ibid., 72.

reproduced on the cover of *Jungle Fever*, which shows a naked Jones inside a cage, on hands and knees and with teeth bared toward the camera. This oft-reproduced image first used in promotional material for an event in 1978 also appears within the book, this time along with the sign "Do Not Feed the Animal."[49] On one hand, the portrait is entirely demeaning: Jones is explicitly identified as a violent and ruthless animal, one who nonetheless is encaged and stripped of any agency to feed herself. As Francette Pacteau notes, Jones "is barely human, even unequivocally bestial" in this particular depiction.[50] And while this is the conclusion we may understandably draw from the still image (with or without the linguistic sign), in fact it was Jones's own idea to perform a stunt in which she pretends to fight a real tiger, emerging victorious, and ending in a similar position as in the still image. Goude finds the act "scary" and thereafter limits his work with Jones to the medium of still photographs that he can control more easily during production and unilaterally manipulate post-production.[51] While the photograph may well have been Goude's idea, Jones turns the static representation into her own dynamic performance in what becomes an act of defiance against the artist. As soon as Jones starts literally moving in a way that Goude did not design, she becomes a source of discomfort and danger to him.

Goude has thus depicted Jones as primitive animals, but he has also famously presented her as sophisticated machines, most famously on the album cover artwork for *Slave to the Rhythm*, as well as in televised commercials for Citroën. Using Donna Haraway's notion of the cyborg feminist, Janine Bradbury astutely argues that Jones's memoir—and the singer herself—can be identified as cyborgic.[52] Jones thus has been positioned at different times as both animal and machine, and here it is crucial to recall that the discursive process of marking a human as "not human" has been heuristically categorized as acts of animalization or mechanization.[53] Further, fans of her

---

[49] Goude, *Jungle Fever*, 116. On the image, see Kershaw, "Postcolonialism and Androgyny," 20–21.

[50] Francette Pacteau, "Dark Continent," in *With Other Eyes: Looking at Race and Gender in Visual Culture*, ed. Lisa Bloom (Minneapolis: University of Minnesota Press, 1999), 99.

[51] Goude, regarding the tiger-fight sequence: "I couldn't see where all this stuff was leading. It was certainly fun, but also very tiring and very difficult to control. So I decided to go back to my still pictures where I was the undisputed boss." Goude, *Jungle Fever*, 103. On Goude rendering Jones as an unchanging "emblem of stable meaning," see Montez's insightful chapter "Theory Made Flesh? Keeping Up with Grace Jones," in Keith Haring's Line: Race and the Performance of Desire (Durham, NC: Duke University Press, 2020), especially 95–98.

[52] Bradbury calls Jones a "a polysemic, post-human cultural icon who, like the cyborg itself, is transgressive, mutable and resists definition." Bradbury, "Grace Jones," 66.

[53] Nick Haslam, "Dehumanization: An Integrative Review," *Personality and Social Psychology Review* 10, no. 3 (2006), 252–264.

music and image also often cast her as something otherworldly and alien, in an apparent attempt at a positive appraisal.[54] Jones is, then, likened not only to both animal and machine, but also to a superhuman entity. She is made to be sub-human, super-human, and non-human, and through it all she continues to insist that she is, of course, simply human.

Humanizing Oneself, Humanizing Others

While Jones has not otherwise publicly spoken out against Goude, the memoir acknowledges just how ingrained his objectification of her had become. Dolph Lundgren, her next lover after Goude, understood that she needed to be cared for "as a person, in the real world, where I breathed, and cried, and bled."[55] Jones reasons that Lundgren thus saved her life, underscoring just how harmful her long-term romantic and professional relationship with Goude had been. That she returns so often in the memoir to remind us that she is human also attests to the likelihood that, just as Mas P made her feel less than human as a child, so too did Goude compel her to reiterate the fact of her humanhood.

And yet, in Jones's assessment, Goude ultimately came to understand that he cared for her not just as his artistic creation but as her own person:

> I think he realized he loved me when it was too late. He loved me as an object during our relationship, and he explained that to me. Later, he realized he loved me as me, but by then I was too aware of being loved as an idealized object, and I didn't want to be loved like that.[56]

In fact, even before she left him for Lundgren, Jones claims Goude had venerated her humanity, albeit inconsistently. In planning *One Man Show*, Jones recalls Goude sharing in her own concerns: "I was a human being, and more than anything *we* were seeing how far you could stretch being human before it became something else altogether" (emphasis added).[57] This concern continued after they parted ways, and for the cover of the album *Living*

---

[54] She has also, for example, been identified as embodying Afrofuturism. See Bennett Brazelton, "The Futures of Grace Jones: Queer, Black, Dystopian, Eternal," *Fire!!!* 5, no. 2 (Spring 2020): 53–82.
[55] Jones, *Grace Jones*, 265.
[56] Ibid., 263.
[57] Ibid., 261.

My Life, Jones declares that "[Goude] was still slicing and dicing me, manning me up, changing my shape, worrying about my humanity, savoring what you can do to a face without hurting it."[58] Jones's memoir crafts Goude into a person who recognizes and values the humanity of another—the rights of being human—which in turn underscores his own humanity, the quality of being humane. Thus Jones presents him as someone who delights in the appearance of another while being careful not to cause her harm. Not insignificantly, this depiction also makes the artist into a more sympathetic figure, one who cannot be dismissed as the racist misogynist he proudly appears to be in *Jungle Fever*. It simultaneously recalibrates the power dynamic between Goude and Jones, positioning them on level footing as both equally human.

Goude's humanhood is also conveyed through familiar characteristics that can be described as human shortcomings. Such flaws are relatable to readers, in kind if not in specifics, like his jealousy of director Ridley Scott that causes Jones miss out on a role in the film *Blade Runner* (1982). Such characteristics also present him as an imperfect and occasionally irrational man.[59] Emotions that complicate his relationship with Jones are in fact underscored in her memoir in an obvious contrast to his self-presentation in *Jungle Fever*. In the passage quoted earlier, Jones notes that Goude wrote his book "when he was angry and frustrated" with her. We are told that later, presumably when he had calmed down, "he trie[d] to take back what he said."[60] Such references to the volatility of Goude's emotional state undermine the validity and sincerity of the declarations made in his own book, suggesting, for one, that he was only facetiously claiming to have "created" Jones. It also confers an emotionally affected intent upon Goude that makes him more than (or less than, depending on the viewpoint) the detached, genius artist that he sets himself up to be. It would clearly be simple for Jones to reduce Goude to a onetime lover and discount his actions to racist fetishism as he himself unabashedly does in *Jungle Fever*, but she provides him with a motivation here that is familiarly human. When he reacts with understandable fear during an armed robbery and giggles nervously while Jones remains calm, readers cannot help feeling for him, even while being impressed by Jones.[61] If humanization is achieved by portraying others in ways that encourage empathy

---

[58] Ibid., 226.
[59] Ibid., 270–272.
[60] Ibid., 227.
[61] Ibid., 218.

and legitimize support, Jones accomplishes this, at least partly, with Goude.[62] By symbolically objectifying Jones and other women in *Jungle Fever*, Goude had effectively dehumanized them, but in her memoir, Jones does the opposite to him. Indeed, we are to understand that while he may have been but one of many lovers and collaborators, just like each of them Goude is neither anonymous nor replaceable. Thus, when describing their first meaningful encounter, Jones highlights its felicity for them both, as well as their interdependence. Indeed, they met precisely "when [they] *each* needed someone... someone who could deepen us, who we could change with, who we could become."[63]

Acknowledging that both she and Goude wished to change (and succeeded in doing so) is particularly significant. Of the seven elements of human objectification that Nussbaum identified, Jones most strongly resists the characterization of inertness.[64] The memoir repeatedly highlights movement and transformation as a constitutive component of her personality, which she declares is founded on an innate and continuous "impulse to change."[65] By attributing this same characteristic—of the ability and willingness to change—to others like Goude, Jones discursively shares her humanity. It has been argued that in the act of dehumanization, the identities of the self and the other are both significant, and thus the process should be treated as dialogical.[66] In the same way, I propose that the process and act of humanization can be equally dialogical. Despite being cast as super-human, sub-human, and/or non-human, Jones is avowedly human, as she persistently reminds readers. But she simultaneously emphasizes that her lovers, collaborators, friends, and even foes are human. Indeed, while never underplaying the pain that her stepgrandfather Mas P caused for her and her siblings, from the time she first refers to him in the memoir, Jones acknowledges that the much younger man had married her grandmother not thinking he would ever be in a position to raise five small children.[67] Without excusing or forgiving his actions, they are contextualized, and while remaining clear that she could not help considering him a "monster," Jones still recognizes his motivations

---

[62] Steve Kirkwood, "The Humanisation of Refugees: A Discourse Analysis of UK Parliamentary Debates on the European Refugee 'Crisis,'" *Journal of Community & Applied Social Psychology* 27, no. 2 (March/April 2017): 117.
[63] Jones, *Grace Jones*, 203. Emphasis added.
[64] This is not to suggest Jones was aware of Nussbaum's concept of objectification.
[65] Ibid., 355.
[66] Seamus A. Power, "Towards a Dialogical Model of Conflict Resolution," *Psychology & Society*, 4 (2011): 53–66, cited in Kirkwood, "The Humanisation of Refugees," 123.
[67] Jones, *Grace Jones* 17.

and desires as a person.[68] Thus, Mas P was human, no matter how seriously flawed. That this reminder is provided to us by Jones, whom he had made to feel as if not even human herself, is testament to her unwavering commitment to recognizing a shared humanity.

In the case of Goude, Jones complicates his image by presenting more than his objectification of her body and underscoring the entirety of their relationship together—including, as we saw earlier, his significant role as the father of her only child. While above I referenced the memoir's opening text and paratextual material as elements that undermine Goude's professional and artistic influence upon the memoir, the emphasis on his fatherhood should not be belittled. In fact, perhaps for Jones, it is the ultimate acknowledgment of his humanity, as well as of her own—after all, highlighting Goude's role as the father of her child underscores her own motherhood. While the memoir is rife with explicit declarations that Jones is human, it is perhaps at these moments when she speaks of others as human that she seems to be most human herself. Grace Jones, as an icon so often portrayed as somehow not quite human, ultimately reminds us of the simple yet undeniable fact of a shared, communal existence.

Bibliography

Anderson, Carolyn G. "En Route to Transnational Postmodernism: Grace Jones, Josephine Baker and the African Diaspora." *Social Science Information* 32, no. 3 (1993): 491–512.

Bradbury, Janine. "Grace Jones: Cyborg Memoirist." In *Music, Memory, Memoir*, edited by Robert Edgar, Fraser Mann, and Helen Pleasance, 65–80. New York: Bloomsbury Academic, 2019.

Brazelton, Bennett. "The Futures of Grace Jones: Queer, Black, Dystopian, Eternal." *Fire!!!* 5, no. 2 (Spring 2020): 53–82.

Cheng, Anne Anlin. "Skins, Tattoos, and Susceptibility." *Representations* 118 (Fall 2009): 98–105.

Fiennes, Sophie, dir. *Grace Jones: Bloodlight and Bami*. London: Spirit Entertainment, 2017.

Gammage, Marquita. *Representations of Black Women in the Media: The Damnation of Black Womanhood*. New York: Routledge, 2016.

Goude, Jean-Paul. *Jungle Fever*. Edited by Harold Hayes. New York: Xavier Moreau, 1981.

Guilbert, Georges-Claude. *Madonna as Postmodern Myth: How One Star's Self-Construction Rewrites Sex, Gender, Hollywood, and the American Dream*. Jefferson, NC: McFarland, 2002.

---

[68] Ibid., 40.

Haslam, Nick. "Dehumanization: An Integrative Review." *Personality and Social Psychology Review* 10, no. 3 (2006): 252–264.
Jones, Grace, and Paul Morley. *Grace Jones: I'll Never Write My Memoirs*. New York: Gallery Books, 2015.
Kershaw, Miriam. "Postcolonialism and Androgyny: The Performance Art of Grace Jones." *Art Journal* 56, no. 4 (Winter 1997): 19–25.
Kirkwood, Steve. "The Humanisation of Refugees: A Discourse Analysis of UK Parliamentary Debates on the European Refugee 'Crisis.'" *Journal of Community & Applied Social Psychology* 27, no. 2 (March/April 2017): 115–125.
Lobato, Ramon. "Amazing Grace, Decadence, Deviance, Disco." *Camera Obscura: A Journal of Feminism, Culture, and Media Studies* 22, no. 65 (May 2007): 134–139.
McDowell, Colin. "Goude Heavens." *Sunday Times*, November 6, 2005. https://www.thetimes.co.uk/article/goude-heavens-t6l8sb5807t.
Montez, Ricardo. "Theory Made Flesh? Keeping Up with Grace Jones." In *Keith Haring's Line: Race and the Performance of Desire*, 83–108. Durham, NC: Duke University Press, 2020.
Nussbaum, Martha C. *Sex and Social Justice*. New York: Oxford University Press, 1999.
Olney, James. "'I Was Born': Slave Narratives, Their Status as Autobiography and as Literature." *Callaloo* 20 (1984): 46–73.
Pacteau, Francette. "Dark Continent." In *With Other Eyes: Looking at Race and Gender in Visual Culture*, edited by Lisa Bloom, 88–104. Minneapolis: University of Minnesota Press, 1999.
Power, Seamus A. "Towards a Dialogical Model of Conflict Resolution." *Psychology & Society* 4 (2011): 53–66.
Royster, Francesca T. "'Feeling like a Woman, Looking like a Man, Sounding like a No-No: Grace Jones and the Performance of Strange in the Post-Soul Moment." *Women & Performance: A Journal of Feminist Theory* 19, no. 1 (March 2009): 77–94.
Thompson, Robert Farris. "Notes on the Art and Life of Keith Haring." In *Keith Haring: The Political Line*, edited by Dieter Buchhart, 47–57. San Francisco: Delmonico, 2015.
Weidhase, Nathalie. "Ageing Grace/Fully: Grace Jones and the Queering of the Diva Myth." In *Women, Celebrity and Cultures of Ageing: Freeze Frame*, edited by Deborah Jermyn and Su Holmes, 97–111. London: Palgrave Macmillan, 2015.
Yelin, Hannah. "'I Am the Centre of Fame': Doing Celebrity, Performing Fame and Navigating Cultural Hierarchies in Grace Jones' *I'll Never Write My Memoirs*." *Celebrity Studies* 12, no. 1 (2019): 119–131.
Young, Lola. "Racializing Femininity." In *Women's Bodies: Discipline and Transgression*, edited by Jane Arthurs and Jean Grimshaw, 67–90. London: Cassell, 1999.

12
Power in the Eye of the Beholder

Authoring Text and Image in the Female Rock Memoir

Silvia Hernández Hellín

Over the last three decades, as the celebrity autobiography has gained recognition as an established genre, numerous music-related volumes have appeared. These autobiographical narratives are commonly—almost expectedly—illustrated with pictures of the subject's life. Such is the case with the so-called female rock memoir, a form that recounts stories of women who made their mark in the rock industry. There are, however, three authors whose use of photography seems to call out for a distinct analysis: Patti Smith, Viv Albertine, and Liz Phair all incorporate images that do not conform to the celebrity memoir practice of displaying career-related portraits of the authors and their lives. Instead, they illustrate their narratives with pictures taken by themselves of people, objects, or places that are relevant to their life story. In doing so, these three women raise questions about the boundaries between fact and fiction, the faultiness of memory, and the need to contextualize photographs, all the while seeking to maintain control over their image.

Introduction

Photography increasingly shapes the world we live in: we are constantly bombarded with images, still or moving, be it through devices like our smartphones, our televisions, or our computers, or simply while walking on the street. The ubiquitousness of images has even permeated our everyday reading lives. Newspapers, textbooks, children's books, and manuals are nowadays almost invariably illustrated, and readers increasingly expect auto/biographical accounts to be complemented with visual evidence. As Liz Stanley notes, "we are accustomed, we surrender to, the power of visual representation, photographs in particular, of auto/biographical subjects."[1] This is especially true for celebrity memoirs, in which the author's image acquires a greater significance, to the extent that it can sometimes stand for his or her persona. Traci Freeman observes how "[v]isual components... are almost always present in some form, whether they be a selection of pictures from the celebrity's childhood or photographs of celebrities encountered in the subject's life."[2] Keith Richards, Richard Hell, Carrie Brownstein, Bruce Springsteen, Kim Gordon, Kathy Valentine, and Elton John are among the best-known musicians to have published memoirs in the last decade, and all incorporate photographs into their books, either embedded in the narrative illustrating particular moments of the story, or appended in the form of a photo album.

Juxtaposing text and image in life-writing frequently results in a greater sense of veracity. Very often, pictures authenticate what words can, at best, suggest; put simply, pictures fulfill the promise made by words. Most critics seem to agree: "Photography seduces us with . . . its high standard of accuracy";[3] "Photography furnishes evidence";[4] "Since its invention, photography has been understood as truer than other representative images."[5] Photography's presence in auto/biography, however, may take different forms. According to Fabien Arribert-Narce, a photograph can be simply evoked, it can be described in greater or lesser detail, and/or it "can be materially reproduced . . . and co-present with a certain number of texts, be they captions, descriptions or narratives."[6] Photographs may also be present but not alluded to, only tangentially related to the text, and not necessarily as supporting evidence.

Depending on how authors incorporate them into their texts, then, photographs may take on differing meanings. As Stanley notes, however powerful images may be, they are not all-powerful: "they require interpretation and this interpretation may be mediated by words which surround,

---

[1] Liz Stanley, *The Auto/biographical I: The Theory and Practice of Feminist Auto/biography* (Manchester: Manchester University Press, 1992), 20.
[2] Traci Freeman, "Celebrity Autobiography," in *Encyclopedia of Life Writing*, ed. Margaretta Jolly, vol. 1 (Chicago: Fitzroy Dearborn, 2001), 189.
[3] Catherine Liu, "Getting to the Photo Finish: Photography, Autobiography, Modernity," *South Atlantic Quarterly* 101, no. 3 (2002): 524.
[4] Susan Sontag, *On Photography* (New York: RosettaBooks, 2005), 3.
[5] Linda Haverty Rugg, *Picturing Ourselves: Photography & Autobiography* (Chicago: University of Chicago Press, 1997), 12.
[6] Fabien Arribert-Narce, "Photographs in Autobiographies: Identities in Progress," *Skepsi. Graft & Transplant* 1, no. 1 (2008): 49.

literally, particular photographs."[7] Text and photography, then, complement each other and result in an enhanced product. Along similar lines, Timothy Dow Adams explains:

> The common sense view would be that photography operates as a visual supplement (illustration) and a corroboration (verification) of the text—that photographs may help to establish, or at least reinforce, autobiography's referential dimension. In the wake of poststructuralism, however, I argue that the role of photography in autobiography is far from simple or one-dimensional. Both media are increasingly self-conscious, and combining them may intensify rather than reduce the complexity and ambiguity of each taken separately.[8]

The intricacies of illustrated memoirs, then, can be understood only through the combined interpretation of text and photography; it is in the relationship between the two that the meaning of the work is revealed.

The female rock memoir is typically a chronological account that traces the artist's beginnings in music and the subsequent pursuit of her career. It therefore tends to be illustrated with childhood and family photographs, pictures from the author's teenage years, pictures of the author with friends (usually musicians or people related to the industry in some other way), and pictures that directly connect the author to the music scene (e.g., performing onstage, backstage with her bandmates, recording in the studio, or posing for photoshoots).[9] While the stories of women in rock have too often been told from a male perspective, women are now taking the reins of the male-dominated genre of auto/biographical literature and drawing attention to the significance of female experience in the equally male-dominated world of rock music.

These women reclaim their stories not only through text, but also through photography. Female rock memoirists appropriate the photographs other people—mostly men—have taken of them and insert them into a narrative

---

[7] Stanley, *The Auto/biographical I*, 1, 25.
[8] Timothy Dow Adams, *Light Writing & Life Writing: Photography in Autobiography* (Chapel Hill: University of North Carolina Press, 2000), xxi.
[9] Viv Albertine's *Clothes, Clothes, Clothes, Music, Music, Music, Boys, Boys, Boys* (2014); Kim Gordon's *Girl in a Band* (2015); Chrissie Hynde's *Reckless: My Life as a Pretender* (2015); Carrie Brownstein's *Hunger Makes Me a Modern Girl* (2015); Debbie Harry's *Face It* (2019); and Kathy Valentine's *All I Ever Wanted* (2020) all display photographs that fall into most or all of these categories.

of their own: in providing new contexts for the photographs, they cease to be objects and become subjects. Depending on how and where photographs are placed alongside a textual narrative, the statement they make will vary: the way they are arranged (chronologically or not, close to or far from the narrative moment they illustrate), whether or not they are referenced in the text, whether or not they are captioned. The focus is no longer on the content of the photographs alone, but also on the interactions between text and photography. While pictures per se may reveal information that might complement the written narrative, it is what surrounds them (the actual story, captions, or references) that really provides them with a distinct meaning. The photographs illustrating female rock memoirs, even when taken by someone else, are now reinterpreted through the words of the women portrayed. In fact, not only do these women recontextualize these images, but they also use them to reinscribe themselves as active participants in rock history. Susan Sontag claims: "What is written about a person or an event is frankly an interpretation. . . . Photographed images do not seem to be statements about the world so much as pieces of it, miniatures of reality."[10] The photographs in the female rock memoirs, then, allow women to prove that they were also there, contributing in myriad ways to the development of rock music.

Female rock memoirists often share in their accounts their concern with public image and the way it affects self-representation, whether touching upon the subject or sharing extensive reflections on it. In *Reckless: My Life as a Pretender* (2015), Chrissie Hynde writes about her express refusal to be sexualized in photo shoots: "I wouldn't allow any photos to be taken of me on my own, even though as the singer, which implies 'sex symbol,' it was expected. But I held my ground. The Pretenders were the four of us, and I was pathologically insistent that we be perceived as such."[11] Despite the fact that most women resort to other people's photographs of them to illustrate their autobiographical accounts, they seem to be willing to challenge the narratives that others attempt to impose upon them, whether through words or images.

Debbie Harry's *Face It*, published in 2019, displays a collection of portraits of her made by her fans down the years, which prompts a reflection on perception and the act of portrayal. Toward the end of the book, Harry reveals that the title of the memoir indeed arises from the many interpretations other people have made of her image as well as from her need to come to terms with

---

[10] Sontag, *On Photography*, 2.
[11] Chrissie Hynde, *Reckless: My Life as a Pretender* (London: Ebury Press, 2015), ch. 30, Kindle.

her own understanding of this. Harry explains: "*Face It* became my title of choice for three main reasons: 1) from all the fan art portraits I have collected over the years, 2) because of all the photos taken of me, 3) and finally, because I had to face it in order to do this memoir."[12] In choosing to incorporate these artworks alongside the more typical celebrity memoir photographs, she not only enriches the visual aspect of her narrative, but she also points to how subjective perception really is. Harry actually notes how, even though many of these images are modeled after famous photographers' shots of her, each reveals something about its author: "when I look at my fan art collection I can see little bits of the artist drawn into their attempts to reproduce my face that they don't even know are there."[13] Harry, then, does not seem to be troubled by the subjectivity in other people's representations of her. Quite the opposite, she acknowledges this fact and uses it in her favor: by incorporating so many distinct reproductions of her face, she is minimizing the importance normally placed on the other's perception.

While the use of photography (and the examination of its implications) is certainly widespread among the female rock memoirs, there are texts in which photography no longer plays a merely testimonial role. Some memoirists choose to illustrate their accounts with pictures taken by themselves, thus taking full control of their narratives and producing hybrid texts in which testimony and aesthetics coexist in each photograph. Such is the case with Patti Smith's *M Train* (2015) and *Year of the Monkey* (2019), Viv Albertine's *To Throw Away Unopened* (2018), and Liz Phair's *Horror Stories* (2019), texts that are markedly different from their counterparts in that they do not offer the conventional chronological account of the authors' rise to stardom. Smith, Albertine, and Phair choose to prioritize narratives that for the most part downplay the celebrity aspect of their stories rather than emphasizing the ordinariness of their experiences. The same happens with the photographs they incorporate: where images of themselves would have been expected, these women instead complement their narratives with photographs of places, objects, or other people taken by themselves.

In authoring the text as well as the photographs in their books, Smith, Albertine, and Phair become subjects—multifaceted artistic subjects—able to reclaim every aspect of their image through their interdisciplinary work. These women prioritize their vision over other people's. According to

---

[12] Debbie Harry, *Face It* (London: HarperCollins, 2019), ch. 9, iBooks EPUB.
[13] Ibid., ch. 10.

Adams, "[i]n one sense all photographs are self-portraits, particularly in the case of professional photographers, in that they tell us something about the photographer's eye—his or her way of framing the world . . . [is] particularly telling."[14] Similarly, Sontag argues that "photographs are evidence not only of what's there but of what an individual sees."[15] This means that, even when female rock memoirists provide their own context for other people's photographs of them, the photographer's gaze (what they choose to highlight through framing, perspective, color, lighting, or the poses in which they choose to capture their subjects) is still present in the representation of these women. Only those women who author the photographs that illustrate their texts can assume full control over their image, become makers instead of objects dependent on the too-often male gaze. It is in these "visual/textual interfaces," as Sidonie Smith and Julia Watson call them, that women may raise questions on "gendered subjectivity and agency in self-representational acts."[16] With distinct aims in mind, Smith, Albertine, and Phair replace the typical portraits of their faces and bodies with images of the world around them, thereby directing the reader/viewer's attention toward the many aspects that inform self-representation beyond physical appearance.

Patti Smith: From Autotopography (*M Train*) to Autofiction (*Year of the Monkey*)

Patti Smith's three autobiographical prose narratives, *Just Kids* (2010), *M Train* (2015), and *Year of the Monkey* (2019), all feature some form of illustration (mostly photographs, but also documentary evidence such as letters or manuscripts). It is with *M Train* and *Year of the Monkey*, however, that the author really consolidates her photographic gaze. These two books display black-and-white Polaroids, mainly taken by the author, which tend to be slightly out of focus or oddly framed; there seems to be no attempt to beautify these images, but rather they are presented as ordinarily as possible. There are hardly any portraits of Smith, with images of objects or places outnumbering portraits of any kind. Even though the photographs in *M Train* and *Year of the Monkey* seem to follow the same aesthetic line,

---

[14] Adams, *Light Writing & Life Writing*, 227.
[15] Sontag, *On Photography*, 68.
[16] Sidonie Smith and Julia Watson. *Interfaces: Women, Autobiography, Image, Performance* (Ann Arbor: University of Michigan Press, 2002), 15.

when put into context they perform differing functions. In the former, Smith defines herself through pictures of objects that belong either to her or to artists whom she deeply admires; in the latter, photography often becomes a fictional element illustrating a narrative where the boundaries between fiction and nonfiction are already blurred.

The twenty-two pictures of objects in *M Train*, which account for three-quarters of the photographs in the book, are tightly connected to the concept of autotopography. In her definition of this term, Jennifer A. González argues that "just as written autobiography is a series of narrated events, fantasies, and identifications, so too an autotopography forms a spatial representation of important relations, emotional ties, and past events."[17] According to González, items such as photographs, souvenirs, or heirlooms act as "physical extensions of the psyche," in that they represent varying intangible memories of our past experiences and can thus ultimately be seen as autobiographical objects. This is also the case with more utilitarian objects, which may no longer serve a useful purpose but have become so attached to one's psyche that they end up becoming representative of oneself.[18] Although *M Train* can chiefly be understood as a narration in which Smith writes about herself (as in an autobiography or memoir), it is also a space in which she "displays"—both in writing and through the pictures that accompany the text—many of the objects that link her present self to the past by means of the memories they evoke (as in an autotopography).

The photographs in *M Train* can be seen as autotopographical on two different levels. First, the objects captured in the pictures are ordinary items that, with the passing of time, are valued not for their original or practical use, but rather for the significance they have acquired (that is, for what they have come to represent), thus becoming autobiographical objects. Such is the case with a table and chair from Smith's favorite café, her coffeemaker, or her copy of Murakami's *The Wind-Up Bird Chronicle*. There are also pictures of objects that belong (or, more properly, used to belong) to artists whom Smith admires: Roberto Bolaño's chair, Frida Kahlo's bed, Herman Hesse's typewriter, and Virginia Woolf's walking stick. These objects are actually biographical of their owners, but the pictures themselves are autobiographical of Smith: the fact that she has decided not only to take those pictures but also

---

[17] Jennifer A. González, "Autotopographies," in *Prosthetic Territories: Politics and Hypertechnologies*, ed. Gabriel Brahm and Mark Driscoll (Boulder, CO: Westview Press, 1995), 134.
[18] Ibid., 133.

to hold on to them and include them in one of her books reveals much about the author and her devotion to artists and their belongings.

This is the second level on which the Polaroids in *M Train* are related to the concept of autotopography: the photographs themselves ultimately become autobiographical objects and, together, they form a museum of Smith's self à la Orhan Pamuk. Polaroids, as opposed to today's digital images that seldom exist outside our electronic devices, exist as physical objects, as actual repositories of the past; it is precisely their singularity as physical objects that grants them their special status.[19] According to Sontag, photographs are artifacts but "their appeal is that they also seem . . . to have the status of found objects—unpremeditated slices of the world. Thus, they trade simultaneously on the prestige of art and the magic of the real."[20] Smith herself writes in the book:

> Spanish pilgrims travel on Camino de Santiago from monastery to monastery, collecting small medals to attach to their rosary as proof of their steps. I have stacks of Polaroids, each marking my own, that I sometimes spread out like tarots or baseball cards of an imagined celestial team.[21]

The pictures she takes acquire a certain holiness, as do the objects she photographs: she describes a chess table as "the holy grail of modern chess,"[22] Friedrich Schiller's table as "innately powerful,"[23] or a well she finds on Washington Square in New York City as "the object that had transformed and reenergized the atmosphere. A true object of desire."[24] However ordinary these items may seem, they hold a special value for Smith. In photographing them and incorporating the pictures into her life narrative, Smith is elevating them to the category of autobiographical objects and is therefore defining herself through them. She chooses to replace images of herself with images more revealing of her private self: the heirlooms she has decided to keep, the artists she admires, the books she reads.

In *Year of the Monkey*, photography plays a very different role. In a narrative in which the line between fiction and nonfiction is blurred to the point

---

[19] Peter Buse, *The Camera Does the Rest: How Polaroids Changed Photography* (Chicago: University of Chicago Press, 2016), introduction, iBooks EPUB.
[20] Sontag, *On Photography*, 54.
[21] Patti Smith, *M Train* (New York: Vintage Books, 2015), 200–202.
[22] Smith, *M Train*, 40.
[23] Ibid., *M Train*, 103.
[24] Ibid., *M Train*, 273.

where the reader is left wondering if any of the events actually happened, photography is used to emphasize the surreal nature of the story. The correspondence between text and image is therefore neglected, resulting in the need to reassess the role of photography in autobiography. As Arribert-Narce explains:

> the effects produced by a picture depend on its various interactions with texts. Captions and narratives can problematize its interpretation and can even make it fictional if there is an obvious discrepancy between what is said and what is shown.... Photographs can thus be used as elements of fiction or can even produce a "fiction effect" if their spectators realize that they do not match the text.[25]

Such is the case, for instance, with the picture of Ayers Rock,[26] Uluru, a location that is constantly mentioned throughout the book. At first glance, it looks like an ordinary landscape picture but, when put into the context of the story, something bewilders us: while in the list of illustrations the photograph is credited to Patti Smith, in the story we are told that she has not yet set foot in Ayers Rock. An appended list of illustrations, then, can be part of the text that helps us contextualize images: in this case, it serves to problematize the narrative, to question the veracity of the story as told.

On a different occasion, Smith writes about a trip to Salton Sea she takes with a friend. The way this episode unfolds, together with the dubious existence of her friend, leads us to question the veracity of the adventure. However, there is a picture of an outpost captioned "Outpost, Salton Sea"[27] that illustrates this surreal excursion. Were it not there, the reader might assume Smith is narrating one of her dreams (which she often does in the book), but the fact that there is a picture alters our understanding of the scene: "An event known through photographs certainly becomes more real than it would have been if one had never seen the photographs."[28] In our photographic culture, we seem to be more willing to trust the incontestable picture rather than the questionable word. Works like *Year of the Monkey*, in which the boundaries between fact and fiction are blurred through text and

---

[25] Arribert-Narce, "Photographs in Autobiographies," 50.
[26] Patti Smith, *Year of the Monkey* (New York: Alfred A. Knopf, 2019), 18.
[27] Ibid., 70.
[28] Sontag, *On Photography*, 15.

photography, however, urge us to reconsider our understanding of the interplay between these two media.

Viv Albertine: Reconciling with Memory in *To Throw Away Unopened*

Viv Albertine's *To Throw Away Unopened* reminds us of Smith's *M Train* and *Year of the Monkey* in that it incorporates black-and-white pictures of apparently ordinary objects. This time, however, the focus is on the photographs' connection to memory. The memoir, dedicated to her late parents, Kathleen and Lucien, to a large extent deals with the relationship between them, as well as with the author's own relationship with them. Most of the photographs are connected in some way to Kathleen or Lucien, especially to the former, since her death is the common thread that ties the whole narrative together.

There are two pictures in particular that are crucial to the story: one of a trunk found among her father's belongings after his passing,[29] and one of a travel bag found among her mother's belongings after hers.[30] Inside her father's trunk, the writer discovers, among other things, two folders: one containing letters to his then wife and his children, and another containing his diary from the latter years of his marriage. From this moment on, Albertine incorporates into the narrative excerpts from both the letters and the diary. This discovery turns out to be extremely revealing for Albertine, who, until this moment, has completely disregarded her father's side of the story.[31] The fact that her childhood memories differ so much from her father's record of events disconcerts her to such an extent that she starts wondering whether her father fabricated his account, or her mother's constant accusations against her father actually ended up clouding her childhood memories: "I don't trust my memories now. Most of what he'd written in his diary was true, but I couldn't believe that Mum had planted false memories in our brains."[32] As for the travel bag, it turns out to be an Aer Lingus zip-up flight bag with white Tippex instructions on the front that give the memoir its title: "To Throw

---

[29] Viv Albertine, *To Throw Away Unopened* (London: Faber & Faber, 2019), 98.
[30] Ibid., 184.
[31] In Albertine's first memoir, *Boys, Boys, Boys, Music, Music, Music, Clothes, Clothes, Clothes*, we learn that, after her father abandons the family, it takes her fifteen years to work up the courage to see him again—at which point she realizes she barely knows him—and never gets to really connect with him.
[32] Albertine, *To Throw Away Unopened*, 170.

Away Unopened."[33] In it, Albertine finds the diaries her mother had kept before divorcing Lucien. The photograph of the bag serves as an introduction to the part of the story where the author discloses her mother's version of the events, realizing that her childhood memories were not faulty: "Lucien hit us with the belt, he didn't just threaten us.... He lied in his diary. My memory of it isn't false."[34] All these findings ultimately help Albertine make peace not only with her memories, but with her parents also.

Of the twenty-six pictures in the memoir, nineteen of which are credited to Albertine, none are captioned, but they are all referenced in the text. We shall not overlook, however, those photographs in *To Throw Away Unopened* which are not physically reproduced but which are present through the author's description of them. One of them is a picture of her father that she describes in detail:

> The black-and-white photograph inside the green book was dated 1945. He gazed out of the picture and up to the left, eyebrows raised, large brown eyes drooping at the outer edges, making him look sad and sensitive. Thick fair hair brushed back from a young forehead, high cheekbones, neat ears, mouth pursed as if he was about to kiss someone or say something French. A dimple in his chin. Overcoat collar turned up, a sliver of white shirt, thin black tie. The image could have been a frame from a 1940s French film.[35]

Even though we readers do not get to see the photograph, Albertine's description of it is so detailed that we can almost mentally picture her father. On two different occasions, Albertine also mentions a photograph of a child (David) from her mother's previous marriage. First, she provides the reader with a brief description: "A soft-focus, black-and-white picture of a two-year-old boy smiled out of the circular frame inset with tiny pearls."[36] Later in the narrative, she looks at this photograph again and is struck by the memory of her grandmother reproaching her mother for abandoning David: "As I studied his face I remembered seeing my mother cry one other time.... I looked up at the window, a pain twisting in my chest. Funny how your body records important events without you knowing. I played out the scene in my head."[37]

---

[33] Ibid., 184.
[34] Ibid., 215.
[35] Ibid., 100.
[36] Ibid., 182.
[37] Ibid., 209.

Despite the fact that, again, the photograph is not incorporated into the book, the memory it evokes in Albertine is what really allows us to connect with what the writer is attempting to convey.

Photography in *To Throw Away Unopened* is therefore closely linked to the act of recollection on different levels. On the one hand, the pictures of items connected to Albertine's parents become, as in Patti Smith's *M Train*, autobiographical objects through which the author may remember them, especially her mother. A red, heart-shaped purse, a set of Christmas figurines, a collection of uniform labels—these items that Albertine incorporates into the narrative through photography ultimately become portals to her mother. "Objects that remind me of my mother," she writes, "have become important to me lately, as if by cherishing the things she liked I'm carrying her inside me like she once carried me."[38] On the other hand, Albertine speaks of photography as a catalyst for memory, observing how photographs can trigger memories she thought had faded. Ultimately, whether materially present, described in detail or simply evoked, pictures help the author navigate her memories as well as her narrative.

Liz Phair: The Need for Context in *Horror Stories*

Liz Phair's *Horror Stories*, published in 2019, differs from Smith and Albertine's accounts in that it does not follow a particular story or period. Instead, it consists of seventeen independent chapters depicting vignettes from her life that are marked by feelings such as guilt, pain, and fear. Each of these chapters is prefaced with a black-and-white photograph that is neither captioned nor referenced in the text, but is somehow connected to the narrative. Interestingly, the use of photography in this memoir is highly reminiscent of social media. On the one hand, if we were to arrange the pictures into a single grid, the result would be very similar to what we would nowadays find on an Instagram profile: pictures of the person in question as a child, pictures of the places she has traveled to, pictures of her taken by herself ("selfies" in social media jargon), or pictures of some part of her body whose perspective implies that she herself is the author of the photographs.[39]

---

[38] Ibid., 266.
[39] Interestingly, the chapter in which Phair discusses her various experiences with sexual harassment and abuse is titled "Hashtag" (again, social media jargon), in reference to the #MeToo movement initiated in the context of social media.

On the other hand, when we factor in the narrative and examine the correspondence between text and image in *Horror Stories*, we notice that there is a contradiction between what is told and what is shown. This contradiction seems to work in a similar way to social media, where the pressure to fit in or to be successful is such that users tend to share only the positive aspects of their lives (even when these are far from idyllic). While Phair does not hesitate to share some of the darker moments in her life with the readers, the photographs in the book transmit a very different feeling: glamour, traveling, music, joy. And yet, behind those pictures there are stories of infidelity, sexual assault, heartbreak, suicide . . . that is, horror stories. In the prologue to the memoir, Phair acknowledges:

> We spend so much time hiding what we're ashamed of, denying what we're wounded by, and portraying ourselves as competent, successful individuals that we don't always realize where and when we've gone missing. . . . Our impulse is always to hide the evidence, blame someone else, put the things we feel guilty about or that were traumatizing behind us and act like everything is fine.[40]

In *Horror Stories*, Phair chooses to share some of the more embarrassing, sour, and disheartening episodes of her life and, whether intentionally or not, through her use of photography, she also lays bare the need to contextualize images.

Contradiction is present from the first chapter, titled "She Lies," where a picture of three pairs of hands with a sparkly ornate manicure precedes the story of the time when Phair, on a night out during her first semester in college, saw a girl who had passed out on the bathroom floor and did nothing about it. The picture, which may or may not have been taken on such night, is in stark contrast with the story it is supposed to illustrate. Something similar happens in chapter sixteen, "Customer Experience," in which Phair shares the story of the time when, after being cheated on by a former boyfriend, she started flirting with a Trader Joe's clerk, who ended up inviting her to his wedding. The story ends up with Phair learning, about a year later, about this man's suicide. Strangely enough, the picture that introduces this chapter is one of a hand (presumably Phair's) with painted nails holding a glass of what looks like a cocktail. An image that is normally associated to a time of

---

[40] Liz Phair, *Horror Stories: A Memoir* (New York: Random House, 2019), prologue, iBooks EPUB.

celebration actually precedes a chapter in which the author examines issues such as lack of self-confidence, loneliness, and self-loathing.

In *Horror Stories*, Phair not only resorts to the correspondence—or, in this case, the lack of it—between photography and text to raise questions about what should or should not be shared; she also reflects on matters of identity, self-perception, and public image. Phair examines, for instance, how celebrity creates tension between her private and public persona. In "Customer Experience," she writes about how the effect her status has on people prevents her from fully being herself:

> Celebrity, however minor, turns people's heads. I try to be the person that I am, but my public image hangs around me like a fog. I can see it in people's eyes as they're talking to me. Once they figure out what I do for a living, they start working out how they can benefit from knowing me, calculating how much access to other celebrities having me in their life would bring them.[41]

She also reflects on the lack of control over her own image whenever she is being photographed by a stranger: "I've been doing a lot of photo shoots lately, and I feel like my identity's being robbed";[42] "They're looking at pictures of me, but the girl in those photographs is someone else. . . . That's the hardest part about being your own product: It's difficult to know what's you and what isn't";[43] "Sometimes, during photo shoots, I get downright hostile because I think the photographer is trying to expose me. They say they want to capture the real person, but I don't know who that is, so how can *they*? My persona is so fragile it tears like tissue paper in the rain."[44] The way Phair sees it, placing herself before a camera turns her into a product at the service of someone else's perception of her.

This all sheds light on why Phair chooses to illustrate her memoir in a nonconventional way, incorporating fewer images of herself and actually using photography to raise questions about the role image plays in our society. In the chapter titled "Magdalena," Phair openly challenges our understanding of looks, something that seems to be inevitably associated to celebrity, especially to female celebrity:

---

[41] Ibid., ch. 16.
[42] Ibid., ch. 4.
[43] Ibid., ch. 4.
[44] Ibid., ch. 9.

What exactly are we evaluating when we think about our looks? Is it what's actually there or how people respond to us that shapes our opinion of ourselves? Can you describe someone's looks without picturing the way they move, the sound of their voice, or their personality? If you break it down into parts, just the physical attributes—brown hair, brown eyes, round face, short, fat, pigeon-toed—is that really how they look, or is it just shorthand for your much more nuanced and complex way of identifying them? . . . Even something as objective as a photograph shows the bias of whoever was holding the camera. And as a viewer, you add your own reaction to the image.

So what are looks? Seriously, what are they?[45]

Phair's reflection on the subjectivity of looks explains, to a certain extent, her decision not to illustrate her life narrative with pictures that would more typically be found in celebrity memoirs. Although in the book she writes about photo shoots in which she is asked to wear nothing but trousers and suspenders over her nipples or a low-cut dress with a rope criss-crossing her body, there is no room for such pictures in *Horror Stories*.

Conclusions

Writing one's story certainly is an empowering experience, more so when one's narrative has long been constructed by others. Female rock memoirists use their accounts to set the record straight, thereby shedding light on the female experience and taking control of their narratives. This control, however, is sometimes limited when we factor in the visual narrative. Only those authors who place themselves behind the camera can make the deliberate choice of what to portray, therefore assuming real power, agency, over their narratives (both textual and visual).

This, in addition, allows them to illustrate complex stories in which the interplay between text and image is much more intricate; it grants them further power over their texts and the text-image dialogue. Photography elevates the status of the objects portrayed in *M Train*; it heightens the fact-versus-fiction duality present in *Year of the Monkey*; it acts as a catalyst for memory in *To Throw Away Unopened*; and it raises questions about the need

---

[45] Ibid., ch. 4.

to contextualize images in *Horror Stories*. Through their use of photography in memoir, Smith, Albertine, and Phair advocate a new way of incorporating photography into an autobiographical text: no longer necessarily as corroboration of the written word, no longer necessarily portraying the author, and no longer the product of someone else's gaze. This, in turn, opens up new possibilities for female self-representation, in regard not only to literature but to life in general: women need not model themselves after society's idea of them; there is room for contradiction, transformation, even hesitation, in the act of self-representation; there is no such thing as the female identity but rather myriad female identities.

Where female self-representation has often been associated with narcissism, Smith, Albertine, and Phair decide, for the most part, to remove their physical selves from the photographs, emphasizing the instability and plurality of the self as well as the complexity of attempting to frame it. As Valérie Baisnée-Keay reveals, "images of women and by women remain at the center of a political and cultural struggle: the struggle for women to resist objectification and to have a 'say' in their own representations."[46] These women's texts thus stand at the crossroads between the personal and the political, both taking part in female representation while also seeking to resist and defy cultural stereotypes concerning the representation of women.[47] In an act of empowerment, they place themselves behind the camera and provide us with a visual narrative of their own, thus challenging preconceptions about the role of photography in the female rock memoir in particular, and in auto/biography in general. These women who have always been best known for their role in the world of rock music now (re)present themselves—using both text and image—as multifaceted artists producing hybrid works of literature.

Bibliography

Adams, Timothy Dow. *Light Writing & Life Writing: Photography in Autobiography*. Chapel Hill: University of North Carolina Press, 2000.
Albertine, Viv. *Clothes, Clothes, Clothes, Music, Music, Music, Boys, Boys, Boys*. New York: St. Martin's Press, 2014.
Albertine, Viv. *To Throw Away Unopened*. London: Faber & Faber, 2019.

---

[46] Valérie Baisnée-Keay, "Introduction," in *Text and Imagen in Women's Life Writing: Picturing the Female Self*, ed. Valérie Baisnée-Keay et al. (Cham: Palgrave Macmillan, 2021), 2.
[47] Ibid., 15.

Arribert-Narce, Fabien. "Photographs in Autobiographies: Identities in Progress." *Skepsi. Graft & Transplant* 1, no. 1 (2008): 47–56.

Baisnée-Keay, Valérie. "Introduction." In *Text and Image in Women's Life Writing: Picturing the Female Self*, edited by Valérie Baisnée-Keay et al., 1–18. Cham: Palgrave Macmillan, 2021.

Buse, Peter. *The Camera Does the Rest: How Polaroids Changed Photography*. Chicago: University of Chicago Press, 2016.

Freeman, Traci. "Celebrity Autobiography." In *Encyclopedia of Life Writing*, edited by Margaretta Jolly, vol. 1, 188–190. Chicago: Fitzroy Dearborn, 2001.

González, Jennifer A. "Autotopographies." In *Prosthetic Territories: Politics and Hypertechnologies*, edited by Gabriel Brahm and Mark Driscoll, 133–150. Boulder, CO: Westview Press, 1995.

Harry, Debbie. *Face It*. London: HarperCollins, 2019. iBooks EPUB.

Hynde, Chrissie. *Reckless: My Life as a Pretender*. London: Ebury Press, 2015. Kindle.

Liu, Catherine. "Getting to the Photo Finish: Photography, Autobiography, Modernity." *South Atlantic Quarterly* 101, no. 3 (2002): 519–539.

Phair, Liz. *Horror Stories: A Memoir*. New York: Random House, 2019. iBooks EPUB.

Rugg, Linda Haverty. *Picturing Ourselves: Photography & Autobiography*. Chicago: University of Chicago Press, 1997.

Smith, Patti. *Just Kids*. London: Bloomsbury, 2010.

Smith, Patti. *M Train*. New York: Vintage Books, 2015.

Smith, Patti. *Year of the Monkey*. New York: Alfred A. Knopf, 2019.

Smith, Sidonie, and Julia Watson. *Interfaces: Women, Autobiography, Image, Performance*. Ann Arbor: University of Michigan Press, 2002

Sontag, Susan. *On Photography*. New York: RosettaBooks, 2005.

Stanley, Liz. *The Auto/biographical I: The Theory and Practice of Feminist Auto/biography*. Manchester: Manchester University Press, 1992.

13
Cosey Fanni Tutti, Age and Place

Abigail Gardner

Introduction

Cosey Fanni Tutti's memoir, *Art, Sex, Music* (2017), starts with a birth story: "'Yours was a difficult birth' my mother told me. I was born with my left elbow bent and my fist firmly wedged against my chin like Rodin's The Thinker. Then she added, with a smile, 'You've been difficult ever since.'"[1]

This recollection establishes Tutti as "difficult," and her memoir continues to cast her in this way by reflecting on a life of artistic disruptions and transgressions centered on art, sex, and music. Cosey Fanni Tutti is a musician, producer, has been a performance artist, porn actor, and stripper, and is now also a memoirist. She is arguably, what Tara Brabazon[2] has called, a "difficult" woman, where "difficult" means someone who does not fit in or adhere to established or expected codes and conventions. Extending ideas that I explored in *Ageing and Contemporary Female Musicians*,[3] this chapter focuses on Tutti's 2017 memoir, *Art, Sex, Music*, in relation to the importance of place in aging and memoir, specifically with regard to transgression and being "difficult." It does this by arguing that the *medium/place*, or format, of a written memoir combined with the *temporal/place*, or timing, of the vantage point of an older literary voice does something to the status of the transgressive performances of her youth. There is a change in register enabled by reflection and distance that allows for the processing of such transgressions. In parallel to this process, where there is a modicum of acceptance that is enabled by the written text and time passed, there is a continuing tension, or awkwardness that cannot be wholly suppressed. Tutti's memoir goes some way to valorizing a non-phallocentric place, by writing into popular cultural

---

[1] Cosey Fanni Tutti, *Art, Sex, Music* (London: Faber & Faber, 2017), 1.
[2] Tara Brabazon, *Ladies Who Lunge: Celebrating Difficult Women* (Sydney: University of New South University of New South Wales Press, 2002).
[3] Abigail Gardner, *Ageing and Contemporary Female Musicians* (London: Routledge, 2019).

history the "fanni" of the opera. This "fanni" is about feminine power in relation to sex, sound, and the body, a noisy body, a body of sound, now made legible through twenty-first-century memoir.

Placing Cosey Fanni Tutti

The name "Cosey Fanni Tutti" is a pun on Mozart's 1790 opera *Così fan tutte*, which translates into English as "Everyone does it like this." This in itself is a swipe at conventionality, be it in relation to femininity, sexuality, or music, as Tutti experimented with all of those in ways that were arguably disruptive of contemporary conventions of mid-1970s codes of gender, sex, and sound.

The change of the "i" to the "ey" makes the word similar to the English adjective "cosy," which means comfortable and familiar. This is juxtaposed with the next semantic disruption; adding the "i" to the second term takes us into the realm of the humorous, risqué, maybe discomforting joke. "Fanni" (written "fanny") in British English is slang for vagina. This "born difficult" woman is "invaginating"[4] Mozart's canonical music text. A leading member of the pre-punk avant-garde music and art scene, Tutti preempted punk's linguistic assaults on propriety and representation, specifically around women and sex. Her memoir traces this "improper" journey from childhood through artistic development, relationships, health crises, and death, and this chapter considers it through two ideas, "discomfort" and "distance."

Looking through these prisms enables me to extend ideas I explored in *Ageing and Contemporary Female Musicians* around the age-appropriacy of the female rock memoir. There, I looked at the role of the aging authorial voice within Anglo-American rock music and considered the importance of genre, temporal, and modal "place" in aging and memoir. I was concerned with how the act of "looking back" was part of an attempt to add to a collective popular cultural history previously untold narratives of women who had been involved in creative music practice largely in the independent music scenes in the later 1970s through 1990s. These concerns concentrated on the "mode" of shifting from music performance to literary exposition and what that might facilitate in terms of reception, specifically in relation to aging. The argument was, in brief, that appearing "as" text and framed "as"

---

[4] Roshanak Kheshti, *Modernity's Ear: Listening to Race and Gender in World Music* (New York: New York University Press, 2015).

memoir allows older women to speak, but on certain conditions. First, these conditions are that, ideally, the memoir be advertised through the younger body of the female musician, which erases her present, aged body. Second, the sexual experiences of the musician can only be let out into culture and discussed after a suitable period has elapsed; this period is what I called the "menopausal gap." Safely on the other side of this gap, the written memoir acts as a valid place for reflection and narration; it is an accepted place in time and format, from which difficult women might speak.

This argument is an extension of the debates around listening that tackle a perceived supremacy of the visual within Western culture from (Feminist) Sound Studies.[5] Anahid Kassabian, for example, historicizes this split by arguing that the "Enlightenment [had an] obsession with vision and perspective."[6] This obsession, Salome Voegelin suggests, is inherently "masculine."[7] Within this oppositional discourse of visual (distance) versus aural (proximity), there is a fear of sound as something that can breach the self. The spread of sound, its ability to seep into spaces and forge through barriers, is something that Jean-Luc Nancy elaborates on in relation to the visual, which he argues is "tendentially mimetic, and the sonorous tendentially methexic (that is, having to do with participation, sharing, or contagion), which does not mean that the two might intersect,"[8] but there is something radical in his use of the term "methexic." This positions sound as something that can't be contained. It lends it a radical flow. Sound can spill out, spatially and temporally. It may be unruly. It invites a certain "being with"[9] from the listener. It requires a geographic and temporal co-presence, a folding into. Imagine the difference between reading Tutti's memoir about performances that included bodily penetration and noise and being there. That difference is the gap, that gap is about the difference between places in time and places in medium.

When I say "place," I am repurposing the geographical notion of place that Murray Forman uses to understand the dynamics of place and affective

---

[5] Jean-Luc Nancy, *Listening* (New York: Fordham University Press, 2007); Anahid Kassabian, *Ubiquitous Listening: Affect, Attention and Distributed Subjectivity* (Berkeley: University of California Press, 2013); Veit Erlmann, ed., *Hearing Cultures: Essays on Sound, Listening and Modernity* (Oxford: Berg, 2004); Salome Voegelin, *The Political Possibility of Sound: Fragments of Listening* (New York: Bloomsbury Academic, 2019).

[6] Kassabian, *Ubiquitous Listening*, xvi.

[7] Salome Voegelin, *The Political Possibility of Sound: Fragments of Listening* (New York: Bloomsbury Academic, 2019), 159.

[8] Nancy, *Listening*, 10.

[9] Michael Bull, in *Hearing Cultures: Essays on Sound, Listening and Modernity*, ed. Veit Erlmann (Oxford: Berg, 2004), 188.

belonging in hip-hop. Here he uses Grossberg's ideas that "places are the sites of stability where people can stop and act, the markers of their affective investments."[10] Tutti's memoir is one such place. It allows her to "stop and act," to claim her own history within the conventions of the memoir narrative. And in doing so it enables her to add "herstory" to "history." Halberstam asks a rhetorical question in her analysis of why women's histories of punk matter: "Why are these other histories of punk so important? Because without them, punk becomes a rebellion without a cause, a boy's club of heroic art school dropouts and another master narrative within which white guys play all the parts."[11] Tutti's career started before punk, but Halberstam's argument is relevant because Tutti's memoir goes some way to wrest a continuing narrative away from the "boy's club" and places herself and her body center stage.

Who Is Cosey Fanni Tutti?

Cosey Fanni Tutti was born Christine Carol Newby into a working-class family in Hull, England, in 1951. Her memoir is chronologically linear and traces the development from her childhood to her recent past. In it, she describes her strict family, her time at school, where she was a rebel, and her early encounters with sound and music making. The surrounding "stuff" of her life is sketched in to show how she was always a bit different, as well as being "difficult." Her early fascination with sound was inspired by her father's interest in electronics, and she recalls how he bought her and her sister a Grundig tape recorder, which she loved recording on.[12] Rather than singing, it was splicing tapes and messing with sound that fascinated her. There is no room for experimentation or fascination in the working-class environment she lives in; she writes about herself and a friend wanting more than the dullness that working-class jobs and expectations required, and she notes that she had the "necessary determination to get it."[13] Exposed to late 1960s pop culture on TV, to pop music through gigs and clubs, she began to start singing in bands, later becoming involved in the hippie scene in Hull,

---

[10] Murray Forman, *The Hood Comes First: Race, Space and Place in Rap and Hip-Hop* (Middletown, CT: Wesleyan University Press, 2002), 25.
[11] Jack Halberstam, "Go Gaga: Anarchy, Chaos and the Wild," *Social Text* 31, no. 3 (2013): 129.
[12] Tutti, *Art, Sex, Music*, 21.
[13] Ibid., 42.

dropping acid and moving into a commune there in 1970 called the "Ho Ho Funhouse." Soon after, she met Genesis P'Orridge, a key member of the Hull avant-garde scene with whom she proceeded to have a long and complex relationship. With P'Orridge, she was a key member of the music and art collective "COUM Transmissions," which went on to form Throbbing Gristle. She writes of how all the while that she was a member of this art/music outfit, she experimented in the studio with loops and pedals, playing with electronics and sound.

It is notable how these accounts remain somehow lesser to the narrative of self-discovery and survival, of her explicit use and infiltration of the sex industry,[14] relationship issues with P'Orridge, and later, of a miscarriage.[15] She writes candidly about sex and the body, and these stories fit with the way that pre-punk (and punk) used transgression as a vehicle for commentary on gender roles and expectations around femininity and sexuality.[16] Tutti was arguably the first woman to perform under a sexually provocative stage name, and in this, prefigured bands and musicians like the Slits, Penetration, and the Nipple Erectors. Her body was the site of her performance, and in COUM she explored its role in articulating aesthetic and performance boundaries. COUM shows were about "extreme and obscure actions,"[17] and they had become notorious for a show at the ICA early on in their career in 1976, called "Prostitution." The description here written by Genesis P'Orridge recalls what happened at that gig:

> In Los Angeles, in 1976, at the Institute of Contemporary Arts (LAICA), Cosey and I did a performance where I was naked, I drank a bottle of whiskey and stood on a lot of tacks. And then I gave myself enemas with blood, milk and urine, and then broke wind so a jet of blood milk and urine combined shot across the floor in front of Chris Burden and assorted visual artists. I then licked it off the floor, which was a not-clean concrete floor.
>
> Then I got a 10-inch nail and tried to swallow it, which made me vomit. Then I licked the vomit off the floor and Cosey helped me lick the vomit off the floor. And she was naked and trying to sever her vagina to her navel with a razor blade—well, she cut it from her vagina to her navel with a razor

---

[14] Ibid., 169.
[15] Ibid., 316.
[16] Angela McRobbie, *Feminism and Youth Culture: From Jackie to Just 17* (London: Palgrave, 1990); Dick Hebdige, *Subculture: The Meaning of Style* (London: Routledge, 1979).
[17] Tutti, *Art, Sex, Music*, 168.

blade, and she injected blood into her vagina which then trickled out, and we sucked the blood from her vagina into a syringe and injected it into eggs painted black, which we then tried to eat. And we vomited again.[18]

This is performance as confrontation, almost *grande guignol* in its embrace of masochism, sadism, body horror, and an ironic degree of humor. Tutti's use of her body, exposing it, subjecting it to violence, both in COUM and later, through her work as a stripper and a porn actor, reveals something Cixiousian. Tutti's work and her description of it throughout the memoir indicate how she was engaged in some kind of pre-punk feminine écriture,[19] through sound and performance art. Contemporaneous with the ICA show, in 1976, Helene Cixous wrote, "your body is yours, take it,"[20] which Tutti did. She used her body to "write" herself, to make her body "heard,"[21] to use it as an instrument of interrogation. Imagine the middle 1970s; the women in "popular" music who had been given space, who were listened to, were folk singers (Joni Mitchell, Joan Baez), pop singers (Lulu, Dusty Springfield, Shirley Bassey), soul singers (Aretha Franklin, Diana Ross). Tutti was part of a transgressive ensemble, and from within it she started to upset by first refusing to be ashamed of her body, its secretions and sensualities. She did not have the "stupid sexual modesty"[22] that Cixous despaired of. Tutti did not ignore the body; she put it at the forefront of what COUM were trying to and I think it is, to a degree, a form of feminine writing, insofar as Cixous defines it: "It will be conceived of only by subjects who are breakers of automatisms, by peripheral figures that no authority can ever subjugate."[23] Tutti did this by working in pornography and against the 1970s' feminist politics, claiming her own space. She writes "I didn't identify with 1970s feminism: it didn't speak for me or the diverse and complex nature of women, I was a free spirit and didn't want yet more rules and guilt thrown at me about my actions."[24] COUM's ICA show and Tutti's role within it, coupled with her reflections on her experience as a stripper, reveal that she is acting out the return of the repressed whereby "When the 'repressed' of their culture and their society

---

[18] http://www.brainwashed.com/tg/coum.html.
[19] Hélène Cixous, "The Laugh of the Medusa," *Signs* 1, no. 4 (1976): 875–893
[20] Ibid., 876.
[21] Ibid., 880.
[22] Ibid., 885.
[23] Ibid., 883.
[24] Tutti, *Art, Sex, Music*, 171.

returns, it's an explosive *utterly* destructive, staggering return, with a force never yet unleashed."[25]

In 1977, COUM developed into Throbbing Gristle, an avant-garde "noise" band, whose work was founded on with tape loops and synthesizers. So Tutti's "upset" in another way by embracing technologies that were somehow discursively situated as something different to playing an instrument, or using her voice as such. Again, Tutti talks about her interest in making sound through electronic means, rather than through working with or "playing" an instrument. She recalls her first visit to Macari's, the famous London guitar and amp store on Charing Cross Road, where she tried out FX pedals and writes: "The other guitarists were all doing renditions of 'Stairway to Heaven' and there was me saying to the assistant, 'No, I don't need to tune my guitar first—I'll just plug in. I kind of know what sound I'm looking for.' "[26] Here, Tutti is not "fitting in" to preconceived notions of how to play, she is making her own set of steps. This might be traced back to earlier in her memoir when she recalls how she found the recording part of the music process the most interesting:

> When I was about ten years old my dad bought me and my sister a Grundig tape recorder. Everyone we knew had record players and we wanted one too—we so wanted to be like our friend and go round buying records and spinning them on our own record player at home. But the Grundig was Dad's sensible alternative.... The recording part was what I loved most. My sister was too shy to do it but I recorded myself a lot.[27]

Throbbing Gristle also played around with "fit." They "messed" with aesthetic expectations of genre and sound. This album cover of their work *20 Jazz Funk Greats* shows them posing on top of a cliff, smiling in casual gear, all in color. Open the album sleeve and you are in a monochrome world and at the bottom of that cliff, a notorious suicide spot in the Southeast of England known as Beachy Head. Listen to it, the Pitchforks' greatest industrial music album, and you will soon find that the music is not jazz funk, not at all. In an interview with Red Bull Music Academy in 2012, Tutti says of it:

---

[25] Cixous, "The Laugh of the Medusa," 886.
[26] Tutti, *Art, Sex, Music*, 244.
[27] Ibid., 21.

We did the cover so it was a pastiche of something you would find in a Woolworth's bargain bin. We took the photograph at the most famous suicide spot in England, called Beachy Head. So, the picture is not what it seems, it is not so nicey nicey at all, and neither is the music once you take it home and buy it. We had this idea in mind that someone quite innocently would come along to a record store and see [the record] and think they would be getting 20 really good jazz/funk greats, and then they would put it on at home and they would just get decimated.[28]

Their view on what they wanted audiences to experience again revolves around the idea of discomfort, that the music does not "fit" with the record cover and that they might, through this disjuncture, discomfort their audience somehow.[29]

Discomfort and Distance

I want to step outside of Tutti's memoir a little now in order to frame it within the idea of discomfort and distance by narrating two stories that I would argue go some way toward understanding what is going on in the memoir, of Tutti's and others at the same time. The first story is about some steps, and the second, about a tennis star, and they go some way to highlight the importance of distance or "gap" in relation to women whose work discomforts. I am acknowledging Sara Ahmed's work on comfort from her 2014 book on emotion and politics, where she used the idea of a comfortable chair that you did or didn't fit in, that did or did not make your body feel at ease.[30] She was talking about queer bodies not fitting into heteronormative spaces. I am thinking about young bodies only being allowed to speak when older, about the comfort that distance brings, but also, and in parallel, about the embrace of discomfort that Cosey Fanni Tutti's work vocalizes.

There are five very steep steps up to my front door in the provincial town of Cheltenham, where I live in the UK. They are the setting for the "first day at school" photographs for each of my three children, now grown up. For

---

[28] Emma Warren, "Hot on the Heels: An Interview with Cosey Fanni Tutti," *Red Bull Music Academy*, 2012, https://daily.redbullmusicacademy.com/2012/11/cosey-interview.
[29] Marie Thompson, *Beyond Unwanted Sound: Noise, Affect and Aesthetic Moralism* (London: Bloomsbury Academic, 2017), 145.
[30] Sara Ahmed, *The Cultural Politics of Emotion* (Edinburgh: Edinburgh University Press, 2014), 148.

years, I had to haul pushchairs up these stairs, and bumped them down them. Now, my eighty-year-old mother-in-law is unwilling to visit the house as she cannot get up those steps. These steps were not designed for me as a young mother, nor for an eighty-year-old who walks with a cane. They do not fit us. This, though, is the landscape we have had to negotiate to reach home; we have put up with it, learned how to negotiate it, but is not comfortable.

The second story is about tennis star Naomi Osaka written by an opinion journalist, Marina Hyde, who writes satirical pieces on current affairs for the UK broadsheet newspaper *The Guardian*. In 2021 she wrote an article about Osaka, who had been in the news for opting out of the post-match media rounds in the French Open. Citing precarious mental health as her reason for non-attendance, Osaka was the focus for Hyde's analysis of the discomfort her actions had caused the relevant tennis authorities. She writes how

> The weird thing is that we DO want athletes [*female musicians*] to have mental health issues [*sexual lives*]—very much so in fact—but we only want them to reveal them at a time and a place that suits us. Namely, after they've retired, and in a book. Then we can profess ourselves fascinated to have learned that an athlete walked out for this or that fixture absolutely broken inside. The key thing is that you couldn't tell from the outside—that's the bit we love. The hidden pain, the belated literary reveal.[31]

And here it is, that gap in time that allows for the processing of "discomfort." In *Ageing and Contemporary Female Musicians*, I put forward the idea of "The Menopausal Gap," the safe distance afforded to women "of a certain age" to broach messy issues of the interior, emotional, or sexual lives. Hyde's analysis of the appropriate place *in time* for women to talk about such issues, here mental health, is the same. There is a suitable gap between the event and its broadcast. We are spared the "messiness." Elizabeth Grosz argued (1994) how the leaking body has been positioned within Western culture as an object of disgust, meaning that the fluids from women's bodies (menses, vaginal discharge, placenta) were cleaned up, ignored, derided, taboo. They did not fit with the patriarchal ideal of the sealed male body; they leaked and oozed. This also applies to the *oozing out* of anguish and anxiety, where women's

---

[31] Marina Hyde, "Sport Loves Athletes with Mental Health Issues—If They Just Shut Up and Play," *The Guardian*, June 1, 2021, https://www.theguardian.com/commentisfree/2021/jun/01/sport-athletes-mental-health-tennis-naomi-osaka.

mental "leakages" have been construed as madness, hysteria, insanity. Their dementia disrupts the patriarchal logos. They are out of control.

Memoirs in a Rock and Pop Landscape

In *Ageing and Contemporary Female Musicians*, I started thinking about how rock memoirs are an established literary genre that function as part of a broader ecosystem of popular music. They extend the reach of the musician and make them a cultural player in a broader cultural landscape. With an already identified audience, they make up part of a metatext of music, images, and words that are the cultural configuration of that artist. They function as one element in the star-making economy that popular music has, like the film industry, been reliant on. Their tales of stardom are usually characterized by early struggles (with musical ability, with drugs, alcohol, family), rejections (both by the industry and in relationships), and ultimate survival. There is, in them, a degree of familiarity as we know their stories already, but the memoir offers us the inside perspective. They take us off stage, behind the scenes and function in a similar fashion to the pseudo-documentary music video that Railton and Watson described (2011).[32] They allow us, the fan, an interested audience, a glimpse into the off-stage stories and offer an "access-all-areas" account. Like the documentary video, they offer an authenticating narrative that shores up ideas of the star and memories of performances.

Tutti's memoir is similar to others published around the same time, and includes confessional moments, tales of how she first approached music, how her relationship with P'Orridge was central to Throbbing Gristle, and tales of health crises. Her memoir operates, as Susanna Radstone suggests, as a personal history that seeks to articulate or repossess the historicity of the self; "Memoir places the self relative to time, history, cultural pattern and change. It is different to confession, which is ontological ... memoir is historical or cultural"[33] and so offers a revision or rearticulation of the past. Radstone's analysis of the distinction between the two forms offers a platform from which to gauge how far these memoirs are not only individual confessional

---

[32] Diane Railton and Paul Watson, *Music Video and the Politics of Representation* (Edinburgh: Edinburgh University Press, 2011).
[33] Francis R. Hart, "Notes for an Anatomy of Modern Autobiography," *New Literary History* 1, no. 3 (Spring 1970): 491 quoted in Susannah Radstone, *The Sexual Politics of Time: Confession, Nostalgia, Memory* (Oxford: Routledge, 2007), 17.

tales from the female rock star but that they are a rewriting of history. They carve out, in retrospect, a history of women in rock that includes trauma, the body, sex, and relationships; the matrix of their creative life. They center the embodied, traumatic, and creative feminine self. In a review of her 2017 album release, Simon Tucker refers to her memoir saying that

> There's no *product* here. It's not built for disposable consumption. Cosey's 2017 memoir *Art Sex Music* was an often-unflinching portrayal of what it is like to live in a coercive controlled relationship that had spilled over into violence. The book was not another *rawk* star yawn fest but an honest chapter in the art/life existence that is Cosey Fanni Tutti.[34]

I read all the rock memoirs by women musicians that came out, and there were a lot of them: Viv Albertine of the Slits, Kim Gordon of Sonic Youth, Carrie Brownstein of Sleater Keaney, Kristen Hersch of Throwing Muses. It was, arguably, partly a nostalgia trip. And so I argued that the women who were writing them, these aging female literary voices, were part of a popular cultural nostalgia for the youthful "age" of punk and post-punk that has been mirrored by contemporary cultural reflections on the era from the world of art and media.

These memoirs fit into a popular music industry that is part of a broader retromanic[35] culture defined by the urge to repackage, reunite, and revive acts from its past.[36] The return of musicians from the 1970s and 1980s not only on stage, but in museums and exhibitions across Europe, the UK, and the United States, and as part of interactive exhibitions, as Ros and I wrote in our book on aging and popular music across Europe, illustrates the veracity for such repeated encounters across different platforms. How, then, might we read the "return" of younger women through the written memoirs of their older selves? Significant visual tensions remain over how voices like Tutti's are now packaged. Older voices are being sold via their younger bodies. Look at the cover of her memoir again (and all the others). These are women in their forties, fifties, and above, but it is their youthful images that continue

---

[34] Simon Tucker, "Cosey Fanni Tutti: *Art, Sex Music* Book Review," *Louder than War*, April 4, 2017, https://louderthanwar.com/cosey-fanni-tutti-art-sex-music-book-review/.

[35] Simon Reynolds, *Retromania: Pop Culture's Addiction to Its Own Past* (London: Faber & Faber, 2011).

[36] Simone Driessen, "Larger than Life: Exploring the Transcultural Fan Practices of Dutch Backstreet Boys Fandom," *Participations, Journal of Audiences and Reception Studies* 12, no. 2 (2015): 150–196.

to market them. While their literary voices are heard, their aging bodies are erased at by versions of their youthful bodies continuing to represent them. This is apparent in the 2021 concert for ABBA's reunion, whereby youthful avatars of the four members, Anna, Frida, Benny, and Björn, took the place of their contemporary, older selves. It happens in other contemporary media platforms, not least YouTube, where there is a constant erasure of the old/aging by the presence of youth.[37] YouTube's "find engine" may get you the current incarnation of a woman musician or performer, but its "drift engine," the sidebars, will throw up images from the past. This means that the current, aged body is in constant, if not competition, then at least comparison, with its youthful version. How "she was then" is always haunting how "she is now." So on the cover of her memoir, Tutti looks out at us, gaze straight ahead, a headshot; the title of the book, *Art, Sex, Music*, is superimposed over her mouth as if she is duct-taped; here, she is young. And if we think again, the duct tape has removed her voice, she cannot speak. So while this older woman can write and retell, the image that sells her history to the buying public remains one of a silenced young woman, and silenced in a way that is connotative of BDSM practices or of violence.

Tutti's memoir is notable for its visceral and almost palpable recollection of pre-punk art collectives and experimental electronica. I found it a discomforting read, one that took me into abusive relationships, the sex industry, the porn industry; there was, indeed, a degree of violence in there, not least in her own relationship with Gen and her encounters with other men. There are episodes in the book that still unnerve me when I read them, because they are troubling and because they are complex; a male GP assaults her in his surgery while a nurse is present; her heart problem is brushed aside by another GP as "peri-menopausal." She (her words) "infiltrates the sex industry" and she falls pregnant while having a coil implanted. She succeeds in conveying the seediness of the 1970s porno scene, the squatting communities of London, and her repeated subservience to Genesis P'Orridge ("Gen had a thing against vacuum cleaners and wouldn't have one in the house. I had to clean with an old carpet sweeper and broom, usually when he was out").[38]

In her book on Grunge and memory, Catherine Strong writes how "memory can be central to the reproduction or alteration of power relations

---

[37] Abigail Gardner, "PJ Harvey, YouTube and Ageing: An Everyday Story of the Erasure of Age," *Convergence, International Journal of Research into New Media Technologies* 25, nos. 5–6 (2018): 1155–1167.

[38] Tutti, *Art, Sex, Music*, 93.

in society";[39] it can work to shore up or dismantle power structures. Tutti's memoir operates somewhat differently. It exposes her affective engagement with the art, sex, and music she was making in the COUM, Throbbing Gristle, and with Chris Carter. This exposure lays bare her experience as a young, white working-class woman on the art and music scenes of mid-1970s Britain. There is an ownership of all her experiences and an exuberance in their narration that illustrates a complexity that cannot be demarcated into a progressive or regressive interpretation predicated on a polarity. One of the instances that refuse to be commented as anything other than experienced is one violent episode where Tutti narrowly escaped serious injury. Throbbing Gristle were in LA for a time and Genesis P'Orridge tossed a breeze block over a balcony while Tutti was sunbathing. She was furious. He ignored it. Her recollection of this violence, and his dismissal, told from the vantage point of the present, is important because it offers us a chance to listen to moments in her life that were ignored. We can now bear witness. And what we bear witness to in the memoir are her experiences of embodiment, place, and how entwined they were with her music, which came out of her experiences of and reactions to her body, how she used it and how others abused it.

This interweaving of the public and private, the body behind the performance, is a particularly important facet in Tutti's memoir, as it is central to many of the "age stages" she recalls. These stories emerge from her pen as an older woman. And so there is something here to consider around aging pens writing youthful traumas and desires, and hitherto unvoiced youthful lives being folded into the widening histories of punk and independent rock music. Might it be too that there is an acceptability of the aging female authorial voice when it is couched within a literary, rather than a musical tradition? Tutti's memoir is a narrative memory act and, as part of the trend for women's music memoirs, might be understood through Halbwachs's "presentist" view on memory, which sees acts of memory as being about the present's use of the past. From the vantage point of herself as an older woman, she is able to affirm her past and recount her role in one of the key, cult bands of the 1970s. Radstone and Schwarz argue that "Memory is active, forging the past to serve present interests."[40] So I would argue that the voices of those that have docked into the safety of older age with bodies that are messy and menopausal have

---

[39] Catherine Strong, *Grunge: Music and Memory* (Farnham: Ashgate, 2011), 5.
[40] Susannah Radstone and Bill Schwarz, *Memories, Theories, Debates, Histories* (New York: Fordham University Press, 2010), 3.

stories to tell about their selves, their journeys to their present that are now accepted. There is now an audience to hear them, given the compulsion to review and relate pop cultural history[41] across multiple sites such as museums, heritage destinations, remastered albums, and never-before-released film footage (Peter Jackson's 2021 TV series of previously unseen footage of the Beatles in *Get Back*) where the affective attraction of popular cultural pasts are explored and encountered. The present is able to deal with the pasts of difficult women. This does not mean that younger women can tell their stories because they are still too close to the mess of that embodied experience; distance from the body's youth is key.

From Beyond the Menopausal Gap

Tutti does not write about aging in *Art, Sex, Music*, but there are reflections on age-stages, of adolescence, sexual awakening, and adventures. It is important that an aging voice tell these tales. Cosey Fanni Tutti is now a writer as much as a musician, and she is safely past the menopausal gap. This change of authorial mode is essential to women's voices being heard. This gap affords a space from which to speak; allowing older women such as Tutti to write about their past excesses because they now pose no sexual or moral threat. As a post-menopausal writer, she becomes part of a literary tradition that includes older women because, primarily, they are heard and not seen. If we think of her as a performance artist, that second word allows her more space to age (as it does Yayoi Kusama, Louise Bourgeois, Agnes Varda, all artists with power of the representative mediums they work in). Age allows them to be listened to. They have moved from being the object of a scopic regime to being in control. Tutti has experimented with this in her early work as well as using sound to explore her place within an auditory regime, which she continues to do. Tutti is still releasing new material and Tucker's review notes her canonical and continuing importance to music and art:

> Tutti has been at the vanguard of the UK (and beyond) art/music scene for approximately five decades now and anyone who has followed her career knows that she has bled, suffered, lived and breathed her art. From the

---

[41] Sarah Baker, Catherine Strong, Laura Istvandity, and Zelmarie Cantillon, *The Routledge Companion to Popular Music History and Heritage* (New York: Routledge, 2018).

days of COUM Transmissions to the game-changing Throbbing Gristle and beyond via her solo works or the music she has made with her partner Chris Carter, Tutti has never once held back and created something for the sake of it.

On what is basically an instrumental album, Tutti manages to say more about human interaction, desires, and needs than most modern music. It allows for a conversation about the subject of sex.[42]

In addition to her 2017 memoir, Tutti appeared in a 2020 film about the pioneering sound technician Delia Derbyshire (Katz, 2020). In this film, for which she composed the soundtrack, she talks about talking across time to Delia, a woman who was also, like Tutti, entranced by sound and electronics. Derbyshire worked at the BBC Radiophonic Workshop from 1962 to 1967 and is now, although not at the time, credited with composing the music for the cult TV show *Dr. Who*. Tutti was inspired by some of the parallels she found between herself and Derbyshire in relation to being a woman in sound recording in the 1960s and 1970s, and a book called *Re-sisters: The Lives and Recordings of Delia Derbyshire, Margery Kempe and Cosey Fanni Tutti* (2022) traces out the connections across time between herself, Derbyshire, and Kempe, a fifteenth-century mystic and autobiographer whose writing shines a light on a woman's experience in the Middle Ages. These three women are connected by not fitting in, being in spaces of discomfort, and who worked out their own non-conformist paths, finding their steps through.

Conclusion

The rock memoir is two things. First, it is a mechanism that affords women musicians and performers across popular music, rock, and sound to transcribe their lives and document and/or narrate their lived experiences. This adds female and female-identified voices to the "his"tories of rock. Second, it is a textual strategy, a written reflection on times past. It is about, but removed from, the past.

Tutti's story, her tale of her younger self, the noisy, confrontational sound experimenter, can be told now. The memoir is a vehicle of time that relocates her into legibility. This *temporal/place* (the "now"), combined with the

---

[42] Tucker, "Cosey Fanni Tutti: *Art, Sex Music* Book Review."

medium/place (the written), makes her body of work readable. Tutti's art, sex, and music can be listened to now, without fear, without the horror of her being too noisy, too loud, too undressed, too fleshy, too feminine, too powerful. Tutti's art, sex, and music was too close. Now, reflected on through memoir, it has a distance that enables it to be processed.

Bibliography

Ahmed, Sara. *The Cultural Politics of Emotion*. Edinburgh: Edinburgh University Press, 2014.

Baker, Sarah, Catherine Strong, Laura Istvandity, and Zelmarie Cantillon, eds. *The Routledge Companion to Popular Music History and Heritage*. New York: Routledge, 2018.

Brabazon, Tara. *Ladies Who Lunge: Celebrating Difficult Women*. Sydney: University of New South University of New South Wales Press, 2002.

Bull, Michael. "Thinking about Sound, Proximity, and Distance in Western Experience: The Case of Odysseus' Walkman." In *Hearing Cultures*, edited by Veit Erlmann, 173–190. Oxford: Berg, 2004.

Cixous, Helen. "The Laugh of the Medusa." *Signs* 1, no. 4 (1976): 875–893.

Driessen, Simone. "Larger than Life: Exploring the Transcultural Fan Practices of Dutch Backstreet Boys Fandom." Participations, *Journal of Audiences and Reception Studies* 12, no. 2 (2015): 150–196.

Erlmann, Veit, ed. *Hearing Cultures: Essays on Sound, Listening and Modernity*. Oxford: Berg, 2004.

Forman, Murray. *The Hood Comes First: Race, Space and Place in Rap and Hip-Hop*. Middletown, CT: Wesleyan University Press, 2002.

Gardner, Abigail. *Ageing and Contemporary Female Musicians*. New York: Routledge, 2019.

Gardner, Abigail. "Anohni and Transgendered, Trans-Age Transgression." In *Subcultures, Bodies and Spaces: Essays on Alternativity and Marginalization*, edited by Samantha Holland and Karl Spracklen, 153–167. Bingley: Emerald, 2018.

Gardner, Abigail. *PJ Harvey and Music Video Performance*. Oxford: Routledge, 2015.

Gardner, Abigail. "PJ Harvey, YouTube and Ageing: An Everyday Story of the Erasure of Age." *Convergence, International Journal of Research into New Media Technologies* 25, nos. 5–6 (2018): 1155–1167.

Gardner, Abigail, and Ros Jennings. *Aging and Popular Music in Europe*. New York: Routledge, 2019.

Gill, Jo, ed. *Modern Confessional Writing: New Critical Essays*. London: Routledge, 2006.

Gilleard, Chris, and Paul Higgs. Ageing, *Corporeality and Embodiment*. London: Anthea Press, 2014.

Grosz, Elizabeth. *Volatile Bodies: Toward a Corporeal Feminism*. New York: Routledge, 1994.

Halberstam, Jack. "Go Gaga: Anarchy, Chaos and the Wild." *Social Text* 116 (2013): 127–134.

Halbwachs, Maurice. *On Collective Memory*. Chicago: University of Chicago Press, 1992.

Hart, Francis R. "Notes for an Anatomy of Modern Autobiography." *New Literary History* 1, no. 3 (Spring 1970): 485–511.

Hebdige, Dick. *Subculture: The Meaning of Style*. London: Routledge, 1979.

Hyde, Marina. 2021. "Sport Loves Athletes with Mental Health Issues—If They Just Shut Up and Play." *The Guardian*, June 1, 2021. https://www.theguardian.com/commentisfree/2021/jun/01/sport-athletes-mental-health-tennis-naomi-osaka.

Jackson, Peter. *Get Back*. Disney+, 2021.

Kassabian, Anahid. *Ubiquitous Listening: Affect, Attention and Distributed Subjectivity*. Berkeley: University of California Press, 2013.

Katz, Caroline. "Delia Derbyshire: The Myths and the Legendary Tapes." *BBC* 4, 2020. https://www.bbc.co.uk/programmes/m000w6tr.

Kheshti, Roshanak. *Modernity's Ear: Listening to Race and Gender in World Music*. New York: New York University Press, 2015.

McRobbie, Angela. *Feminism and Youth Culture: From Jackie to Just 17*. London: Palgrave, 1990.

Nancy, Jean-Luc. *Listening*. New York: Fordham University Press, 2007.

Radstone, Susannah. *The Sexual Politics of Time: Confession, Nostalgia, Memory*. Oxford: Routledge, 2007.

Radstone, Susannah, and Bill Schwarz. *Memory: Histories, Theories, Debates*. New York: Fordham University Press, 2010.

Railton, Diane, and Paul Watson. Music *Video and the Politics of Representation*. Edinburgh: Edinburgh University Press, 2011.

Reynolds, Simon. *Retromania: Pop Culture's Addiction to Its Own Past*. London: Faber & Faber, 2011.

Strong, Catherine. *Grunge: Music and Memory*. Farnham: Ashgate, 2011.

Thompson, Marie. *Beyond Unwanted Sound: Noise, Affect and Aesthetic Moralism*. London: Bloomsbury Academic, 2017.

Tucker, Simon. "Cosey Fanni Tutti: *Art, Sex Music* Book Review." *Louder than War*, April 4, 2017. https://louderthanwar.com/cosey-fanni-tutti-art-sex-music-book-review/.

Tucker, Simon. "Cosey Fanni Tutti: TUTTI—Album Review." *Louder than War*, January 29, 2019. https://louderthanwar.com/cosey-fanni-tutti-tutti-album-review/.

Tutti, Cosey Fanni. *Art, Sex, Music*. London: Faber & Faber, 2017.

Tutti, Cosey Fanni. *Re-Sisters: The Lives and Recordings of Delia Derbyshire, Margery Kempe and Cosey Fanni Tutti*. London: Faber & Faber, 2022.

Voegelin, Salome. *The Political Possibility of Sound: Fragments of Listening*. New York: Bloomsbury Academic, 2019.

Index

For the benefit of digital users, indexed terms that span two pages (e.g., 52–53) may, on occasion, appear on only one of those pages.

age, 2–3, 15, 17, 30–31, 53, 74, 94–95, 124–25, 126, 180–81, 189, 225–41
agency, 16, 40, 48–49, 52, 107–8, 118–19, 127–28, 131–32, 137, 138–39, 161–62, 178–79, 180–85, 192–94, 201–2, 212–13, 222
aging studies, 2, 15, 17
Albertine, Viv, 1, 7, 9–10, 16–17, 208, 212–13, 217–19, 222–23, 235
all-girl band, 134
American poet, 158, 164
Anderson, Carolyn, 192–93
animalization, 201, 202–3. *See also* dehumanization
Anzaldúa, Gloria, 41, 44–45
Arch Enemy, 187–88, 189–90
authenticity, 8, 11, 13, 14, 106–8, 109, 110–11, 112, 114, 118–19, 141–56, 162–63, 193–94, 199–200
  authenticity in punk, 106–8, 110–11, 112, 114, 115–16
  authenticity in rock, 8, 13, 14, 77–78, 106–7, 108–9
autobiographical memory, 3–4
autobiographical truth, 79–82, 148
autofictional, 25, 28, 36–37
autonomy, 167–68, 173, 201
autotopography, 213–17

Baartman, Saartje (Sarah), aka "Hottentot venus," 201
Backstreet Boys, the (band), 95–96
Bag, Alice, 1, 9–10, 12, 40–53
Bags, the (band) 42, 49, 52
beauty work, 178–79, 181, 183
Benatar, Pat, 14, 122–39
Black Sabbath (band), 184
Blackmore, Ritchie, 184

Blondie (band), 108, 111, 112–14, 115–18
body, 23, 66, 72, 99–100, 101–2, 124, 131–32, 183, 184–85, 193–95, 196–97, 206, 218–19, 222, 225–28, 229, 230–31, 232, 233–34, 235–38, 239–40
Bowie, David, 90–91, 95–97, 98–99, 114, 182
Bradbury, Janine, 193–94, 199–200, 202–3
bricolage, 112, 160–61, 173, 197–98

camp, 90–91, 129, 192–93
cancer, 9–10, 27, 37. *See also* metastatic breast cancer
celebrity, 6–7, 16–17, 112, 156, 179, 183, 189, 192–94, 208, 211–12, 221, 222
celebrity culture, 6–7
Cherie's Corset, 180–85, 188–89
Cherry Bomb, 181, 183
Chicano/a, 12, 40–42, 44–46, 47, 48–49, 52, 53
childhood, 12, 23–24, 27, 28, 30–31, 32, 35–36, 37, 40, 41, 42, 46, 52, 72, 125, 171, 200, 210, 217–18, 226, 228–29
chronicles, 91–92
Coates, Norma, 3, 8
Cobain, Kurt (Nirvana), 101–2
commodification, 119
Conn, Canary, 94–95
contradiction, 12–13, 53, 108–9, 145, 153, 159, 220–21, 222–23
cool, 59, 68–69, 93, 111, 115–16, 118–19, 182
Coon, Caroline, 50
Cosey Fanni Tutti, 1, 5, 17, 225–26, 227–29, 230–31, 232, 234–40
Così fan tutte, 226
COUM, 228–29, 230–31, 236–37
County, Jayne, 1, 13–14, 90–100, 103–4

INDEX

Couser, G. Thomas, 4, 137–38
cowboy, 14–15, 158–60, 163–70, 171–73
cross-dressing, 95–96, 101–2
crowdfunding, 141–42, 143, 151, 155, 156
curation. *See also* bricolage
Currie, Cherie, 1, 16, 177–90
cyborg, 202–3. *See also* dehumanization
cynicism, 109

Davis, Angela, 11
de Beauvoir, Simone, 84
De Certeau, Michel, 107–8
Deep Purple (band), 184
Defries, Tony, 95–97, 98–99
dehumanization, 198–99, 200–3, 205–6. *See also* objectification
Derbyshire, Delia, 239
Dicks, the (band), 92–94
discomfort, 201–2, 226, 232–34, 236, 239
distance, 15, 60, 69–70, 110, 225–26, 227, 232–34, 237–40
DIY, 42–43, 91–92, 93–94, 102–3, 113–14, 147–48
DIY ethos, 102–3, 113–14
dream, 27, 28–29, 30, 32–33, 47, 124, 125, 160, 161, 166–67, 168–70, 171–72, 216–17
dreamscape, 160, 166, 168–69, 171

Edgar, Robert, 4–5, 80, 160–61
empowerment, 128, 137–39, 178–79, 180–81, 186–89, 223
ethics, 13, 26, 28, 35–36, 72–86
  ethics of care, 28, 35–36, 83–84
existential-ethical, 73–74, 85
experience, 3–7, 10–11, 13–16, 23–26, 28–30, 32–37, 40–44, 46, 49, 53, 60, 62–64, 66, 69, 72–75, 80–81, 83–85, 89, 96–97, 98–103, 108–9, 110, 119, 122–24, 126–28, 134, 137, 145, 153–54, 158–59, 161–63, 165, 170, 177–79, 189, 210, 212, 214, 220–22, 226–27, 230–32, 236–39

fame, 6–7, 81, 116, 125, 177–81, 187–89. *See also* celebrity
family, 12, 16–17, 23–26, 28–30, 32, 33, 35–36, 44–45, 52–53, 61–62, 64, 66–68, 74, 78, 79, 112–13, 115–16, 125–234
fan art, 113–14, 211–12
femininity, 62, 115–16, 177–78, 189–90, 199, 226, 229
feminism, 2, 11, 56–57, 129, 134, 149–50, 178–79, 230–31
feminist consciousness, 9–10, 14, 48–49, 122–23, 126, 129
Femme Fatale (band), 51–52
Ford, Lita, 1, 2, 16, 177–81, 183, 184–90
Fowley, Kim, 134, 178–82, 185–86
fragments, 29, 32–34, 37, 160
freedom, 30–31, 62, 63–64, 84, 109, 131–32, 136, 165, 179, 186–89
frontier, 118–19, 160, 171–73

Gardner, Abigail, 15, 17, 162–63, 178–79, 189
gender, 4–6, 8, 10, 13–14, 17, 28, 50, 52, 57, 60, 62–64, 65, 67–68, 78, 89, 90–97, 99–104, 107–11, 118–19, 122–24, 126, 127, 135, 138–39, 146, 148–49, 150–51, 159, 162–63, 166–67, 172–73, 182, 193–94, 212–13, 226, 229
  gender-based violence, 9–10, 40–41, 44
  gender dysphoria, 101–3
  gender ideologies, 110–11
Germs, the (band), 50–51
Gillette, Jim, 184
Gilmore, Leigh, 167, 168, 179
glam, 90–91, 96–97, 111
Go-Go's, the (band) 122–23, 124–25, 134–36, 137–39
Goldman, Vivien, 8–9, 48–49
Gordon, Kim, 1, 12–13, 56–235
Gossow, Angela, 187–90
Goude, Jean-Paul, 16, 192–206
Grace Jones: Bloodlight and Bami, 199–200
Grace, Laura Jane, 13–14, 90–91, 93–94, 99–104
Green, Anna, 72–73
grief, 168, 170
Grossberg, Lawrence, 7–8, 108–9, 227–28
groupie, 51, 185–87

Hanna, Kathleen, 56–57, 67–68, 182, 189–90

Haraway, Donna, 26, 202–3
Harry, Debbie (Deborah), 1, 9–10, 14, 68–69, 107–8, 111–19, 211–12
heavy metal, 147, 186–90
Hell, Richard, 2, 92, 114, 208–9
Hill, Rosemary Lucy, 186, 187
Hirshey, Gerri, 3, 9
Holt, Fabian, 7–8, 74–75
humanization, 204–6
humor, 9–10, 110, 114, 115, 117–18, 226, 230–31
Hynde, Chrissie, 1, 9–10, 211

identity, 12, 15–16, 29, 40–41, 44, 56–60, 62–63, 64, 66, 68–70, 90–92, 93–97, 98–99, 100–2, 107–8, 112–13, 137, 142–45, 148–50, 153–56, 160–64, 168, 171–73, 183, 186–89, 192–93, 198–200, 221–23
  identity construction, 144, 145, 148–50, 153–56, 173, 186–87
image, 2, 11, 14–17, 30–31, 35–36, 62–65, 68, 72–73, 108–15, 117–19, 122–23, 127–29, 131–36, 151, 159–67, 172–73, 177–78, 182, 183, 192–94, 201–3, 206, 208–16, 218–23, 234, 235–36
interpretive continuum, 30–31
intersectionality, intersectional, 2, 6, 10, 25, 124
intersubjective, 80–82, 85
intimacy, 14, 60, 66, 112–15, 142–43, 146, 156
Iommi, Tony, 184
irony, 79, 82, 109, 110, 112–13

Jett, Joan, 117, 179, 181
Jones, Grace, 16, 117–18, 192–206
Jungle Fever, 192–97, 201–5

Kempe, Margery, 239
Kerner, Kenny, 95–96
Kershaw, Miriam, 198–99
KISS, 95–96

lack of credibility, 13
Latino/a/x, 41, 47
Lauper, Cyndi, 14, 122–28, 131–34, 136–39

legacy, 26–27, 67–69, 122–23, 193–96
Lobato, Ramon, 197–98
Lovesey, Oliver, 5, 83
Lundgren, Dolph, 194–95, 203–4
lyrics, 5, 12, 67–68, 74–76, 77–78, 81–83, 92–94, 102–3, 130, 171

macho, 44–45, 53, 103–4, 117–18, 133
male bonding, 61, 100–1
male gaze, 62–64, 89, 131–32, 183–85, 212–13
Manitoba, "Handsome" Dick, 98–99
Mann, Fraser, 4–5, 80, 120, 160–61
Mapplethorpe, Robert, 112–13, 159–60, 165
Marquee Club, London, 90–91
masculine, 8, 14–16, 51–52, 77–78, 93–94, 98–99, 109, 114, 158–74, 177–79, 187, 188–89, 227
  masculinist, 25, 107–8, 118–19
  masculinity, 95–97, 102–3, 158–59, 172, 173, 199
Max's Kansas City, New York, 90–91, 117
McDonnell, Evelyn, 178–79, 181, 182, 189–90, 191
McLaren, Margaret, 183, 191
McNeil, Legs, 93–94, 98–99
memory, 2–5, 11–12, 13, 16–17, 18, 20, 28–31, 38, 47, 54, 57, 67–68, 72–74, 76, 77, 79, 80, 82, 83–84, 86, 115, 119, 120, 126, 159–62, 163, 168–70, 172–74, 206, 208, 217–19, 222–23, 236–38, 240, 241
menopausal, 237–38
  "menopausal gap" 226–27, 233–34, 238–39
  peri-menopause, 236
  post-menopausal, 238
Meretoja, Hanna, 23–27, 29–33, 35–36, 73–74
metastatic breast cancer, 27
#MeToo (movement), 2, 11, 119
Mexico, 43, 45–46
  Mexican, 43, 44–48, 53
Midnight Cowboy, 165–66
misogyny, 16, 96–97, 103–4, 126, 127–28, 178–79
Miyake, Issey, 195–96

mother, 12–13, 23, 27–31, 34–37, 40–41, 43, 44, 46–49, 52–53, 57, 61–62, 64–66, 74, 78, 79, 115–16, 125–31, 217–19, 225, 232–33
   Motherhood, 64–66, 78–79, 128, 188–89, 206
Munster Records, 95–96
musical in-between, 12, 23–26, 32–36, 37
music genre(s), 4–5, 7–8, 74–75, 107, 119, 146
music industry, 3, 9, 11, 14, 17, 83–84, 96–97, 98–99, 107, 119, 122–23, 126, 127, 128, 142, 150–51, 155, 177–79, 180, 188–90, 235–36
music memoir, 4–5, 7, 80, 81, 83, 116–17, 160–63, 172–73, 179, 237–38
myth, 83, 91–92, 103–4, 117, 158–59, 162–63, 164, 171–73, 178–79, 186–88, 192–94, 201. *See also* mythical; mythology
mythical, 14–15, 160
mythology, 119, 160, 162–64, 195–96

narrative, narrative ethics, 13, 72–86
   narrative-in-between, 23–24
   self-narrative, 144, 148–53, 155–56
neoliberalism, 178–79
New Wave, 14, 102–3, 107, 117–19, 122–23
New York punk scene, 117
Ngozi Adichie, Chimamanda, 8–9
nostalgia, 81–82, 159–60, 163–64, 235, 241
Nussbaum, Martha, 201, 205–6, 207

objectification, 117–18, 129, 131–32, 183, 201, 203, 205–6, 223. *See also* dehumanization
objects, 16–17, 50–51, 59, 62, 189, 208, 210–11, 212–15, 217, 219, 222–23
objects of desire, 50–51, 183, 186
O'Brien, Lucy, 1, 3, 11, 19, 39, 50, 54, 62–63, 64–65, 71
One Man Show, 198–99, 203–4

Pacteau, Francette, 201–2, 207
Palmer, Amanda, 14, 141–56
patriarchy, 91–92, 98–99, 103–4, 180, 187
   heteropatriarchy, 92, 93–94
   patriarchal capitalism, 119

patriarchal heteronormativity, 14–15, 160
   patriarchal society, 4–5, 9, 51–52, 82
   patriarchal world, 10, 15–16
performance of authenticity, 14, 142–43, 146, 149, 152–53, 155–56
performative, 3–4, 15, 73–74, 85, 96–97, 146, 153, 161–62, 178–79
peritext, 112
Phair, Liz, 1, 16–17, 208, 212–13, 219, 220–23
photographs, 15–17, 47, 112–13, 173, 199–202, 208–23, 224
photography, 15–17
place, 9–10, 17, 18, 61–62, 72–73, 85, 104, 108–9, 116, 120, 122, 124, 139, 147, 148, 154, 155, 161, 163, 164, 170, 182, 185–86, 189–90, 223, 225–41
Plath, Sylvia, 36–39, 78–79, 82
Pleasance, Helen, 4–6, 80–81, 107–8, 120, 160–61, 206
poetry, 157, 160–61, 163, 171
pop music, 52, 78, 106–7, 228–29
P'Orridge, Genesis, 228–29, 234–37
possibility, 26, 29–30, 33, 78, 82, 84, 138–39, 196–97
postfeminism, 178–79
Postfeminist, 129, 178–79, 183, 187
postmetropolis, 54
postmodernism, 109, 197–98, 206
Previn, Dory, 12, 23–34, 36–37
prostitution, 180–81, 191, 229
protopunk, 93–96
public persona, 2, 179, 180–81, 184–85, 188–89, 221
punk, punk ethos, 50–51, 103–4
   punk manifesto, 93, 98–99, 105
   punk rock, 11, 18, 19, 50–51, 54, 56–58, 71, 90–91, 96–97, 105, 147
Pussy Riot, 8–9, 18, 49, 54, 56–57, 70

Queens of Noise, 177–79, 191
queer, 14–15, 93–94, 96–97, 98–100, 103–4, 158–74, 232
queerness, 90–91, 93–94, 96–97, 98–99, 100

race, 6, 10, 18, 89, 93, 100, 193–94, 198, 199, 202–3

Ramones, the (band), 51–52, 92, 93–94, 114, 117
rape, 9–10, 115, 127–29, 184–85
recognition, 13, 84, 102–3, 109, 149, 150–51, 192–93, 208
Reed, Lou, 76, 93–94
relationality, 32, 108, 116
retro, 111, 131–32
Riot Grrrl, 182, 189–90
rock and roll, 60, 62–65, 68–69, 103–4, 114, 119, 134–35, 163, 178–79, 181, 182, 184–86, 188–89
rock chick, 16, 70, 177–91
rock music industry, 107, 119, 177–78, 180, 188–89
rock naturalism, 109
Rosenvinge, Christina, 12–13, 72–85
Runaways, the (band), 16, 134, 177–86, 189–90

Savage, Jon, 90–91, 105
screaming, 28–29, 141, 187–90
self-representation, 69, 167, 211, 212–13, 222–23
sex industry, 178–79, 229, 236
sexism, 11, 13, 14, 89, 103–4, 122–23, 126, 127–28, 131–32, 134–39
sexual abuse, 9–10, 13, 119
sexuality, 11, 13, 51, 89, 92, 93–97, 103–4, 107–8, 129, 178–79, 180–81, 182, 193–94, 226, 229
   heterosexuality, 90–91
   homosexuality, 91–92, 93, 96–97
Shepard, Sam, 159–60, 166, 171
shredding, 177–78, 187, 189–90
Simmons, Sylvie, 112, 114, 120
singer, 16, 38, 52, 95–99, 107, 111, 112, 117–18, 122, 124, 127–34, 177–79, 182, 183, 184, 187–88, 189–90, 202–3, 211
   chick singer, 124, 136, 137–38
singer-songwriter, 18, 26–27, 72, 74, 83, 85, 86, 162–63
situated knowledge, 26, 38
Smith, Fred Sonic, 168–69, 170
Smith, Patti, 1, 2, 5, 7, 11, 14–17, 36–37, 51–52, 68, 81–82, 117, 158–73, 208, 212–17, 219, 222–23
Smith, Sidonie, 4, 6, 143

Snider, Dee, 185–86
social media, 143, 154, 219, 220
songwriting, 12, 13, 23–24, 32, 35–36, 72–74, 77, 79, 82–85, 130, 132–33, 138–39
Sonic Youth, 56–64, 67–69, 70, 76
Spheeris, Penelope, *The Decline of Western Civilization*, 52
squatting, 236
Starwood, the, 180–81
storytelling, 4–5, 24, 30–31, 32, 38, 73–74, 86, 137–38
stripper, 225–26, 230–31
subculture, 89, 90–99, 101–4, 117–18, 146, 187–88
survival, 13, 16, 32, 33, 37, 41, 52–53, 72–74, 79, 82–84, 124–25, 126, 178–79, 186–87, 188–90, 229, 234
Swan, Astrid, 12, 23–24, 27

Throbbing Gristle (band), 228–29, 231, 234–39
Thurston Moore, 58
transgender punks, 13–14
transgressive, 17, 161, 163–66, 171, 225–26, 230–31
transsexual, 94–99
trauma, 11, 12, 24–37, 44, 53, 72–73, 79, 82, 114, 115, 177–79, 188–89, 220, 234–35, 237–38
   childhood trauma, 12, 24, 30, 52
   trauma narrative, 12, 24, 29–30
trust, 46, 81, 84–85, 135, 142–43, 144, 147, 152–56, 216–18
truth, 13, 37, 72–74, 76, 79, 80–82, 93–94, 100–1, 106–7, 141, 148, 155, 161, 166–67, 179, 194

Valentine, Kathy, 1, 14, 20, 122–28, 134–39, 140, 208–9
value, 5–6, 18, 106–9, 122–23, 142–43, 145, 146, 150–51, 155–56, 157, 172–73, 196–97, 215
veracity, 209, 216–17, 235–36
Vig, Butch, 102–3
violence, 9–10, 12, 25–26, 28–30, 35–36, 40–42, 44–53, 101–2, 180, 184–85, 230–31, 235–37
   domestic violence, 40–41, 44–45
   See also gender-based violence

visual, 30–31, 38, 62, 74–75, 92, 96–97, 110, 112–13, 117–19, 122–23, 132–33, 193–94, 202–3, 207–13, 222, 223, 227, 229, 235–36
visuality, 112–13
voice, 74–75, 83–84, 109, 114, 118–19, 120, 124, 130–32, 137–38, 139, 141, 149, 160, 164, 166–67, 170, 172, 192–94, 222, 225–26, 231, 235–36, 238
   authorial voice, 226–27, 237–38
   literary voice, 17, 77, 225–26

narrative voice, 27
Village Voice, 93, 105

Warhol, Andy, 105, 158
warrior, 11, 186, 187–89, 194–95
Watson, Julia, 3–4, 6, 41–42, 80–81, 148, 152, 183, 191, 212–13
White-Guz, Alissa, 189–90

Yelin, Hannah, 6–7, 178–79, 182, 191, 193–94